Working with Venues for Events

This is a book for aspiring event managers, providing both a theoretical and a practical guide to selecting and working with venues as part of the event planning process.

The book explores the different types of venues available to event managers, from unique venues such as historical buildings and theatres to sporting and academic venues, analysing the specific characteristics, benefits and drawbacks that distinguish them. It also illustrates how venues function and are managed, incorporating key aspects of venue management including staffing, marketing, legislation, production, scheduling and administration. Sustainability, ethics and technology are also integrated throughout, along with a vast range of industry examples of different venue types and events from around the world.

Comprehensive and accessible, *Working with Venues for Events* offers students an essential understanding of how event managers can successfully negotiate, work with and plan for a successful event in a variety of venue settings. This is an invaluable resource for anyone with an interest in events management.

Emma Nolan has 25 years' experience as an event management practitioner and an academic. This includes working in visitor attractions, theatres and local authorities and delivering events for a variety of clients including political parties, the TUC and the NHS. Emma moved into academia in 2008 and worked at the University of Winchester as a Senior Lecturer in Project and Event Management for several years. Emma is a Senior Fellow of the HEA, has an MA in Education and is currently working towards her PhD at the University of Chichester, UK.

Working with Venues for Events

A Practical Guide

Emma Nolan

Routledge
Taylor & Francis Group

LONDON AND NEW YORK

First published 2018
by Routledge
2 Park Square, Milton Park, Abingdon, Oxon OX14 4RN

and by Routledge
711 Third Avenue, New York, NY 10017

Routledge is an imprint of the Taylor & Francis Group, an informa business

© 2018 Emma Nolan

The right of Emma Nolan to be identified as author of this work has been asserted by her in accordance with sections 77 and 78 of the Copyright, Designs and Patents Act 1988.

British Library Cataloguing-in-Publication Data
A catalogue record for this book is available from the British Library

Library of Congress Cataloging-in-Publication Data
A catalog record for this book has been requested

ISBN: 978-1-138-94452-7 (hbk)
ISBN: 978-1-138-94453-4 (pbk)
ISBN: 978-1-315-67182-6 (ebk)

Typeset in Frutiger
by Florence Production Ltd, Stoodleigh, Devon, UK

I would like to dedicate this book to my husband Damien and my dear friend Jay for their support and encouragement with this endeavour and many others.

CONTENTS

FIGURES

IMAGES

TABLES

CASE STUDIES

INDUSTRY EXPERT'S VIEW BOXES

INTERNATIONAL EXAMPLES

Chapter/section		Image	Case study	Industry expert	Country
1.1	The Ancient Theatre of Epidaurus	x			Greece
1.1	The Ancient Theatre of Epidaurus		x		Greece
1.2	One Marylebone		x		UK (London)
1.3	The Pipe and Glass Inn, Yorkshire, England	x			UK (Yorkshire)
1.3	Shakespeare's Globe Bankside, Bankside, London, England	x			UK (London)
1.3	Unique Venues of London		x		UK (London)
1.4	Ascot Race Course	x			UK (Berkshire)
1.5	The Original Crystal Palace	x			UK (London)
2.2	The Sydney Opera House	x			Australia
3.1	The Las Vegas Strip	x			USA
3.1	Singapore, a Thriving Destination in Asia		x		Singapore
3.1	Destination Management			x	USA
3.2	A Partner Programme organised by Ruth Pretty Catering		x		New Zealand
3.3	A Familiarisation Trip		x		South Africa
4.1	The Milano Congressi - MiCo	x			Italy
4.1	The Milano Congressi		x		Italy
4.2	A Venue With Interconnecting Rooms: Croke Park		x		Dublin
4.3	Callow Event Management		x		UK (Belfast)
4.4	Croke Park	x			Ireland
4.5	The Sensoji Temple	x			Japan
5.1	Marina Bay Sands	x			Singapore
5.1	Marina Bay Sands		x		Singapore
5.2	The UNON *Sustainable Events Guide*		x		Nairobi
5.3	The Melbourne Convention and Exhibition Centre		x		Australia
5.4	GL Events Venues and ISO 14001 Certification		x		France
6.1	Inclusive Design		x		UK (London)
7.1	Highland Resort Hotel and Spa, Fujiyoshida City, Japan	x			Japan
7.2	The Gainsborough Bath Spa	x			UK (Bath)
7.3	The Petronas Twin Towers, Kuala Lumpur, Malaysia	x			Malaysia
8.1	Ronnie Scott's Jazz Club, London	x			UK (London)
8.1	Meeting Tomorrow Hybrid Events		x		Australia
8.2	Ronnie Scott's Jazz Club		x		UK (London)

PREFACE

I consider myself very fortunate to have worked in the events industry for over 25 years as both a practitioner and an academic. Like many others, I never set out to become an events professional, this sort of happened by chance. In 1993, while I was a student at university, a friend's dad, a front of house manager at an open-air theatre, helped me to find a summer job in the box office. I thought that this would be a fun way of earning some much-needed cash to see me through my studies. Little did I realise at the time, that this job would set me on a career path that has led me to where I am today. I found working in a theatre exhilarating as every day was an event day; full of hard work, lots of preparation but also anticipation and excitement and I was hooked. Before I graduated I realised that this was the industry for me.

I went on to employment in other theatres, visitor attractions and multi-purpose event venues in both the public and private sector and worked with a range of clients and suppliers on many different types of events. My love of working in the events industry grew as did my admiration for the profound impact that all kinds of events from weddings to conferences to sporting competitions can have on our lives.

In 2008, I had the opportunity to become a lecturer and to share my passion for the industry, my knowledge and my skills with the next generation of event managers. I have found academia to be as challenging and rewarding as working on live events! Teaching students is a joy and a privilege and it is wonderful to watch and support others as they start to develop their own career path in an industry that I'm proud of. I want to inspire students to promote and champion the events industry and challenge some of the stereotypes and misconceptions about the profession and the study of event management.

One of the challenges of teaching the subject is that as a relatively new academic discipline, it has limited resources in some areas. I noticed a few years ago that there are very few textbooks that are dedicated to exploring and discussing the role of the venue in the event planning process. As the venue is one of the key stakeholders in any event, and can greatly influence and shape an event, this felt like an omission, but also an opportunity. With the help, support and encouragement of my academic colleagues and the team at Routledge I decided to write a book about venues.

What I set out to achieve was to create a useful handbook for event management students and new practitioners. A book that will guide you through the process of looking for, choosing and working with a venue as well as planning a venue based career. As someone who has worked in a number of venues, I wanted to draw on my knowledge and experience of venue management to provide a useful, insider's guide to understanding how venues operate. To that end, I hope that I have achieved this and that you will find this book to a be a handy companion to your studies and to your first steps into the wonderful world of event management.

ACKNOWLEDGEMENTS

I would like to thank all the people who have contributed to this book and brought it to life through their insights and stories. Many thanks to all the industry experts and the many individuals and organisations who agreed to take part and be profiled in case studies. I would also like to thank Professor Pru Marriott at the University of Winchester for her encouragement and to my two fantastic research assistants, Carl Matthews and Eryn White, for all their hard work.

ABBREVIATIONS

AV	Audio visual
BOH	Back of house
CVB	Convention and visitor bureau
DMO	Destination management organisation
FOH	Front of house
MICE	Meetings, incentive travel, conferences and exhibitions
PAYG	Pay as you go
REVPAR	Revenue per available room
RFID	Radio frequency identification
RFP	Request for proposal

The evolution of venues

LEARNING OUTCOMES

By the end of Chapter 1, you should be able to:

* Appreciate the history of event venues
* Categorise venues according to their primary function
* Understand the benefits and challenges of using different types of venues
* Recognise patterns in past, current and future venue development

1.1 INTRODUCTION

The twentieth-century event manager has a diverse range of venues to choose from as the backdrop to their next event. Today visitor attractions, theatres, museums, universities and sporting complexes compete for event business against hotels and purpose-built conference and exhibition space. Most venues are multipurpose in function and can accommodate all manner of events. Today parties, celebrations, festivals, cultural events, meetings, weddings

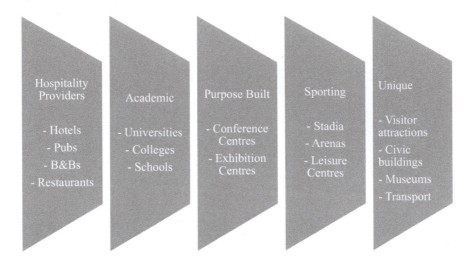

Figure 1.1 Venue categories.

Table 1.1 Venue characteristics

Venue type	Typical characteristics
Hospitality providers	• Catering facility on site • Accommodation on site • Competitive hire charges • Additional facilities (pool, spa, golf course etc.) • Rural and urban locations • Disproportionate number of bedrooms compared to capacity of event space
Academic venues	• Number of well-equipped rooms/lecture halls • On-site sporting facilities • Some accommodation, but this may not be high quality • Competitively priced • Restricted availability
Purpose-built venues	• Excellent access (e.g. service roads/dock doors/entrances) • Good floor loading limits and ceiling heights • Blank canvas for theming • Superior electricity network • Large lighting and sound rigs • Potentially expensive (to hire/to decorate) • Large capacities (but unsuitable for intimate gatherings)
Sporting venues	• Varied and generous capacities • Competitive rates • Restricted availability • Strong transport links • Limited ambience for small events
Unique venues	• Wow factor • Restricted availability • Limited access/on-site facilities • Restrictions on theming/decoration • Restrictive spaces • Expensive

and sporting competitions can all be successfully hosted in many venues. However, comparatively few of today's buildings were originally designed and built to accommodate events. Most were constructed for a very different purpose and have since entered into the events industry in order to secure a secondary source of income. By reviewing key moments in history we can identify and understand how different types of venues have emerged and developed. Venues that have a similar background and the same primary function today also typically share features such as architectural design and layout. They also have shared characteristics such as when they are and are not available for events and what the event manager can and cannot do within the space. This chapter will provide you with insight into what to expect from working within different types of venues and how to use this to your advantage when designing and delivering an event. We will briefly review key developments in society that have led to the construction of various types of venues and look at the characteristics that they share. The chapter includes tips on how these can be both beneficial to the event manager but can also present them with a particular set of challenges to be aware of. The chapter includes case studies and illustrations of a range of venues and takes a look ahead to the future of venue development for the events industry. The categories of venues that will be covered in this chapter are illustrated in Figure 1.1 with a summary of their key characteristics shown in Table 1.1.

1.2 VENUES ROOTED IN EARLY CIVILISATIONS

The tourism, leisure, **hospitality** and events industries are deep rooted in our history and culture. Some of our most ancient civilisations – the Egyptians, Mayans and Aztecs – explored leisure pursuits and developed sporting rituals and competitions (Masterman, 2009). The Greeks and the Romans developed purpose-built venues to accommodate their large-scale sporting events and of course many of these amphitheatres and colosseums can still be visited. Some of the more well-preserved venues are not just visitor attractions but are still in use today such as the Ancient Theatre of Epidaurus.

CASE STUDY 1.1 THE ANCIENT THEATRE OF EPIDAURUS

The Ancient Theatre of Epidaurus is situated within the archaeological site of the Sanctuary of Asklepios, in an elevated valley surrounded by mountains in the Peloponnese area of Greece, approximately 2 hours from Athens.

The theatre was originally constructed in the fourth century BC and was later extended in the mid-second century BC. It was built to stage plays and performances but it was also used for athletic and artistic competitions. The theatre seats 14,000 within an auditorium that is nestled into the natural curve of Mount Kynortio at an incline of 26 degrees. Fifty five rows of bench seating are set out across two sections separated by a semi-circular aisle. The theatre has a circular orchestra pit and a two-tier stage building (skene) from which backdrops can be suspended. Due to the perfect geometric design, the theatre has excellent acoustics and unlike many other theatres of the same period, the Romans did not alter it. Therefore although the venue has been carefully restored in recent years, it still retains its original design.

continued

Image 1.1 The Ancient Theatre of Epidaurus.

Credit: Ivan Bastien/ Shutterstock.

From the time it was constructed the theatre was used regularly until the invasion of the Goths in AD 395. In the following century Theodosios the Great banned all activities at the Sanctuary and for nearly a millennium the theatre was left abandoned and fell into disrepair. In 1881, the Archaeological Society began to excavate the site and discovered that the auditorium was in a reasonably good condition although the stage building had completely eroded. The rediscovery of the famous theatre generated much public interest and revived a passion for classical drama. This led to a 10-year long project intended to restore and relaunch the venue once it had been made safe and suitable for performances. The project was a success and by 1936 the Greek government had introduced yearly festivals with performances of ancient drama being staged once again at Epidaurus. The theatre became a popular venue once more with leading musicians and playwrights keen to experiment with using the space for various theatrical and musical performances.

In the 1950s the Greek government launched the Athens and Epidaurus Festival and granted the National Theatre exclusive use of the venue for major operatic, dance and musical productions. This partnership cemented the theatre as a leading venue in the Greek arts sector. The festival is still running today and continues to draw in a broad audience to attend traditional and contemporary performances and productions.

In 1988, the theatre, along with the entire Sanctuary of Asklepios, was made a UNESCO World Heritage Site and since then further restorative work has taken place at the venue to include replacing seats and repairing the auditorium's ancient drainage system. Today the theatre is a bustling visitor attraction drawing in thousands of international visitors every year. It continues to be well used by actors, actresses, directors, composers, choreographers and set designers alike for a variety of classical and modern productions.

Source: 'Athens and Epidaurus Festival' available from http://greekfestival.gr

Both the Greek and Roman way of life led to the creation of a primitive tourism industry. The ancient Olympic Games that took place in Greece from 776BC to AD393 became extremely popular drawing in visitors from across the country and creating a demand for accommodation. And as the Roman Empire extended and established into the fifth century, two branches of tourism developed as a consequence of the acquisition of more and more overseas territories. Firstly, these territories needed to be managed, leading to the creation of **business tourism** – as a number of Romans needed to travel across the Empire for business related purposes. In parallel, Roman seaside resorts were developed for a prosperous Italian society looking for holiday destinations and thus creating a domestic tourism sector. Rome, the capital city, emerged as a significant tourism destination due to its stature as the heart of the empire. Consequently a number of venues were built including inns and taverns to service the needs of local residents and visitors (Page, 2012).

1.3 VENUES FROM THE MIDDLE AGES

The demise of the Roman Empire was followed by the start of the Middle Ages. This time in history saw the spread of Christianity which replaced the pleasure seeking Romanesque way of life with feudalism whereby society was divided into the land governing nobility and the working class tenants. For the working class majority of the population, leisure time was limited and often confined to religious celebration. Although outdoor festivals took place, these were usually organised as gatherings that were to strengthen allegiance to the church and the state who dually controlled the population (Andrews and Leopold, 2013). As the only communal venue within a rural community, the church would serve to accommodate not just religious devotion but also primitive meetings and gatherings.

In more recent years, the decline in the number of Christians has led to the closure of many churches. However, a number of entrepreneurial investors have bought and transformed churches into vibrant and quirky modern day venues while retaining and preserving some of their historic features.

The Middle Ages also saw the development of additional branches of tourism including religious tourism, as pilgrimages to holy sites became very popular, and health tourism to spa towns and cities such as Buxton and Bath. This led to further creation of hospitality-providing venues such as inns and taverns. These venues were multipurpose in function as they gave the local community a watering hole but they also supplied much needed accommodation for travellers and served as ideal venues for meetings, celebrations and social gatherings. Only in more recent times have we labelled these venues as pubs and although many counties across the UK claim to be home to the oldest pub in the country, ultimately it is very difficult to attribute this accolade to a particular venue. Nonetheless many historic inns and taverns have survived for centuries and continue to operate today as pubs with facilities for many types of small events. These venues are still very appropriate for meetings and parties as they typically have private function rooms which can frequently be hired at no charge, providing the bar and food service facilities will be well used and a number of them continue to offer accommodation too. Image 1.3 is of the Pipe and Glass Inn located in East Yorkshire. The pub is a former coaching inn and parts of the venue date back to the seventeenth century.

However, the construction of the more sophisticated hotel accommodation that we are used to today is rooted in what happened in the nineteenth century when the Industrial Revolution was at its peak.

CASE STUDY 1.2 ONE MARYLEBONE

One Marylebone, formally Holy Trinity Church, was built in 1826–28 to the designs of Sir John Soane to celebrate the defeat of Napoleon. Soane (1753–1837) was arguably England's finest architect in the neoclassical style. His architectural works are distinguished by their clean lines, massing of simple form, decisive detailing, careful proportions and skilful use of light sources. His best-known work is the Bank of England, a building that has had a widespread effect upon commercial architecture. Grade I listed by English Heritage, One Marylebone is one of only three London churches by Soane; it was the most expensive and now considered to be the most architecturally distinguished. His use of the neoclassical is evident in the portico of the church and his constant desire to work with light is most evident in the first floor galleries. Apart from the loss of the original chancel, the basic structure of Soane's church survives complete and is of huge national architectural and historical significance.

Image 1.2 Soane Hall, One Marylebone.

Source: One Events.

One Marylebone opened its doors as a hireable events space in 2008 and quickly became one of the leading unusual venues of London. It has been beautifully refurbished to the original designs of Sir John Soane, and the venue boasts two exclusive hireable spaces plus landscaped garden, moments from Regents Park. The grandeur of One Marylebone has attracted blue-chip brands from a variety of industries with a focus on fashion, beauty and the arts. Hosting a range of events including Christmas parties, exhibitions, charity and corporate events and weddings, the possibilities are endless at this unique venue.

The Soane Hall is the jewel in the crown of One Marylebone; at over 27 feet in height, the prestigious space is both impressive in size and beauty. Although full of character with its opulent mosaics and stained-glass windows evoking everlasting elegance, the space remains flexible allowing clients to either enjoy it in its natural state or transform it to fit any requirements of style and branding. The first floor contemporary and light galleries are the perfect setting for pre-dinner drinks or can be used on their own for a multitude of events.

Able to host standing receptions for 800 and sit-down dinners for 350 or more intimate parties for under 100, One Marylebone is one of London's most flexible venues.

Source: http://one-events.co.uk/

Image 1.3 The Pipe and Glass Inn, Yorkshire.

Source: Tony Bartholomew/VisitBritain.

1.4 THE INDUSTRIAL REVOLUTION AND VENUE DEVELOPMENT

The rapid expansion of industry during the late eighteenth to mid-nineteenth centuries saw a hardworking nation driving forward these developments, becoming more and more eager to enjoy the fruits of their labour away from the workplace. Many business leaders were not keen to promote leisure time seeing it as a distraction from creating a more and more profitable economy (Page, 2012) but despite this the 1871 and 1875 Bank Holiday Acts introduced four new UK public holidays thus creating more opportunities for workers to have days off. The newly created public railway, as well as popular waterways, gave them the opportunity to have a day out, and visiting coastal areas became a particularly popular pastime. Those who could afford it would extend their visit to a holiday and consequently Victorian resorts quickly developed with a range of venues to accommodate visitors. Hotels were built along seafronts, and theatres, assembly rooms, dance halls and winter gardens were created to satisfy social pleasures. And so a number of underdeveloped towns such as Torquay, Blackpool and Eastbourne were transformed into vibrant, popular and prosperous resorts built around a variety of venues including hotels and visitor attractions.

1.5 HOSPITALITY PROVIDERS

There are obvious benefits to using hospitality providers as venues for modern day events. Hotels, bed and breakfasts (B&Bs), pubs, inns, restaurants and cafes will have a fully operational catering facility on site and venues with accommodation are beneficial for **residential events** (where attendees need to stay overnight). Most hospitality providers have separate rooms for functions taking place within the venue and for fully catered events, these spaces can often be hired for free. However there is sometimes a disparity between the capacity of the function and the number of bedrooms at the venue, meaning that some hotels, for example, can accommodate large events but can only provide bedrooms for some of the attendees. The reverse can also be true, where bed stock is greater than the capacity of the principal function room which means that if you are organising a residential event it is important to compare the capacities of both. A number of hotels and some B&Bs will have additional facilities such as a pool, spa and golf course which may be useful in attracting people to the event. However, they can sometimes provide an unwanted distraction. Similarly hospitality providers can be found in rural locations as well town and city centres and therefore they can suit, or be unsuitable for, a number of different types of events. Our twenty-first century appetite for tourism fuels an ever growing number and range of hospitality providers and today's travellers can share facilities in basic hostels and campsites or choose to go glamping in yurts. It is also worth noting that the cruise sector is now more popular than ever with an ever increasing number of operators sailing to even the most remote areas of the world. Cruise ships are 'floating hybrids of hotels, conference centres, and full-service resorts' (Fenich, 2012, p. 66) which offer an alternative but comprehensive venue option for event planners.

In terms of ownership, there are a number of privately owned, independent hospitality venues in operation today. They can often provide very competitive rates to event managers for both function space and bedroom accommodation and will be prepared to enter into a negotiation of the charges. Larger establishments are more likely to be a part of a national or international chain although frequently they operate as franchises. A franchised hotel will be run by an individual or a group of individuals but it will operate under a well-known name or brand and in accordance with their policies. Chains and franchised hotels can sometimes offer appealing rates to event managers who will provide them with a regular income but at times they can be restricted as to how far they are able to negotiate hire charges. Many hotels offer **day delegate rates**, a per capita (per person) charge to cover function room hire, catering and basic equipment. In other words, the event manager will pay a set amount which is calculated by the number of people attending the event. This charge will include the use of one main room for the event, one light meal for attendees, additional teas and coffees and use of stationery and AV equipment.

1.6 UNIQUE VENUES: HISTORICAL BUILDINGS

As we've already seen in this chapter, in primitive societies the Church dominated daily life and churches were the primary venue for indoor events. However, as towns and cities were developed in subsequent years, the state took control of meeting spaces by including the construction of guildhalls as part of urban development. One of the first guildhalls was built in London in the twelfth century. It was commissioned by the then Lord Mayor of London at a time when this role came with a level of power and prestige equivalent to royalty. The Mayor and members of the Guildhall essentially controlled the various trades that were responsible for making London the wealthiest city on earth for a time and they needed a suitably grand venue to convey their prestige. Many guildhalls are still in existence today and they continue to serve this primary purpose; to provide a meeting space for those in power. These civic venues are frequently the location for council meetings and government events but they are generally also available for private hire for most types of events. One of the benefits of using this type of historical venue is that they can often be quirky, full of original features and still covey a sense of power. This can influence the ambience of an event and add a sense of gravitas to proceedings. On the downside, historical venues can sometimes have very poor access, narrow stairways and strict rules against the use of decorations. Frequently they are listed buildings, which means that they cannot be altered without special permission which can be difficult to obtain. Consequently, some listed buildings are not as accessible or flexible as their modern day counterparts.

1.7 UNIQUE VENUES: THEATRES AND CINEMAS

In 1576 James Burbage built the first purpose-built playhouse which he called The Theatre. This open air venue was succeeded by other thatched venues including the Rose and the most famous Elizabethan playhouse of all, The Globe. The Globe has since been replicated near its original location on London's Bankside and as a faithful reproduction the venue has a thatched roof, with the majority of the audience standing around the stage in an area that is open to the elements.

Going to the theatre was a popular Elizabethan activity enjoyed by the masses not just the nobility. Most playhouses were open air venues and plays were performed during the day when there was enough sunlight to warm the audience and light the stage. Over time the interest in theatregoing propelled the use of covered spaces and theatres developed from outdoor venues to mostly indoor, lit venues. However, the English Civil War, which started in 1642, saw the closure of theatres. At first this was a means of preventing public disorder but the closures were upheld by Oliver Cromwell and the Puritan movement who objected to theatre going as they perceived it to be an unsavoury leisure pursuit.

By the mid-nineteenth century there was further campaigning for the end of activities that were considered to be inappropriate such as fox hunting and prize fighting, and at the same time the Museums Act of 1849 and the Recreation Grounds Act of 1852 promoted the use of more acceptable leisure activities (Haywood et al., 1995). Music halls were also erected and these large venues were privately owned by budding entrepreneurs eager to capitalise on a buoyant leisure industry. By the early twentieth century, technology had progressed to create another new industry – film production – and the oldest cinema still in operation today in its original location is the Korsør Biograf Teater in Korsør, Denmark, which first opened its doors on 7 August 1908 (Guinness World Records, 2016).

Image 1.4 Shakespeare's Globe, Bankside, London.

Source: VisitBritain.

1.8 USING UNIQUE VENUES

Theatres and cinemas are of course still very frequently attended venues today but a number have now extended their use and can be hired for private functions. Similarly, we have a growing number of music venues, visitor attractions and museums who have also diversified and use events to provide them with a secondary source of income. These unusual event spaces have a big 'wow factor': a meeting held in a zoo or a party held in a theme park is likely to create a lasting memory for event attendees. As such there is great demand for unusual and unique venue spaces for all kinds of traditional and one-off events. By carefully integrating the unusual venue into the event experience, the event manager has the potential to deliver a truly unique and outstanding event (and potentially one that needs very little additional expenditure on props or theming). However, unusual venues present the event manager with a range of challenges. Firstly, most of these venues have very limited availability. A number of visitor attractions, for example, can only be hired in the evening and for short periods of time and conversely theatres and cinemas can generally only be hired for daytime use. Access to the venues may be very restricted, with limited entry points for equipment or staging and this problem will be compounded by a short 'get-in' period.

A number of unusual venues, such as museums, will have very strict rules for the protection of their artefacts and exhibits. This may prevent the event manager from moving existing equipment or furniture and they may be restricted as to what they can put on walls. The capacities of some unusual venues may be quite generous in total, but many are designed to move small numbers of people around the site quickly (e.g. attractions) and therefore these spaces may be restrictive for networking or socialising. The large capacity of theatre-style seating, AV and blackout facility makes theatres and cinemas ideally suited not just to private screenings but also to conferences. However, **auditoria** are not suited to networking events. Although traditional theatres have excellent staging and AV facilities, they are generally unsuitable to anything more than a staged production (Matthews, 2016, p. 172). Furthermore, many unusual venues do not have a regular need for AV equipment or staging, meaning that these event staples will have to be hired in at an extra cost. And despite the many drawbacks of using unusual venues, their enduring popularity and full diaries means that they are able to charge premium rates to event managers for the privilege of having private use of the space. Even state owned theatres, art centres and community venues are likely to be managed by a commercial team that will maximise the return on the investment of public money (Bladen *et al.*, 2012, p. 280).

1.9 SPORTING VENUES

As we've already seen, there is much evidence of a commitment to sport from our most ancient civilisations onward. The eighteenth century in particular saw a number of developments in sport such as the introduction of rules and practices and the launch of regular tournaments and competitions. The first horse racing meeting at Ascot was held in 1711 and the construction of the first permanent building at its Berkshire location in 1794 was a step towards establishing the site as the permanent home of the world famous Royal Ascot racecourse. Similarly the first Lords cricket ground was opened in Dorset in 1787 and moved to its permanent London address in 1814, and the first tennis championship to be held at the now iconic All England Lawn Tennis Club in Wimbledon took place in 1870. And of course the newly constructed rail system meant that people could travel to attend sporting events which cemented the popularity of these new competitions for years to come.

Schools and universities have also had an instrumental role in the development of sport and sporting competitions. Masterman (2009, p. 6) illustrates this with the example of how basketball was originally devised in the US by James Naismith in 1891 as an indoor game that he developed for a school for Christian workers. And in the UK physical education had been introduced into the school curriculum in 1870, originally as a type of military drill (Haywood *et al.*, 1995) but as different sports evolved they replaced the drills as teachers favoured them as a way to engage and discipline students and encourage them to develop responsibility to others while aiming for excellence.

Image 1.5 Ascot racecourse.

Source: Grant Pritchard/VisitBritain.

The modern Olympics that began in the late nineteenth century is perhaps responsible for some of the world's largest and most significant site and venue development in the last 100 years. Cities that host this mega event will typically leverage the event to create large-scale urban regeneration (Bladen *et al.*, 2012) and post-event, the host city may benefit from a legacy that includes improved transport systems, additional housing and a number of world class sporting venues and stadia. It can be argued that cities with the most enduring Olympic legacy are those which have carefully strategised for long term usage of their venues to extend beyond their original sporting purpose. Barcelona is a great example of such a success story and much of the infrastructure built for the 1992 Olympics continues to serve a consistently popular destination for tourism and events.

1.10 USING SPORTING VENUES

Our twenty-first century appetite for sport continues to fuel venue development and in the UK alone there are now more than 100 stadia (venues with a capacity of at least 10,000) not to mention a huge number of smaller, local leisure centres, grounds and arenas. While some of the smaller venues are government owned and operated, more recently we've seen a trend towards private governance of sporting venues due to lack of availability of public funds (Schwarz *et al.*, 2015). Therefore although the main function of these venues is to support sports training and sporting competitions many are run as commercial ventures and they are increasingly marketed to event managers. In fact in the last decade new stadia have been designed with flexibility of use in mind to facilitate the generation of additional and regular income to insure their long term economic viability (Bladen *et al.*, 2012).

In general, sporting venues have much to offer the events industry. The outdoor seating and pitch area of a stadium combine to create a generous capacity for large scale music concerts, while some of the smaller rooms used for match day hospitality are suitable for meetings, parties and more intimate events. Generally these spaces are not used outside of sporting competitions and tournaments and therefore any additional revenue that they generate is a bonus to their owners. As such it may be possible to negotiate excellent rates for hiring the facilities. Typically sporting venues have strong transport links, and despite their often suburban locations, they have adequate facilities (entrances, toilets etc.) to cope with the influx of large crowds. The availability of these venues may be a little restricted, but there will usually be plenty of scope to host events outside of key competition times and around training sessions. However, many stadia have restrictions on the number of music events that they can host each year, particularly if the venue is in a residential area. And although the larger sporting venues are ideal for large scale events, they can be a little soulless for smaller meetings or celebrations held on non-match days without the ambience and frisson created by thousands of fans. The key problem with using arenas and stadia is that it is a real challenge to create the wow factor for small, intimate events (Matthews, 2016).

1.11 PURPOSE-BUILT EVENT VENUES

The Industrial Revolution was an enormously productive chapter of history. As well as directly influencing the development of a valuable domestic tourism industry, this period of prosperity led to the emergence of the meetings, incentive travel, conference and exhibition (**MICE**) industry and with it the creation of a number of purpose-built convention and exhibition centres.

Image 1.6 The original Crystal Palace.

Source: © Victoria and Albert Museum, London.

This era of fortune created new industries and with them professionals who needed to meet, converse and exchange ideas. The parallel development of transport systems mobilised workers, enabling them to travel to attend business related meetings and exhibitions. Rogers and Davidson (2016) affirm that the US was the first country to embrace the concept of building purpose-built event spaces and indeed the first convention bureau was launched in Detroit in 1895 in order to provide a dedicated accommodation and venue finding service to delegates and conference organisers. However, it could be argued that the UK was even quicker to capitalise on the value of the MICE industry by holding the Great Exhibition of 1851 to celebrate industrial achievements. This exposition lasted 6 months during which over 6 million visitors viewed the 100,000 exhibits in a purpose-built exhibition space; the original Crystal Palace.

The exhibition was a huge success in terms of visitor numbers and the profit it generated. Having attracted visitors from abroad it became the first ever international **trade show** (Bowdin *et al.*, 2011) which paved the way for the introduction of similar showcase venues in the following years including Alexandra Palace (1862) and Earls Court and Olympia (1887/86).

It was the development of commercial air travel in the twentieth century that was to have the greatest impact on this new MICE industry, but it would also have a devastating effect on the domestic tourism industry. The post-war introduction of the affordable package holiday abroad was hugely popular and swiftly and effectively destroyed domestic tourism as British holiday makers began to vacation abroad. Although British cities started to benefit from new inbound international tourism, London, Oxford, Stratford-upon-Avon and other historic locations became particularly popular, the coastal resorts could not attract international visitors nor compete with the package holiday. The result was that many Victorian resorts entered into a period of decline. Lots of theatres, hotels and winter gardens were abandoned and fell into disrepair and low morale and unemployment in these areas rose.

Conversely air travel propelled the exponential growth of the MICE industry enabling greater than ever numbers of people to travel internationally as well as domestically to attend business related meetings and events. As such the demand for suitable venues, and of course hotel rooms for delegates, was outweighing supply. This led the UK government to put into action a two pronged strategy to invest in the growing MICE industry. Firstly government funding was used to create purpose-built large, modern conference and exhibition venues in city centres and by the end of the 1970s the Wembley Conference Centre had been built in London and the NEC (National Exhibition Centre) opened its doors in Birmingham. Secondly the government had decided to invest in a number of failing coastal resorts by supporting hotel refurbishment and by creating purpose-built conference and exhibition space in order to lure business tourism into coastal areas. Consequently the Brighton Centre was built in 1977 and this pioneered much further development of south coast resorts including Bournemouth, Eastbourne and Torquay. Since the 1970s the business tourism industry has continued to grow year on year and so has the development of purpose-built event space in both coastal areas and inner cities. In the UK Manchester, Glasgow and Harrogate now compete with Blackpool and Southport for a piece of the very lucrative business events industry.

1.12 USING PURPOSE-BUILT VENUES

Purpose-built venues have generally been designed for conferences or exhibitions but their size, layout and facilities can make them excellent spaces for a range of events. As these venues have been specifically designed to suit the needs of the events industry, they have typically been built with excellent access. Most purpose-built venues have rear **service roads** and large **dock doors** big enough to allow large pieces of equipment or vehicles inside. **Floor loading limits** and ceiling heights will typically be greater than in any other types of venue and there will be a number of entrances and exits. Exhibition halls in particular will be huge and empty spaces which provide the event manager with a completely blank canvas for each event. On one hand, this can facilitate the adaption of the room to any given theme that the creative event organiser can come up with. On the other hand, this means that there is potentially a great cost involved in transforming a large, empty shell into a meaningful and enticing event space. Hiring purpose-built space can seem costly, particularly in comparison to other venues. However, designated event venues often have a superior electricity network (essential for most exhibitions) and large lighting and sound rigs which would otherwise come at an additional cost and take a lot of time to install, extending to the venue hire period. Many purpose-built venues have been designed to accommodate complex trade or consumer exhibitions as well as large international association conferences and the capacity of their largest room may well run into thousands of people. Although many of these venues also have smaller rooms generally these venues may not be suitable for more intimate gatherings. All in all, the 'range of services already in place is the real plus for convention centres' (Matthews, 2016, p. 171) and their supreme functionality contributes to their enduring success.

1.13 ACADEMIC VENUES

There are more than 130 universities operating in the UK alone who primarily offer higher education but typically also have a specialist events team dedicated to promoting the use of their campuses to event planners. Furthermore, there are a vast number of schools and colleges who have a thriving internal events programme ranging from parent/teacher evenings to summer fetes and most of these establishments can also be hired for private meetings, events and even weddings. It's not surprising that these academic venues are great locations for educational events such as conferences, due their primary function of supporting the development of knowledge, and this can add a certain level of prestige to these types of events. Additionally most university campuses will be made up of a large number of lecture halls and seminar rooms, all equipped with lecterns, microphones, projectors and screens which may suit a range of events. Additionally, partly due to the historical connection between education and sport, most of these establishments have extensive sporting facilities too such as gyms, tennis courts and pools. And of course universities are residential venues with many bedrooms for students on or near the campus. The combination of much indoor and outdoor space, plenty of AV equipment and (in many cases) decent en-suite accommodation, academic venues are well suited to a number of types of events. Furthermore, as much of these facilities would otherwise go unused out of term time, grateful university managers are only too glad to find a secondary use for their venue the rest of the year and offer competitive hire charges. Consequently academic venues can sometimes represent great value for money but the drawbacks of using these types of venues is firstly that availability is usually restricted to outside term-time only. Catering and accommodation may be readily available but the needs of students don't always match the expectations of others and they may fall short of what the event manager would like to offer event attendees.

1.14 THE EVENTS INDUSTRY TODAY

In the later part of the twentieth century the popularity and the value of events began to be particularly well documented and understood with national agencies such as the BVEP (Business Visits and Events Partnership) and international organisations such as ICCA (International Congress and Convention Association) regularly reporting on the volume and value of events, particularly with reference to the MICE sector. This has no doubt drawn the attention of a number of other venues that have since developed their space and operational strategies in order to target the events industry. Indeed an increasing number of sporting and academic venues as well as boats, bridges, parks, museums and other unique venues and open air locations are seeking to work with event planners. This trend represents the principal contribution to the diversity of venue supply in the twenty-first century (Rogers and Davidson, 2016). Additionally, the introduction of the Marriage (Approved Premises) Regulations in 1995 which allows civil weddings to be held in various venues other than churches, has led the way for many types of venues to secure a license to conduct marriages meaning that today it is possible to get married in all sorts of venues from the Sydney Opera House to Florida's Disneyworld.

In fact today there are an increasing number of consortia dedicated solely to promoting unique venues as event spaces that can be hired for all types of private events. Similarly there are trade shows, directories and websites which focus on one type of venue whether that be academic venues, sporting venues, hotels or purpose-built exhibition and/or conference centres. Hotels continue to be very popular venues with event managers and the UK Events Market Trends Survey (UKEMTS) consistently shows hotels to host more events than any other category of venue. This could be due to their event experience as most hotels regularly host a variety of events. This could also be down to the ease of use for event managers as catering will be done in-house and the hire charges are clear and self-explanatory. However, many industry professionals would suggest that event attendees are less enthusiastic about attending events in hotels as they can be seen as rather ordinary and sometimes drab venues. Instead there is a growing interest in using unusual venues because they allow the event manager to be more creative with the space available to them (Colston, 2014).

1.15 THE FUTURE OF VENUES

Much of the recent expansion of venues with event space has been driven by developments in the Middle East and South-East Asia where a number of 'new' destinations are entering the conference sector in particular (Davidson and Hyde, 2014). Consequently the number of hotels and purpose-built event spaces around the globe is greater than ever and dated venues face a mounting pressure to modernise. These spaces continue to be rivalled by academic, sporting and unusual venues seeking an increasing greater secondary income from the events industry. The introduction of pop-up venues has also added a new and interesting dimension to the ever growing number of options. This term refers to temporary structures that range from basic tents to multi-room constructions which are extremely flexible as they can be created to specific sizes and styles (King, 2015).

Private investment in venues is also increasing, with more examples of the awarding of naming rights. This is when private investors put so much capital into new venues that they are able to alter the name of the venue and examples of this include the O_2 Arena, the Emirates Stadium (home to Arsenal football club) and the now privatised Barclaycard Arena in Birmingham (formerly the National Indoor Arena).

Developing sustainable event space has become an increasing priority for venue and event managers and venues, new and old, face an ever growing pressure to meet event organisers' environmental targets. Similarly, globalisation and advances in technology have changed the way many attendees want to experience events today. Consequently these two trends are impacting the way venues are developing and planning for the future to ensure that the needs and expectations of event organisers and their clients can be met.

1.16 THE EVOLUTION OF VENUES – THE VENUE MANAGER'S PERSPECTIVE

As a venue manager it's important to be aware of the history and evolution of your venue. Understanding why the building has particular architectural features, internal layout and geographic location for example, can be useful when it comes to advising potential clients – event managers – on how to make good use of the space. A good venue manager will be able to offer tips and suggestions on how to incorporate the unique characteristics of the venue into the event programme or how the history and background of the building can enhance a contemporary event.

As a venue manager you will be acutely aware of the importance of making sure that the venue stands out in a densely competitive environment. It's essential to be able to make sure that the venue is marketed in a way that it is recognisable as a hireable event space. This can be quite a challenge if the venue has not been purpose built for the events industry but has evolved over time into a multipurpose space. For many venue managers this can mean overcoming the perception, or even misconception, that people may have about the venue. And as a venue manager you may find that you are frequently tackling a lack of awareness that the venue is even open to events business. For many venue managers, these challenges are

CASE STUDY 1.3 UNIQUE VENUES OF LONDON

Unique Venues of London was founded in 1993 and it is an organisation whose members are unique and specialist properties that derive a secondary income from the events industry. UVL aims to be the leading collection of venues and the voice for venues whose primary purpose is other than events.

To become a member of UVL you must be a venue with one of the following primary functions:

1. Art gallery, museum, art collection
2. Historic house, castle, palace, iconic building
3. Attraction
4. Performing arts, theatre, recording or film studio or set
5. Religious buildings and grounds
6. Society, college, academic institution, political or military HQ
7. Retail
8. Home of sport

Eligible members are judged on the calibre of their event spaces rather than their status or reputation and the event spaces must be available for commercial external hire. Members pay an annual subscription fee based on their turnover and in exchange they will have access to networking opportunities and training events. They will be featured in a comprehensive marketing campaign which includes the UVL brochure, website with a venue search facility and UVL's attendance at national and international trade shows.

Source: https://www.uniquevenuesoflondon.co.uk

compounded by a limited marketing budget. However, there are an increasing number of marketing consortia and sales initiatives that bring together venues with a common history or shared principal function. A good example of this is the organisation Unique Venues of London.

Recognising and embracing the history of your venue is an important step towards successfully marketing the space to potential clients. Joining a membership association or working with other similar venues, can be a useful way of accessing marketing channels that would otherwise be too expensive and it can be an effective way to promote the use of the space to event professionals. When working with event managers, draw their attention to the distinct features of the venue. Be honest about the challenges of working within your venue but discuss with them how the venue has evolved into a modern day space which is suitable for a range of events.

1.17 SUMMARY

Today's event manager has potentially thousands of viable venues to choose from for their next event. Purpose-built event venues compete with an ever increasing number of other types of buildings and sites, keen to work with event managers. Therefore choosing the right venue for any event is going to be a difficult decision. Understanding how and why venues have evolved can provide event managers with an insight into what makes them viable for events. Although every venue will be unique and will present the event organiser with its own set of advantages and challenges, each of these categories is identifiable not just by the main function of the venue but also by typical venue characteristics and traits. Recognising and understanding some of these commonalities can provide some time saving shortcuts when beginning the process of shortlisting suitable locations for events and it can also be inspirational in terms of incorporating the venue into the design of an event and maximising the use of the space in order to both meet the needs of the event and enhance the attendee experience.

The events industry, which is now recognised to include all manner of gatherings from meetings and exhibitions to festivals and celebrations, is one of the most valuable global industries and continues to expand year on year. Venues are not only an integral and essential part of this growing industry, but interest in venue management and investment in venue development is at an all time high. Twenty-first century venues may be brand new, state of the art spaces or ancient buildings with quirky features and an interesting history but collectively they provide event managers with spaces that can be used, moulded and adapted to provide perhaps the most important element of their event. Given that choosing an appropriate venue is one of the most important decisions that an event manager will make, and taking into account how much choice there is now available to them, it's unsurprising that choosing the right venue has become a complex and challenging problem. The following chapters will provide the event manager with insight, tips and information in order to help steer you through this decision and the subsequent process of working with a venue.

ACTIVITY 1.1

Compare and contrast types of events with types of venues and consider the potential benefits and drawbacks of each pairing. For example, if you were to stage a concert in a historical building, a fashion show in a church or a wedding in a visitor attraction what challenges might the venue present you with and how might the venue compliment the event?

1.18 FURTHER READING

The following sources are particularly useful for further reading on the subject of types of venues:

Purpose-built venues

Rogers, T. (2013) *Conferences and Conventions: A Global Industry* (3rd edn). London: Routledge.
Rogers, T. and Davidson, R. (2016) *Marketing Destinations and Venues for Conferences, Conventions and Business Events* (2nd edn). London: Routledge.

Unique venues

Whitfield, J. (2009) Why and How UK Visitor Attractions Diversify their Product to Offer Conference and Event Facilities, *Journal of Convention and Event Tourism*, 10, (1), 72–88.
Attractions Management magazine, available at: http://www.attractionsmanagement.com/

Sporting venues

Schwarz, E., Hall, S. and Shibli, S. (2015). *Sports Facility Operations Management* (3rd edn). London: Routledge.

The following sources are particularly useful for further reading on the subject of the history of different types of events:

Andrews, H. and Leopold, T. (2013) *Events and The Social Sciences*. London: Routledge.
Laing, J. and Frost, W. (Eds), (2015) *Rituals and Traditional Events in the Modern World*. London: Routledge.

Incorporating venues into the design of events

LEARNING OUTCOMES

By the end of Chapter 2, you should be able to:

- Understand the influence of stakeholders over the design of an event
- Appreciate the role of the venue in the creative design process
- Recognise the ways in which the characteristics of a venue can be used in event design
- Identify ways in which to create a sensory experience within a venue

2.1 INTRODUCTION

Event management is a complex and often lengthy process involving both design and production techniques to first identify the concept and create the event programme and then bring it to life. There is very limited event management literature which focuses on the role of the venue in the design stage, but what exists points to contradictory ideas. On one hand, it is suggested that the design phase must include thorough consideration of the use of space and flow of movement (Berridge, 2007), therefore it would seem that the venue must be predetermined. On the other hand, it can be argued that the creative design process should not be subjected to restrictions or barriers and therefore the venue should be selected to complement the event design once this stage of the process is complete. As Powell (2013, p. 59) explains, 'think: event first, venue second'. However, there is a consensus that having the 'right' venue for any event is crucial to the event's success because it provides the backdrop to all activities and as such the venue will make a significant contribution to the theme and ambience of any event. Furthermore, the venue's structure will influence the shape of the event, and the venue's facilities (entrances, toilets, etc.) will be used by attendees and will therefore impact their experience throughout. Consequently, choosing an appropriate venue and incorporating key aspects of the venue into the design of the event are crucial stages of event management, regardless of whether this happens as part of the initial design process or as part of the development or revisions of the original design. Therefore, this chapter will guide you through the early stages of event planning, focusing on the role of the venue in the process of designing the event.

2.2 EVENT DESIGN

Within academic literature there are different views of what design means within an event management context and there have been several attempts to describe event design. Getz (2012, p. 226) suggests that event design is a part technical and part creative act that has the purpose of 'facilitating unique, satisfying and memorable experiences'. Bladen *et al.* (2012, p. 56) propose the definition of event design as involving 'the conception of an intended event experience with the intention of delivering it through event production'. While Berridge (2007, p. 104), who has devoted a whole book to exploring event design, compares it to stage production whereby the designed elements of an event are those that are visible to attendees like the stage scenery and the costumes worn by actors. There is a general agreement that the event design phase precedes event production. This means that as the event manager you will begin by identifying the event concept which is the basic idea for the event and then create the content of the event and develop an event programme. Event production is the next phase of event management which involves bringing the concept and the programme to life and delivering the event. Figure 2.1 illustrates this basic event management process.

Figure 2.1 The event management process.

2.3 CREATIVITY

Every event that you will design and produce will be different and how much creative influence you have over the design phase of the event will vary and may be influenced by the wishes of the client and the resources available to you. However, as the event manager you will always have some creative input into the design of the event and in some cases you may have complete freedom to design and produce a truly original event based wholly on your own ideas.

There are diverse views on what creativity is and whether it is inherent or whether it is a skill that can be learnt, but within event management both Getz (2012) and Matthews (2007) say that some of us are more creative than others and this may be largely influenced by our upbringing. Despite this, there is much evidence to suggest that we can all develop our levels of creativity. We can do this by surrounding ourselves with creative people and by using triggers (activities, words, pictures, etc.) to stimulate idea generation. Goldblatt (2007) suggests visiting an art gallery, attending a live performance or even enrolling in a dance class to stimulate the creative thought process. Matthews (2007) also advocates brainstorming (perhaps with random words or images), developing mood boards and attending other events as useful activities to trigger a creative response.

There is no clear view on whether or not (or to what extent) the venue should feature in the process of generating ideas for the event programme. It could be argued that pictures of venues can be used as triggers in a brainstorming session, or attending an event in a venue could stimulate creative thoughts. Going to look around a venue might suggest a potential theme for an event or indicate types of activities that lend themselves to that space. However, Bowdin et al. (2011, p. 246) argue that the brainstorming process works best with no rules. This suggests that having a predetermined venue or budget is a rule which is going to stifle the creative process and therefore the venue should not be considered during the design phase.

Conversely Matthews (2007) affirms that the creative process must be built upon extensive knowledge of the resources available. This may include the venue but it will of course include factors which will determine the venue, such as the budget. Berridge (2007) agrees, arguing that creativity works best when built around a framework which involves a full appraisal of the venue. This therefore suggests that the venue plays a crucial role in the early stages of event design. However, Berridge (2007) also puts forward the view that the venue should complement the theme of the event, thus inferring it should be identified once the design process is underway. And Bowdin et al. (2011, p. 246) confirm that the venue must 'meet the needs of the event', which is perfectly reasonable although the precise shape and nature of these needs is unlikely to be clear until the designed event programme has been fully developed.

As there is no such thing as the completely perfect space for any event, the use of any venue will come with challenges and restrictions which could be seen as barriers to idea generation during the creative design phase. Although these challenges will need to be overcome and the restrictions will need to be adhered to, these will be tackled as part of the production phase of event management.

ACTIVITY 2.1

Imagine that you have been tasked with designing a product launch (e.g. a new car). Brainstorm ideas for the event using triggers, including a variety of pictures from magazines and an online random word generator.

2.4 THE ROLE OF THE VENUE IN EVENT DESIGN

Despite the conundrum of whether or not the venue is a trigger or a barrier to generating creative ideas, the majority of the viewpoints suggest that the venue is such an important part of successful event management that it should be incorporated early into the design phase of the planning process. Goldblatt (2007, p. 49) indicates that the most effective event designer will give much consideration to the 'personality' of the venue and Shone and Parry (2010) confirm that the venue's internal layout and existing decoration should be considered in the initial stage of event design.

The venue itself is a significant contributor to the event programme as it is part of the whole attraction of the event. The architecture, layout, furniture and décor of the venue may complement the programme that you are designing. In other words, as you begin to design the content of the event it can be useful to reflect on how the event might be shaped around one or more potential venues.

ACTIVITY 2.2

Imagine that you have been tasked with designing a product launch (e.g. a new car) in a predetermined venue (which you can choose). Brainstorm ideas for the event using triggers to include photos of the venue and text from the venue's website. Compare your event design with what you produced for Activity 2.1.

Ferdinand and Kitchin (2012) explain that the design of the venue itself will influence not only the experience of the audience, but also their emotions, and therefore the theme of the event should be carefully matched to an appropriate venue. It may be possible to adapt the 'wrong' venue to match the theme of the event, but only providing you have enough time and resources to achieve this (Shone and Parry, 2010). Furthermore, even if you end up choosing a venue which is a little soulless, such as a large purpose-built exhibition space, these can be exciting places to bring to life. A blank canvas presents the event manager with the opportunity to be imaginative, and taking an unconventional approach to personalising a venue is an opportunity to wow both the client and the audience.

Therefore, whether you decide to incorporate the venue into the early stages of creative event design or not, the event programme will need to be flexible enough to adapt to the venue's layout and requirements. Matthews (2016) explains that every venue will come with limitations, some more frustrating than others, such as poor accessibility, inadequate power and limited onsite facilities. This means that in your role as event designer, as you develop the programme you will need to take into account various practical aspects of the venue such as the layout, lighting, colour scheme and décor. But the question remains, when should you incorporate the choice of venue into the event design process? This is perhaps best resolved on an event by event basis, by taking into account the input of the client, the content of the event brief and the event aims and objectives.

2.5 THE CLIENT

As a professional event manager, you will be designing and delivering events for a client. The client may be an individual who requires your help to deliver a personal event such as a wedding or other celebration. Alternatively, the client may be one or several people who belong to, work for or represent a company or an organisation who are going to employ you to deliver an event. In some cases the client may represent several organisations, or you may work with a team of

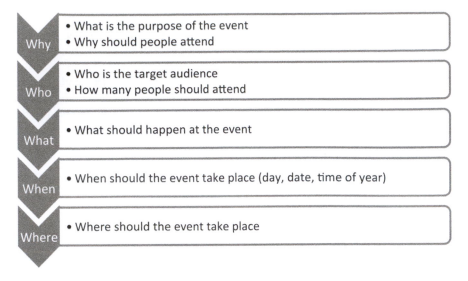

Figure 2.2 The Five Ws.

Adapted from Dowson and Bassett (2015, p. 25).

clients from across several companies who wish to collaborate on one event. Usually at the start of your relationship with the client, the client will provide you with an event brief.

A brief is usually a set of written instructions which outline the concept (the basic idea) and the purpose of the event and, depending on the client's own background and experience of events, they may provide you with a short and vague brief or a comprehensive and detailed set of written instructions. If the client's brief is not very clear then it is a good idea to spend some time with them getting to understand why they want to hold the event and what they would like to achieve. The event concept 'must be capable of achieving the event's purpose, flexible enough to serve the full range of stakeholders and achievable within the range of resources' (Bowdin *et al.*, 2011, p. 239).

A useful tool for discussing and confirming the brief with the client, is Dowson and Bassett's (2015) Five Ws which will help to establish why the event is going to take place, what needs to happen at the event, where and when the event will take place and who should be invited.

Dowson and Bassett's (2015) The Five Ws indicates that the client may have a firm idea of the location and/or the venue that they would prefer for the event. This is a well supported view in the literature and as Bladen *et al.* (2012) confirm, the client may well dictate to the event manager which venue they must use. If this is the case, it is worth talking this over with the client to establish exactly why they want to use this venue. It could be because it is in a convenient location or because it appears to the client to be an appropriate choice in terms of venue type or event theme. It could also be because the client has been there before and in this case in particular, it is important to understand what has motivated the client to preselect the venue for this event and how they envisage their event being staged in this particular location. If they have attended an event in the venue before, was it the same type of event as the one you are organising? Was it held at the same time of year or same time of day? If not, you will need to assess whether or not the venue is suitable and viable for the event that you are planning and discuss this, carefully, with the client. If your client has not provided you with a written brief, Table 2.1 can be used as a template and you can ask the client to fill it in as much as they can.

Table 2.1 Template for the client brief

Name of organisation	
Name of contact	<your name>
Title	<your job title>
Email address	
Phone number	
Concept	<details about why the event should be held/if it's been held before, what should happen at the event and background information about the event/the idea>
Event aim	<key purpose of the event>
Event objectives	<additional purposes>
Target audience	
Date	<add in any specific times/days/dates/seasons to use or to avoid>
Event parameters	<are there any venues, suppliers, activities that can't be used>
Budget	
Additional notes or requests	

As part of the process of getting to know your client it is also worth clarifying their level of authority over the event. For example, some individual clients will be able to make all the final decisions about every aspect of the event from selecting the venue to finalising the programme. If your client is actually several people, they may need to jointly agree decisions before you can proceed. Other clients may need to seek approval from their line manager or sometimes from a group of board members. This of course will mean that the decision-making process may not be straightforward. Most clients will be influenced by their colleagues or friends too and may want some time to think over your suggestions. A client may want to run your ideas past a co-worker or, with a wedding for example, past their best friend or family before coming to a final decision. Therefore, it is a good idea to get a sense of how slowly or quickly decisions will be made by your client quite early on in the event design phase, and how involved they want to be in key decisions such as choosing the venue.

2.6 THE EVENT AIMS AND OBJECTIVES

The initial phase of event planning must begin with a clear understanding of the purpose of the event. This usually means working closely with the client to fully establish their event aims and objectives. In order to design an event that reaches its potential, the event manager must have a clear and comprehensive understanding of what the client wants to achieve by staging the event, and what are the key elements that must be incorporated into the design of the event.

While the written brief is a useful starting point, these instructions can often be unrealistic and having a face-to-face chat with a client is a good way of getting a better idea of what they are trying to achieve. For example, a client may say that they want to hold a party for their staff as a thank you for their hard work during the year. While this is a clear aim, there may be some underlying objectives that are also important to the client. For example, it is worth asking the client what hard work they want to recognise, as the client may wish to draw attention to specific individual or team achievements. Is the event about building morale and, if so, is it important that the senior managers contribute to the event with speeches or awards? Additionally, if the company are paying for the event, then they may wish to use the event for training purposes and might, for example, use the event to introduce new company initiatives or targets. As you work with the client to elicit their objectives, ensure that they are SMART – specific, measurable, achievable, realistic and time-bound.

If the conversation with the client results in the formation of several SMART objectives it is also worth putting them in order by asking the client to determine which of the objectives are essential and which are less important. Few clients have an unlimited budget and most event managers will have to work within a set budget and to a specific deadline, therefore it may be prudent to discuss these limitations early on with the client and prioritise the objectives accordingly.

Table 2.2 SMART objectives

Specific	Make sure that each objective sets out just one, clear action to be met.
Measurable	Make sure that each objective can be measured in some way which will help you to demonstrate to the client that it has been achieved.
Achievable	Refine each objective so that it sets out an action which is appropriate to the resources available to deliver the event.
Realistic	Make sure that each objective is appropriate to the overall aim of the event.
Time-bound	Set time limits for each objective that will work within the overall time scale of the event management process.

2.7 THE TARGET AUDIENCE

Your client may also have a very clear idea of who should attend the event and as part of understanding the brief, it is important to go over this. For example, if you are organising a private event then the target audience might be entirely predetermined and may be personally invited to attend. For example, most couples will specify the guest list to their wedding, although it is still worth clarifying if the guest list includes children or plus ones (where one invitee may bring a guest). If the event is going to be open to the public it is essential that you spend some time with your client understanding whether or not they want to target a specific demographic (age group, gender, etc.). An event can have many target audiences who share different characteristics, but the nature of the intended audience will shape every aspect of the design of the event from the theme to the programme and the venue. So it is important to understand if your client has strong preferences for who they wish to target to attend the event. It is then essential to undertake some research on the intended audience to understand their key characteristics.

The characteristics of the intended target audience may have a significant influence over the choice of venue. For example, as with the client, some members of the audience may have prior experience of or preconceived ideas about venues (good or bad). They may live near to or far away from the venue, and this, as well as how easy it is for them to travel to the venue, is likely to contribute to their decision to attend or not.

Ultimately, as the event manager, it is your job to work towards what your client wants to achieve and this will influence the decisions you make, including choice of venue, above the opinions of the potential audience.

2.8 THE BUDGET AND OTHER PARAMETERS

It is important to discuss the client's budget very early on in the process as this will influence every aspect of event planning, and it will have a clear impact on which venues can be considered and which are going to be too expensive. It is important to begin by clarifying the financial plan for the event. For example, is the overall aim to fundraise or is one of the objectives making a profit? If so, the event must be designed in order to raise money to meet a monetary target. If not, the event manager will still need to manage expenses carefully to ensure the event breaks even, and in either case it is essential to know early on how far the budget must stretch. Important questions to ask include whether or not attendees will pay to attend or will the event be free? Does the budget cover things like food and drink, or will attendees pay for what they consume?

It is also important to clarify with the client whether or not an income can be made from sources other than ticket sales. For example, sponsorship or selling **trade pitches** at the event may bring in additional income before event day, and the sale of mementos and **merchandise** may bring in an income on event day. These and other potential sources of income are shown in Figure 2.3.

The answers to these questions may have a significant impact on choice of venue. For example, if the client is open to the idea (or even very keen) to sell space to traders then this may impact the size or layout of the venue needed to accommodate this element.

At the start of the design process it is also very important to have a frank discussion with the client about any parameters that will influence the event. Parameters are boundaries or

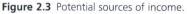

Figure 2.3 Potential sources of income.

limitations that may shape every decision that you make and these can include the client specifying any venues or suppliers that shouldn't be used, any themes or activities deemed inappropriate, whether children can or can't attend and so on.

2.9 STAKEHOLDERS

Any event will be influenced to a greater or lesser degree by its stakeholders. Stakeholders include anyone with an interested in or who may be affected by the event and therefore typical event stakeholders include the client, the venue, the event manager, the attendees, but also local residents and businesses, the local council and potentially the media and the emergency services. Figure 2.4 shows an example of stakeholders for a small-scale community festival.

Figure 2.4 Community festival stakeholders.

Each stakeholder, or stakeholder group, will have a different level of interest in your event and influence over what you do. The Mendelow framework is a useful tool for mapping the amount of interest and influence that stakeholders have with regards to your event and it is based on your judgement as to whether these are high or low. High power, high interest stakeholders are significant and this means that you should work closely with them and involve them in your event planning. The venue is a good example of a high power and high interest stakeholder, because the venue can significantly shape the event. If your stakeholder has high power but low interest they are powerful organisations or people, but they aren't very interested in your event and as such you should ensure that you work within their rules and guidelines. The low power, high interest stakeholders should be kept informed by letting them know about your event and involving them if appropriate and the low power, low interest stakeholders require limited time from you.

High power, low interest (keep satisfied)	High power, high interest (key player)
Low power, low interest (minimal effort)	Low power, high interest (keep informed)

Interest

Figure 2.5 The Mendelow framework.

Adapted from Dowson and Bassett (2015).

The framework is a simple tool which provides a useful mechanism for identifying the connection of each stakeholder with the event and suggesting to what extent you need to involve them in the event planning process.

2.10 THE PROGRAMME

Once the event aims, objectives and parameters have been agreed with the client, you can begin to develop the event programme. Some clients may have a clear idea of what they want and may provide you with details of the activities, performers or themes that they want to feature at the event. Other clients may leave this up to you and allow you to take full responsibility for the creative development of the event programme. It can be useful if a client has a clear idea of what they want as this may save you time developing and presenting your ideas only for the client to then rule them out. On the other hand, designing the event can be the most enjoyable aspect of event management and having full creative control can be exhilarating and may give you the chance to inspire your client as you present them with suggestions that they had never thought possible, or even considered.

2.11 THEMING

Events are part of the **experience economy** which means that attending a live event gives participants a unique experience that they cannot get elsewhere. Therefore, because events are designed, the event organiser can shape and influence that experience. Having a distinct theme can help you to create an experience that your attendees will recognise, understand and engage with. Themes can be tangible or intangible, visual and sensory. As Getz (2012) explains, the use of a particular colour, for example, can be reflected in the décor of the venue as well as the type and nature of entertainment you provide. There could be specific activities or games that participants will be involved in. You could have a fantasy theme such as a fairy-tale or space, a historical theme such as the roaring twenties, a TV or film-based theme and this could be evident in the décor and entertainment. The theme could be connected with an emotion, a celebration of something specific. It could have an intellectual theme and relate to an event that is focused on education or problem solving.

THE INDUSTRY EXPERT'S VIEW 2.1

GETTING CREATIVE WITH WEDDINGS

Marie Haverly, The Wedding Expert, Founder of Isabella Weddings & Events, www.isabellaweddings.co.uk

With every bridal magazine on the shelf in the newsagents offering a generous amount of wedding inspiration you'd be forgiven if you thought that styling a wedding or finding a theme would be easy to achieve. Whenever I meet a couple for the first time they are usually bursting with fabulous ideas of how to let their personalities shine through on their wedding day. Creativity for most lies in the powers of Pinterest or magazine cuttings and inspiration can be found in many places. It is usually easy to start putting ideas down on paper and begin to work through them. However, for some, even this is daunting and trying to put a theme together can be incredibly stressful for those who are not usually creative in their day-to-day lives.

I often meet brides who have lots of ideas but are not sure where and how to source them or re-create the DIY ideas they have found. Not everyone has a creative soul. So I allow them to be honest with themselves, not everyone is arty, I love to be creative but I lack ability in some areas, as do many of us. I will sit down with my couples and run through their ideas, I create a mood-board with them or perhaps start a scrapbook for them so that they can begin to see the theme take form. We start with a large piece of corkboard. Then gather inspiration from bridal mags, print outs, swatches of material, paint testers, a favourite scarf etc., and start pinning these items on the board (maybe not that scarf). It doesn't have to be in any order but, to be a little more organised, section off areas of the board for areas of the wedding – e.g., outfits, colours, style, food and drink. As you start to pin and stick, their style will shine through, it doesn't have to make sense to start with and that's the fun of it. Then we discuss how we are actually going to achieve what they want and whether all of the options are actually practical.

There are many options such as hiring an expert to make or create what a client needs, and you can hire in props to add to a theme or buy everything ready-made. Some, but not all, couples have the time and desire to sit and make 125 chair sashes and if they want to have the hands-on approach then I encourage them to draft in some help and spread the work so it stays fun.

But you don't have to have a theme for a wedding day, so don't fall into the trap of thinking you must have one – vintage, modern, nautical, steampunk. The couple can be themselves and surround themselves with things they love, items that make them happy despite what category they fall into, and enjoy colours that make their hearts smile – this will be a perfect way to reflect their love for each other without feeling like they have to be a slave to a theme.

Image 2.1 An example of a mood board.

Source: Ikonworks photography, www.ikonworks.co.uk, shooting at Emmy London.

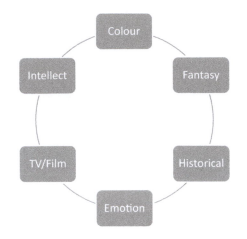

Figure 2.6 Themes.

As the event designer you may wish to develop the programme and then start the process of finding a suitable venue and this is the path Fenich (2012) would suggest, the thinking being that the success of the event rests on matching the characteristics of the event to the venue. Alternatively, the venue may be the inspiration for a suitable theme, particularly if you are going to use a unique venue that is full of quirky features and distinct décor. The additional benefits of this is that although using a unique venue may be costly, the hire charges might be offset by the saving on theming and decoration as explained by Matthews (2016, p. 172):

> Palaces, fortresses, temples, castle, ancient ruins and ancient theatres . . . already hold a certain mystique as ritual spaces and may need little if any additional decorating.

2.12 EVENT PSYCHOLOGY

As part of the event design process it is worth taking some time to consider the role of psychology in shaping an event that will have specific outcomes and will create a memorable experience for attendees. Behaviourism is the theory that how we act is influenced by conditioning and therefore how we behave can depend on how our senses are stimulated. Bladen *et al.* (2012, p. 71) illustrate this with the example of being at an event and smelling food being cooked. When this happens, we will start to feel hungry and start to anticipate being fed. If we see beautifully dressed tables and food being served by well-dressed waiters onto china plates we will expect the food to be of high quality and we are likely to adapt our behaviour to reflect what we believe is normal behaviour in this situation (in other words we will put on manners as if we were at a top class restaurant). Furthermore, operant conditioning suggests that we are aware that our behaviour has consequences and how we behave will result in us being punished or being rewarded. So, if at this event we smell the food, see it being served, sit down, put a napkin on our lap and politely wait for our food, we know we will be rewarded with a delicious meal. If we are rude to the waiter and smash the crockery we know that we may be asked to leave as punishment.

So, what this means to the event manager is that when we design an event which stimulates the senses in a particular way, we will be encouraging attendees to behave in a

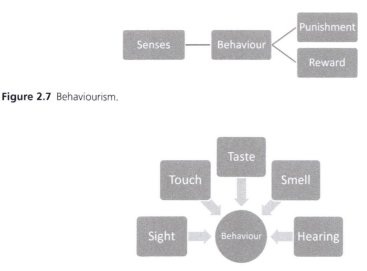

Figure 2.7 Behaviourism.

Figure 2.8 Positive and negative stimuli.

certain way. Both positive and negative stimuli can be used to do this as they will affect behaviour in different ways. Examples of positive stimulation are altering the lighting at an event to control the mood (dimming lights to get people to pay attention to a film or speaker), playing lively music to get people feeling energised or positive.

You can also use negative stimuli to control behaviour. Bladen *et al.* (2012, p. 72) illustrate this by explaining that at most events attendees will have to do certain things that they don't particularly want to – queue to get in, fill in paperwork, etc. Ways to ensure that your attendees comply, and accept these as necessary parts of the event, is to use stimuli such as putting up signage, making announcements and having formally dressed security staff at entrances to reinforce the importance of these processes.

Therefore, as you continue to develop and design your event consider how you can make it a sensory experience for the attendee (so that they will engage with the event and remember it), but also how you can stimulate attendee senses in order to get them to behave in a certain way. How you do this should connect very obviously with your theme and with the event objectives.

2.13 SYMBOLIC INTERACTION THEORY

Symbolic interaction theory suggests that how human beings act is also affected by what meaning we give to everything around us. In other words, what we think about people, objects and less tangible things such as ideas, influences our behaviour. What things mean to us and what we think about them will be shaped by the lives we have lived up to now. Where people have had a common upbringing or common life experiences they may have similar opinions about other people, objects or ideas. This means that as an event manager, you can influence the way people behave at events by using symbols to encourage attendees into thinking in a certain way about other people, objects or ideas and getting them to behave in a certain way. Symbols might include words, logos, icons or pictures, and when deciding what symbols to

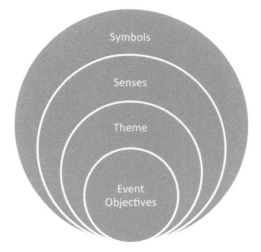

Figure 2.9 Event design.

use at your event (and when marketing your event) you must consider once again your target audience and try to work out what you know about them and what symbols (words, pictures, etc.) are going to resonate with them.

Shone and Parry (2010) suggest that when designing a full sensory event experience, it may be best to choose a venue that can be readily adapted to the theme. Therefore, the process of shortlisting potential venues might overlap with the creative design phase. Distinct unique venues might be appropriate to historical or fantasy themes, for example, and academic venues might work well for educational events that aim to inspire or perhaps need to convey a sense of prestige. If you choose to leave the venue shortlisting until after the event design process is well underway, it is worth remembering that many venues have strict rules prohibiting the use of temporary wall fixtures. Some venues, such as museums, will not remove artefacts and exhibits, and others will restrict the type of decoration or props that can be used on site. Although this is not necessarily a barrier to theming the event, it may mean that as the event manager you have to be particularly creative in how you are going to ensure that the theme is evident in and around the venue. And as you develop your event programme and decide what your attendees will be doing, you will design an event that is built around the event objectives as set down by the client. Build a clear theme around these, add in sensory experiences and symbols that are going to shape the way your attendees behave at your event and ultimately how they connect with and experience your event.

2.14 AMBIENCE

The ambience or the mood of the event is significant, and Shone and Parry (2010) suggest that an event with an appropriate atmosphere may be a great success while an event with a poor ambience is likely to be a great failure. Furthermore, if you are trying to create a particular mood for your event that the venue does not naturally imbue, then you will need to invest in additional decoration to ensure the ambience at the venue and at the event are a match (Whova, 2015). The mood can be designed by the event organiser using various tools, such as lighting and

Image 2.2 The Sydney Opera House.
Source: © Deb Gillespie/Tourism Australia.

sound effects, as well as props, entertainment and food. The contribution of the venue to the overall mood is going to be significant, and to a certain extent this can be shaped and controlled by the event designer. The venue may already complement the theme of the event, but if not, it can usually be transformed in order to match the theme and imbue the right ambience, although this may come at a significant design cost. However, many event designers take a different approach and will visit the venue during the design phase to absorb the pre-existing venue atmosphere and aim to incorporate the 'personality' of the venue into the design of the event for greater effectiveness (Goldblatt, 2007, p. 177). For example, a historical venue may have creaking doors, dark corridors with nooks and crannies that enhance ghostly themed events, while a famous sporting venue may be filled with competition memorabilia that imbues a sense of glorious determination that will complement a celebratory or a competitive event. Some venues, such as the Sydney Opera House, have such a distinctive design and façade that the image of the venue is instantly recognisable the world over.

However, if you are going to design the event and then look for a suitable venue, a degree of flexibility in the event planning is essential as the venue will ultimately provide the foundation for the event and therefore it will determine the layout of the event and influence the social interactions that will take place there (Ferdinand and Kitchin, 2012, p. 58). Additionally, the event designer will need to consider the venue's architecture and position. For example, beautiful outlooks onto lush gardens or busy riverways might be rather mesmerising, but they could provide unwanted distraction or clash with a contrasting theme. Also, although you may have extensive creative control of the rooms you are hiring within the venue, rarely can you command such influence over the exterior of the building, particularly the main entrance. As this provides attendees with their first taste of event day, you may wish to consider what first impression the front of the building creates.

2.15 ARCHITECTURE

As well as the main entrance to the building, there are other aspects of the venue that you may only be able to alter providing you have an extensive budget, permission of the venue and often only if you have exclusive use of the venue for the event. And even in this case, there will still be many aspects of the venue that cannot be altered and that therefore should be considered as part of the event design process whether this is from the outset or further along the creative process.

The entrance hall, foyer or reception area to the venue may be adaptable to your event, but in many cases this will be a shared area of the venue which may mean that you are restricted in theming, decorating or altering this part of the building. The location of each room and the connecting corridors may be areas that you can personalise but the overall layout, width of corridors and ceiling height will generally be beyond your control. The toilets, lifts and staircases are also areas that you may be able to theme but in many cases, these are shared facilities that cannot be personalised. There may be restrictions on covering up or altering the flooring, carpeting and wallpaper or paint in each area of the venue and this may be particularly true of listed buildings. The lighting in each room may be adjustable but this is not always the case. Similarly, some venues have large windows which let in natural light, others are very dark, and some venues will have **blackout facilities** while others don't. Finally, some venues will have fixtures or items of furniture that cannot be removed as well as fireplaces, bannisters, arches, columns and decorative features such as **moulding** or **latticework**. Therefore, a site inspection of the venue to review these, and other important aspects of the venue, is an essential part of the design process and this is discussed in detail in Chapter 6. However, choosing the destination for the event can sometimes be an even bigger and more complex decision than choosing a venue and this will be explored in detail in the next chapter.

2.16 INCORPORATING VENUES INTO THE DESIGN OF EVENTS – THE VENUE MANAGER'S PERSPECTIVE

It can be hugely beneficial to the venue to be involved in the early stages of event design, and for the venue manager it can be an opportunity to market the venue to potential clients as a viable space for their event. Drawing on your unparalleled knowledge of the venue, you will be in the best position to give lots of advice and suggestions on how to develop a theme and an event programme that will be suited to the building. As a venue manager, you will develop an intimate knowledge of the building as all of back and front of house areas will be familiar to you. You will know the layout and have first-hand experience of how people move around the building. You will understand how each room has unique features, acoustics and ambience. From your experience of overseeing events in the venue, you will have an excellent appreciation of what works particularly well in the space in terms of layout, theming and activities. Try to collect photos of successful events held in the venue, and testimonials from satisfied customers. Not only can they be very useful tools that you can use to illustrate the potential of the venue, but as Rogers (2013, p. 143) suggests, this can really impress new clients.

Venue managers are not always invited to contribute to the early event design process and sometimes they can seem unwilling or unable to get involved in the creative process before the venue is booked. Yet, being a proactive venue manager can reap rewards as you will usually have a far better understanding of the potential of the venue as well as its limitations. It's important to be honest with event managers and, for example, to admit when your venue isn't suited to the programme or the theme. However, if there is scope to adapt the venue or to adapt the design then offer to help with the creative process. This might involve inviting event managers to visit the venue, providing them with a hands-on guided tour or the opportunity to attend a similar event. You can show them videos and photos of past events and, drawing on your own experience, and the experience of other venue staff, you can give examples of what could work really well in the space. If the client has yet to make a final decision about which venue to book, every conversation that you have with them is an opportunity for you to promote the venue. So it's worth being involved in the creative design process. Even if you lose out on securing this particular event, the event manager will remember you for being helpful and knowledgeable and may recommend you to others or approach you again in the future as they start to plan another event.

2.17 SUMMARY

Event design and delivery begins with understanding what your client is trying to achieve. Going over the brief for the event and making sure that you have a clear understanding of the event aims and objectives is essential. It is important to discuss with the client the intended target audience, the budget and any event parameters. The client may have already decided which venue to use for the event or they may have very specific ideas about what venues they believe to be suitable or unsuitable for their event. Therefore, you may wish to incorporate the venue into the initial design phase of the event. Alternatively, you may wish to begin to design the event and then choose a venue which complements the concept and programme that you are developing. The creative process of designing an event can be very enjoyable and for many, this element of event management is the most rewarding and the most fun. Designing a sensory event around a clear theme is the starting point for delivering a memorable event that attendees will fully engage with. Whether or not you include the venue early on in the design process, it is important to remember that the venue will be the scaffolding upon which you will build your event and therefore the venue will play a significant role in the event. Consequently, it is essential to ensure your event design is flexible enough to, at the very least, accommodate key architectural features of the building. Alternatively, you may wish to build the event around the venue, taking inspiration from the unique qualities that each venue can offer the event manager.

2.18 FURTHER READING

The following sources are particularly useful for further reading on the subject of event design:

Berridge, G. (2007) *Events Design and Experience*. London: Routledge.
Matthews, D. (2016) *Special Event Production: The Process* (2nd edn). London: Routledge.
Powell, C. (2013) *How to Deliver Outstanding Corporate Events*. Publisher: Author.
BizBash publications (available at www.bizbash.com).
Event MB publications (available at www.eventmanagerblog.com).

Choosing a destination

LEARNING OUTCOMES

By the end of Chapter 3, you should be able to:

- Understand the factors that can influence the choice of event destination
- Recognise the role of intermediaries in connecting destinations and event managers
- Assess the tools available to assist event managers in the search for a destination

3.1 INTRODUCTION

Having established the role that the venue is going to play in the event itself, the process of venue shortlisting and selection can begin. This exercise can be time consuming and complex so the next two chapters are devoted to exploring this and together they will provide plenty of useful tips in order to conduct a more efficient search. The first step in choosing an appropriate venue is deciding on the geographical location of the event. Frequently the event manager's client will have a strong view on where the event should be held. At other times the event may be specifically aimed at a particular audience and this will determine the location. However, the rest of the time the event manager may be required to identify a suitable destination for the event. This may be within a particular region or country but on occasion they may even have the choice of locating the event anywhere in the world. As it is now easier than ever to travel to the remotest parts of the globe, this means that choosing a destination for an event is a mammoth decision in itself and narrowing down the list of possible locations can be a long and difficult process. This chapter aims to provide an insight into key considerations when assessing what a destination can offer, how to tap into local expertise and therefore how to conduct an efficient search for the right location for an event.

3.2 EVENT TOURISM

The events industry has expanded at a phenomenal rate in the last 20 years and such growth means that it is now one of the most lucrative and fastest growing industries in the world. Event tourism is a phenomenon which was first identified in the 1980s (Raj *et al.*, 2013, p. 31). The term refers to the influx of visitors to a location to attend a specific event and this branch of tourism has the potential to generate huge economic activity. Event attendees will spend money in the destination on travel, accommodation, food and drink, shopping, sightseeing and using leisure and entertainment facilities. This is often referred to as the multiplier effect or 'inscope expenditure' (Edwards *et al.*, 2014, p. 409) and both are terms that describe money generated by the event that the host destination would not have received if the event had not taken place there. This form of tourism can contribute to sustaining employment in towns and cities that would otherwise struggle to offer year-round jobs and money generated from event visitors can contribute to the development of local facilities and the creation of business opportunities. Therefore event tourism has the potential to generate a substantial income even in under-developed countries. Additionally, event tourism can promote community cohesion and a range of cultural benefits to residents (Raj *et al.*, 2013). Therefore, it's not surprising that many governments around the world have begun to strategically develop their **infrastructure** in order to attract tourists and event planners and join this competitive and lucrative market. Quinn (2013, p. 72) notes that the scale of investment has been particularly evident in the UK, Australia, South Africa, Thailand and Dubai while Park *et al.* (2014) point to increasing competition from some of Asia's strongest economies including Malaysia, South Korea, China and Singapore.

Even well developed countries have continued to invest in their infrastructure in order to compete with newer destinations and more established event locations in America and much of Western Europe have invested in new or refurbished venues including state of the art hotels and purpose-built exhibition space. Transport systems have been updated to provide additional and faster land connections, and despite the environmental concerns and controversy, airport expansion is a continuing global trend. The rise in the number of budget airlines has led to cheaper air travel and the number of domestic and international passenger flights is at an all-time high. All of these developments have led to a disposition for travelling and an eagerness to explore new territories but for the event manager, this has created the impossible task of choosing from an ever-growing list of potential locations.

3.3 CLIENT REQUIREMENTS AND ATTENDEE PROFILE

To begin the search the event manager may need to review their client's brief to ensure that they have a comprehensive understanding of why the event is to be held, what the client wants to achieve, and whether they have any specific destination and venue requirements.

CASE STUDY 3.1 SINGAPORE: A THRIVING DESTINATION IN ASIA

Since gaining independence from Malaysia in 1965 Singapore has become a thriving tourism and events hotspot thanks to government funding and an ambitious plan to make the country a destination of choice for domestic and international tourists and event planners. In 2016 the government unveiled a new 5-year plan which will see further investment of more than £353 million going into a Tourism Development Fund (TDF). At the heart of the plan is a focus on encouraging the collaboration of destination stakeholders in order to cement Singapore as a leading destination for international visitors and events.

Travel within Asia has been very healthy for a number of years, partly due to the disposition of an emerging Asian middle class. The government's 5-year plan will build on what has already been achieved, as the country already attracts high-yielding tourists from Indonesia, Malaysia (and Australia), but now the plan is to also target visitors from developing countries such as Myanmar and long haul markets in Europe and the US. The MICE sector has arguably had the greatest impact on Singapore so far as although business tourists only account for a fifth of all travellers to (and within) the country, they generate a third of the total tourism income. Therefore it's no surprise that the chief executive of the Singapore Tourism Board (STB) recently announced that as part of the 5-year plan, the STB will continue to support the Business Events in Singapore (BEiS) fund in order to draw in more quality MICE events to the country. This will involve encouraging destination stakeholders to work together including key organisations such as the Singapore Hotel Association (SHA) and the Singapore Association of Convention and Exhibition Organisers and Suppliers (Saceos). An example of how this could work is venues collaborating on joint bids for large scale events, where each venue hosts an element of the event. Money from the BEiS fund could then be used to provide shuttle bus transport for event attendees to take them from venue to venue.

A significant part of the TDF fund will go towards increasing the number of skilled workers in the tourism and events industry. Money will be spent on encouraging Singaporeans to enter into these industries as developing manpower is a key element of the government's 5-year plan. One such initiative will see the STB working with the SHA to develop career strategy plans for Singaporeans and offer bursaries of around £2,500 to help mid-career professionals to develop and learn new skills.

Technology is also under the spotlight and funding has been set aside to facilitate using technology to increase efficiency in hotels. Money has also been ring-fenced to develop a new mobile app which will personalise the visitor experience to the country by giving tourists a single online resource detailing events, services and promotions available to them during their stay. According to the chief technology officer for the STB, this is so that visitors will view the country as a 'single, unified, mega attraction'.

The Singaporean government have made their intentions clear; they want their tourism industry to compete with the best in the world and their financial investment and long term planning shows commitment to their tourism and events industry. The collaboration of destination stakeholders is at the heart of the plan and as Saceos president Janet Tan-Collis confirms 'if we can all agree to work together, I think . . . Singapore can win'.

Source: Ramchandani (2016).

Table 3.1 Key destination requirements

Attendee requirements	Event venue facilities
	Local shops
	Restaurants
	Attractions and sightseeing opportunities
	Local safety
Organiser requirements	Event venue facilities
	Accessibility, especially convenient flights
	Destination infrastructure
	Range of accommodation
	Social and political stability of destination

Source: Park *et al.* (2014).

Alongside this the event manager needs to have a clear idea of who the event attendees are going to be and what their motivation is for going to the event. In their investigation into conference management, Park *et al.* (2014) reviewed the most important destination requirements for attendees and for the event organiser. Table 3.1 summarises their key findings which indicates that a range of destination features is important but that the event venue is equally important to attendees and organiser.

What is expected from the venue is likely to depend on the type of event held there, and this is discussed in more detail in Chapter 4. Although Park *et al.* (2014) suggest that the event manager will have more influence over choice of venue than attendees, it is essential to undertake an analysis of attendees to ensure that both the destination and venue are going to meet their needs and expectations as well as those of the client. These factors are going to be very influential over the choice of destination that the event manager will ultimately make. Questions to consider could include: Will attendees be familiar with the destination or have preconceived ideas about the area? How will they travel to the event? Will they have time to explore the destination and if so what are they likely to want to do there? Will they want to or need to stay overnight in the destination? The answers to these questions may significantly impact the decisions that you go on to make about the destination and the venue, so it is worthwhile taking time to conduct proper attendee research with potential attendees.

Analysing the average profile of event attendees can also provide you with useful information that will help you to make decisions about the destination. Gathering demographic information about attendees, such as their gender, age range and disposable income, might guide you towards particular destinations. Shared demographics can mean shared attitudes, for example younger attendees may have similar opinions towards travelling long distances or older attendees may have common views on their preferred standard of accommodation.

3.4 TRAVEL/LENGTH OF EVENT

If the event is going to be a day in length or less than this will help to limit the search area to destinations within a short travelling distance from most attendees. However, if the event is going to last more than a day this opens up the possibility of holding the event further afield. How much travel time is needed for attendees must be considered carefully. Although they will be making the journey from various starting points, it is worth assessing the average distance and the furthest distance to be travelled and assessing whether or not this seems reasonable. Bladen *et al.* (2012, p. 104) share an important warning to organisers that 'it is a common misconception among event managers that the way in which customers travel to the event is outside of their control and therefore not their concern'. They are quite right because although the event manager may pick the destination and the venue, this decision will directly impact the attendees and therefore it is important to assess the accessibility of the destination.

A key destination requirement for any event is the availability of transport to the venue and also within the local area. As such it is important that you investigate and assess the destination's public transport links as well as its road access. If attendees are travelling from overseas or long distances, look at the destination's location in relation to international and national airports as well as motorways. If the event is going to attract a high number of attendees from particular cities or countries it is worth investigating specific routes, taking into account seasonal variations. For example, some small airports have excellent flight connections in summer months, but can have few operating in the winter. If the event is going to be spread across several venues, or if the attendees may have free time before, during or after the event, it is also worth checking to see what level of public transport is available nearby to facilitate attendees moving around an unfamiliar area.

3.5 ACCOMMODATION

If the event is going to last more than a day, then accommodation in the destination for everyone at the event is going to be vital. Furthermore, many attendees may wish to extend their time in the region before or after the event in order to explore it and in such cases accommodation is going to be needed too. Therefore, it is essential that the event manager checks the type, location, availability and cost of **bed stock** in the destination. Event attendees may seek various types of accommodation for their stay, from hostels and campsites to guest houses and 5 star hotels. Table 3.2 provides a breakdown of the types of hotel and guest accommodation according to the AA, who also inspect and grade visitor accommodation in the UK.

Ultimately, before picking a destination, the event manager needs to have a good idea of what kind of accommodation is needed for attendees, for roughly how many nights and at what time of year. Remember that popular tourist destinations may have plenty of accommodation but prices for an overnight stay might be significantly higher during the summer and national holidays. In some destinations the accommodation can be spread out over quite a large area so this is also important to consider as neither you nor your attendees are going to want to have to travel some distance from the accommodation to the event.

If you are going to organise a large event where much of the audience will be seeking accommodation, it is prudent to work with a DMO (destination management organisation) or CVB (convention and visitor **bureau**) as many offer free accommodation booking services to event attendees. This means that you won't have to source hotel rooms for attendees and neither will you have to make reservations. The DMO or CVB will provide this service to you and your attendees free of charge. This is explained in more detail later in the chapter. Even if you are going to take advantage of such a service, you may well have to organise the overnight accommodation for the key event staff and event VIPs. The VIPs might include the client, and several members of the client's network of friends, family and colleagues. Additionally you may need to make arrangements for speakers or performers or other important suppliers or sponsors. In some cases you or the client may feel that it is appropriate to accommodate all of the event VIPs in one hotel. This can facilitate meetings, discussions and preparations before and during the event that need to take place in the morning or evening, around the main event

Table 3.2 Types of accommodation

Hotels	
Hotel	A formal accommodation offering full hotel service
Country house hotel	A hotel with ample grounds or gardens set in a rural or semi-rural situation; the property has an emphasis on peace and quiet
Small hotel	Smaller establishments having a maximum of 20 bedrooms, and personally run by the proprietor
Town house hotel	A high-quality property of distinctive style with a maximum of 50 bedrooms, set in a town or city centre; possibly no dinner but room service is available instead
Metro hotel	A town or city property providing full hotel services except dinner, close to a range of places to eat
Guest accommodation	
B&B	Accommodation provided in a private house by the owner for up to six paying guests
Guest house	Accommodation for more than six paying guests, with the owner and staff providing more services, e.g. dinner
Farmhouse	B&B or guest house accommodation provided on a working farm
Inn	Accommodation provided in a fully licensed establishment. The bar will be open to non-residents and provide food in the evenings
Restaurant with rooms	A restaurant offering a maximum of 12 bedrooms
Guest accommodation	Any establishment that meets the minimum entry requirements can choose to use this general category

Source: http://www.theaa.com/travel/accommodation_restaurants_grading.html

programme. Therefore you may need to book several bedrooms at your designated headquarter hotel which may be the location of the event itself or a hotel near to the event venue. The event VIPs may also be expecting hotel accommodation of a higher grade than the event attendees therefore as part of scoping the accommodation in potential destinations, have in mind the need for a headquarter hotel.

In many countries the national or local DMO will inspect and grade accommodation according to specific criteria. This provides event planners and guests with standardised benchmarks to use in order to book appropriate accommodation. Table 3.3 shows the set of standards used in the UK by the AA which have been agreed by three national DMOs (VisitBritain, VisitScotland and VisitWales).

Table 3.3 AA accommodation star ratings

One star	Courteous staff provide an informal yet competent service. All rooms are ensuite or have private facilities, and a designated eating area serves breakfast daily and dinner most evenings
Two star	A restaurant or dining room serves breakfast daily and dinner most evenings
Three star	Staff are smartly and professionally presented. The restaurant or dining room is open to residents and non-residents
Four star	Professional, uniformed staff respond to your needs or requests, and there are usually well-appointed public areas. The restaurant or dining room is open to residents and non-residents, and lunch is available in a designated eating area
Five star	Luxurious accommodation and public areas, with a range of extra facilities and a multilingual service available. Guests are greeted at the hotel entrance. High quality menu and wine list

Source: http://www.theaa.com/travel/accommodation_restaurants_grading.html#tabview%3Dtab1

3.6 AMENITIES

If the event attendees are going to spend any amount of time in the destination then it is important to pick a location that has suitable amenities. This includes restaurants, visitor attractions, shops and banks. As with accommodation, event attendees may be looking for particular kinds of facilities that fit their budget and preferences. For many people, attending an event is a gateway to spending time exploring a new destination. However the client will generally prefer them to spend as much time and money at the event as possible and this can mean purchasing food and souvenirs at the venue rather than from a nearby outlet and taking part in event activities rather than visiting local attractions. So as the event manager you will need to make prudent decisions in order to balance the needs of the client with the expectations of the attendees to ensure that both are met. Reflect on the event programme that you are

CASE STUDY 3.2 A PARTNER PROGRAMME ORGANISED BY RUTH PRETTY CATERING

New Zealand husband and wife team, Ruth and Paul, manage Ruth Pretty Catering which provides a full event management service to include creating original menus, providing entertainment such as cooking classes or talks, providing trained staff and sourcing suppliers such as florists, transport providers and photographers. The couple have more than 25 years of experience of working with individuals and businesses on corporate events, weddings, private parties and large-scale celebrations including many weddings. They believe that 'successful catering is as much about impeccable organisation and high quality service as it is about great food'.

Recently they were given a brief from a client to organise and run a half day partner programme for the partners of delegates attending a conference in Wellington. The 20 guests would be mainly female but there would be some males. The programme needed to include a light lunch (as the conference dinner would be held that evening).

The concept they came up with was to demonstrate catering in action by visiting nearby locations and to get the group to take part in a variety of relaxed activities. The itinerary kicked off at 9.30 am as guests were collected from their Wellington hotel and taken by coach for an hour's drive along the Kapiti Coast. On arrival at Ruth and Paul's premises in Te Horo, a short distance inland, the group was greeted with fresh fruit juice and local lavender lemonade. They then took a tour of the catering kitchen, met staff and learnt about how a large catering business operates. They watched top chefs prepare various dishes for upcoming functions and saw a demonstration of some of the kitchen's most used appliances and gadgets including old-fashioned apple peelers and Microplane graters. The guests had time to buy souvenirs in the kitchen shop and stroll around the 2 acre garden which is also used to grow salad leaves and herbs which are used daily by the chefs. Guests were then treated to a glass of wine and finger buffet lunch which included little roasted vegetable pies, baby bagels with smoked salmon, fresh date and almond friands, cheese and seasonal fruits.

The coach collected everyone at 2.00 pm for the return journey to Wellington. The feedback from the group was that they'd had a lovely day out in the country and it had been great to watch an expert in action.

Source: https://www.ruthpretty.co.nz/

developing and assess how much free time the event attendees will have in the destination. If there are going to be long gaps in the programme, or a late start or early finish, then you can anticipate that attendees will spend this leisure time in the destination. As such, they will look for places to eat and shop and things to do either near their accommodation or near to the event venue. Furthermore, people frequently attend events with a friend, partner or as part of a group but not everyone in the group may wish to take part in all of the event activities and may prefer to spend some time exploring the destination instead. Partner programmes are a feature of some conferences for example. This is when the event manager provides a structured or flexible itinerary of leisure or sightseeing activities for the partners of delegates to do during the day. There are number of agencies that will help you to coordinate a partner programme, such as the local DMO which is discussed later in this chapter. But if you are going to organise the partner programme yourself it is important to consider what suitable amenities, transport providers, attractions and landmarks are located in or near to the destination.

ACTIVITY 3.1

Select a destination that you have never visited and research the area's facilities, transport, attractions and landmarks. Put together an itinerary for a partner programme for a group of men and women aged 25 to 45. The itinerary should appeal to this demographic, showcase the destination and fit within an 8 hour period that involves no more than 2 hours of travelling.

3.7 SUPPLIERS

One of the event manager's key challenges when using a venue for the first time is finding reliable suppliers in a new destination. The suppliers that you will need to support the event will depend on the event programme but typical suppliers are illustrated in Figure 3.1.

The venue may provide some of the supplies that you need and in some cases, you will be obliged to use the venues own or appointed supplier and this is discussed in detail in Chapter 7. Most venue managers can provide information and advice on local suppliers and will give you contact information for reliable, local businesses. However if the event that you are organising is going to require a significant amount of specific equipment or supplies this should be investigated as part of the destination selection process. For example, if there are no florists, AV suppliers or caterers in the area it may prove difficult and expensive to properly resource the event that you are planning.

Many suppliers will travel to the event, regardless of where it is going to be held. However, the cost of their travel arrangements, and possibly their overnight accommodation and subsistence costs, may be passed on to you. Therefore using suppliers that are based in or near the destination may be cost effective and as they are likely to know the area, and may have worked in the venue before, they may also be able to offer you useful destination advice and have contacts in the area that you could also use. As part of your efforts to be a responsible event manager, using suppliers in the destination may also help to reduce transport emissions and demonstrates your support for local businesses and your promotion of authentic produce.

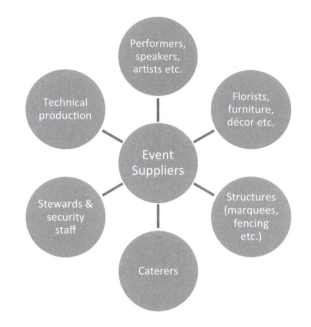

Figure 3.1 Event suppliers.

3.8 TRADE SHOWS AND FAMILIARISATION TRIPS

As we've seen in this chapter so far, when choosing a destination there are a lot of things to consider and potentially a lot of facts and figures to gather. Most of us will automatically begin any search for information using the internet however this is not necessarily the most efficient way to review and choose a destination and there are other methods to consider.

There are a number of national and international trade shows for the events industry that take place annually. Exhibitors can include venues and suppliers as well as national and regional DMOs. These organisations typically promote entire countries as well as specific regions and encourage business into the area. At these exhibitions, stands are often grouped by location meaning it's possible to talk to and compare a range of exhibitors from the same region. As most trade shows take place annually, this is not always the best way to find the venue for the event you are currently planning as you may need something sooner. However, attending trade shows is a great way to network with fellow event planners and meet a range of suppliers face to face that you may work with in the long term if not the short term.

One of the most wonderful perks of being an event manager is taking part in familiarisation, or **fam trips**. Fam trips are business visits to a destination and they are usually organised by the region's DMO. The purpose of a fam trip is to introduce new buyers to the area and to showcase the local venues and facilities in order to encourage event managers to choose the destination for future events. The visit will often last for at least a day or two and will include staying at a hotel, visiting other venues, restaurants and attractions as well as spending time exploring the area. The trip is often completely funded by the DMO so the event manager is provided with complimentary accommodation, meals and entertainment for the duration of their visit. Although the fam trip may be quite structured and packed full of lots of business related activities, it is usually quite a leisurely and relaxed business visit and it can be a very pleasant way to get to experience everything that a destination has to offer.

Table 3.4 List of international events industry trade shows

Trade show	Location	Website
AIME	Melbourne, Australia	www.aime.com.au
FIEXPO Latin America	Lima, Peru	www.fiexpo-latam.com
IBTM Africa	Cape Town, South Africa	www.ibtmafrica.com
IBTM America	Florida, USA	www.ibtmamerica.com
IBTM Arabia	Abu Dhabi, UAE	www.ibtmarabia.com
IBTM China	Beijing, China	www.cibtm.com
IBTM Latin America	Mexico City, Mexico	www.ibtmlatinamerica.com
IBTM World	Barcelona, Spain	www.ibtmworld.com
IMEX	Frankfurt, Germany	www.imex-frankfurt.com
IMEX America	Las Vegas, USA	www.imexamerica.com/
International Confex	London, UK	www.international-confex.com
ITCMA	Bangkok, Thailand	www.itcma.com.sg

CASE STUDY 3.3 A FAMILIARISATION TRIP

The TFI Group is a creative and live event agency and recently one of their employees was invited to take part in a fam trip to South Africa to visit two areas: Sun City and Cape Town.

Sun City is approximately 40 minutes by air from Cape Town and as a destination it combines nature, culture and luxury. Those invited on the fam trip stayed in the five-star Palace hotel which is part of the city's main complex, and took part in a game drive viewing all of the animals on the reserve including zebras, springboks, giraffes, elephants, gnus, and hippopotami.

As well as the Palace hotel, the Sun City complex comprises several fine dining restaurants, golf courses, a conference centre and additional hotels with excellent event space. There are six swimming pools, a water park and additional activities on offer. The various hotels are suited to honeymooning couples, families and larger groups and the ambience across the complex is very relaxed. Rooms are spacious and filled with dark wood and like the rest of the complex, they have been designed to give the impression of being inside the natural South African landscape. There are sounds of waterfalls, green lawns and trees everywhere. However, the visit revealed that the conference centre is quite dark (in keeping with the overall African theme) and it is situated near to a food court, swimming pool and casino which means that it could be considered inappropriate for some events, particularly as people would be walking around in swimming costumes.

The Cape Town itinerary included a stay at the five-star Table Bay Hotel and trips to the top of Table Mountain, a local market, the penguins at Simon's Town, a boat trip around the peninsula, a helicopter ride and wine tasting. Cape Town also has a big conference centre in the centre of town and as a destination is has all the frisson of a bustling city centre. However, here the fam trip revealed that upon arrival in Cape Town, one of the first things visitors will see are shanty towns, which is part of the experience of going to a developing country but does contrast with the five-star luxury.

Everyone on the fam trip agreed that South Africa is a great destination for events as there is a lot of quality accommodation and a wealth of things to do. The weather is superb although the seasonal differences mean that it's summer in South Africa when it's winter

continued

in the Northern Hemisphere. There are overnight flights from Europe and although they are long haul, the limited jet lag makes it an easy destination to travel to.

When taking part in a fam trip there are important things to remember. As an event organiser you need to view the destination differently to any other kind by putting on your 'event manager glasses' and focusing on the event specific considerations. For example, event attendees won't have that many opportunities to wander around and meet and mix with the locals, aside from venue staff. Also, don't forget that on a fam trip your visit is arranged so that you will be taken to see the 'good side' of the destination.

Source: Bret (2016).

Recent global changes in bribery legislation have caused some concern over the ethicality of fam trips. Event managers generally do not pay to attend a fam trip. Therefore it could be argued that giving event managers a complimentary visit, which includes travel to a destination, accommodation (often in a luxury hotel), activities and meals, is the equivalent of a bribe.

CASE STUDY 3.4 TAKING PART IN ETHICAL FAM TRIPS

A fam trip is one of the perks that come with being an events professional and is a valuable opportunity to see a destination up close. If you are invited to attend a fam trip, usually the host will pay your expenses or give you a significant discount. However, to take an ethical role in a fam trip it is advisable to take some steps first.

Firstly you should check to see what your company's policy is on attending fam trips and having your expenses paid by someone else. It's important to be aware of what you can and cannot accept. Secondly, in order to demonstrate professional courtesy you should decline a fam trip invite if you know that you are never going to bring any business to the destination. Next, make sure that you know who is organising or sponsoring the fam trip. For example, is it the DMO, a venue or a mixture of destination stakeholders? If these are organisations that you would be interested in working with, it's worth attending. Remember that you are taking part in a business visit and you are not going on holiday. Therefore go with a view to learning about the destination and spending a lot of time at meetings. Check the planned itinerary to make sure that the visits to venues and activities seem appropriate to the types of events you work on. This way you are more likely to have meaningful discussions with destination suppliers. Find out who else has been invited to attend to make sure that there are no conflicts of interest but also because a fam trip is a great networking opportunity. Therefore plan how to maximise the networking opportunities so that you get to engage with a variety of venues as well as other event managers. Make sure that you will visit venues that are of particular interest to you and that you will have time to talk to the venue managers.

Remember that fam trips are a great way to explore parts of the world at the same time as developing your destination knowledge and your network of contacts. If you can demonstrate respect towards the fam trip hosts and make ethical plans for your attendance, then a fam trip has the potential to provide you, and consequently your clients, with real value.

Source: McNeill (2012).

Therefore most industry professionals only condone fam trips as legitimate business activities if they have a key role to play in marketing the destination to the events industry. The value of the trip is proportionate to the inscope expenditure that will be generated by new events that are held in the destination. However, there is now more and more guidance on how to conduct ethical fam trips and how to be a responsible event manager if you are invited to attend one, as illustrated in Case study 3.4.

3.9 WORKING WITH DMOS

There are an increasing number of DMOs operating across the globe as more and more countries are recognising the value of the events industry and develop strategic plans to target event planners (Park et al., 2014, Quinn, 2013). This growth has meant that destinations face increasing pressure to develop innovative marketing practices in order to showcase a clear identity or brand (Paskaleva-Shapira, 2007, p. 112). The size and scope of DMOs can vary with national organisations promoting an entire country and often working towards achieving government targets related to tourism. Regional DMOs operate in a similar way in order to attract visitors and investment into particular parts of a country. They often focus on encouraging events to take place in areas that do not attract leisure tourists in order to ensure a countrywide spread of the economic benefits of event tourism (Bowdin et al., 2011). Towns and cities that are located in resorts or historical locations will often have their own DMO too.

The key role of a DMO is to:

> act as an intermediary, to serve as a custodian of the destination's information, to be the official voice of the destination's facilities, services and overall 'product'.
>
> (Rogers and Davidson, 2016, p. 234)

In other words, the DMO will promote the destination and provide information about the destination's facilities to visitors and event planners. In this way, the DMOs are 'like a key to the city' (Fenich, 2012, p. 39) and are a valuable resource to the event planner. Table 3.5 lists some of the ways in which national, regional and local DMOs can support event organisers.

Historically most DMOs have been set up as state funded organisations with a key role to play in achieving government targets relating to attracting inbound and domestic tourists. Frequently these organisations have drop in centres in their destination, either located on the high street or in another popular part of the area that can be easily located by visitors. These generally operate under the title of a tourist information centre (TIC) and their public location is to help visitors find hotel or guest accommodation, places to eat and things to do.

Table 3.5 DMO support for event organisers

Organise familiarisation trips
Provide a venue/supplier finding service
Create and manage an accommodation booking service for attendees
Provide maps, brochures and discount vouchers (for restaurants, shops and visitor attractions etc.)
Advertise all or parts of the event
Sell tickets for the event
Offer advice on planning and licensing applications, road closures etc.
Negotiate civic support or additional funding for the event

3.10 CONVENTION AND VISITOR BUREAUX

Many state funded organisations have also expanded to include specialised convention bureaux to focus on attracting business events to the destination as these can be particularly lucrative (Park et al., 2014; Quinn, 2013). A convention bureau is a business version of a TIC as it will assist domestic and inbound business tourists to find accommodation, transport etc. Convention bureaux also assist all types of event organisers in finding venues, accommodation and suppliers within the destination. As much of the work done by a convention bureau happens well before the event and the business visit to the destination, they are less likely to have a high street presence although today many TICs and convention bureaux work together to offer a one stop shop to all tourists (leisure or business) and all event organisers and these are called convention and visitor bureaux or CVBs.

Most convention and visitor bureaux make excellent intermediaries as they have unparalleled knowledge of their destination and they can support event managers in a number of ways very often for little or no charge. They can provide a venue finding service, secure accommodation for event attendees and put an accommodation booking service in place. This is a system that will enable event attendees to book their accommodation via the CVB without the involvement of the event organiser. This will obviously save the event manager a lot of time but it also means that event attendees have access to a comprehensive service and destination expertise as the CVB staff will be able to offer advice on the exact location and type of accommodation available. Also, if a lot of accommodation is going to be required for event attendees, the CVB can often negotiate competitive rates based on securing a block booking and this discount, which could be as much as 40 per cent off the **rack rate** (Lee and Fenich, 2016, p. 161) will be passed on to the individual event attendees.

Many CVBs will provide event organisers with information about the destination to use and to pass on to event attendees. This can include maps and brochures as well as discount vouchers for restaurants, shops and visitor attractions. If the event that you are organising is

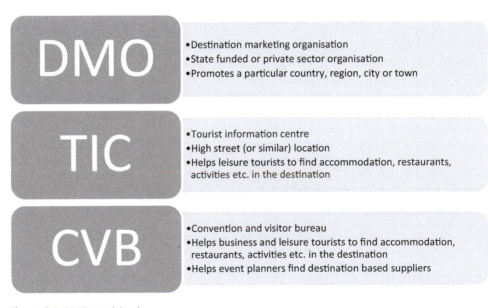

Figure 3.2 DMOs explained.

THE INDUSTRY EXPERT'S VIEW 3.1

DESTINATION MANAGEMENT

Chris Meyer, Vice President of Global Business Sales, Las Vegas Convention and Visitors Authority, www.vegasmeansbusiness.com

The Las Vegas Convention and Visitors Authority (LVCVA) is the official destination marketing organization of Southern Nevada, promoting tourism, conventions, meetings and special events. The LVCVA operates the Las Vegas Convention Center and Cashman Center, and the destination features millions of square feet of meeting, event and convention space. In addition, the LVCVA owns and operates four visitor information and welcome centers.

There are several reasons why I would encourage event planners to work with DMOs as the benefits are plentiful. Firstly, it's a free resource and it is a much more efficient way of finding information than any search engine. Plus, working with a DMO provides you with the quality of human engagement; when you work with a destination-based team you develop a trusted relationship with them and that can really help with unforeseen circumstances that can often occur in event planning. The relationship often begins with the RFP process and at the Las Vegas Convention and Visitors Authority we will respond to RFPs very quickly, often within minutes. Even if it's a complex request that will take time to gather information for, we will acknowledge it straight away. We have an internal system for processing RFPs so the service we offer is very efficient.

Las Vegas has much to offer event planners and we don't hide from the fact that it's a fun destination, but it also offers an elusive experience factor. All event organizers are looking to create that memorable experience and in Las Vegas there are lots of engagement opportunities; it's all about adult freedom, whatever that means to the individual. We do offer lots of advice to event planners. For example, many convention delegates will arrive Sunday or Monday and there will be business events taking place Monday through Friday. So we suggest not tying delegates up with too many activities in the evenings and avoiding a 7am plenary!

One of the challenges of running a DMO is the volume of information that is involved in destination management – we must make sure that we take it all in but also express it in a business-like manner to the planners we work with. Las Vegas is constantly evolving and we are continually learning about the destination. Each of our executives is assigned a hotel liaison – someone based at each venue who will keep our staff up to date about their product. Most venues are proactive in keeping us informed of developments but we will also seek information. We represent the whole of Clark County which means that there is a lot of work involved in keeping up to date of everything that's going on.

In terms of the events industry there are a number of destinations now competing for business including Shanghai, Munich, Frankfurt, London, Barcelona, Hong Kong and Macau. So we are always developing our product. We have increased the size of our convention center 14 times and we are looking ahead at further expansion in the future. My advice to other venue managers is to be competent in your key processes. For example, it can be so important to remember the small things like not turning off the

continued

power during an exhibition. That gives you the baseline to be innovative and nimble. Venues can become stale, so constantly look to what you can improve. At the moment we are working on making the entry and exit process at the venue more efficient. Event participants want safe and quick access into the building and we are constantly looking at ways in which we can make our systems for this even better.

going to be open to the public, the CVB will usually advertise it via all of their suitable channels such as on their destination website and in their brochure. If there is a charge to attend the event, they may even be able to sell tickets via their website and their public information centres. There may be a cost for this service, or a **commission** arrangement, but this may still be worthwhile pursuing.

As the CVB will usually have unrivalled knowledge of the destination, they can often provide event organisers with useful information about local suppliers such as caterers, florists and photographers. Typically they will work closely with public and private transport providers who serve the area and have good working relationships with national train, bus and coach companies. As such they can offer expert advice to event organisers on the best travel routes to the destination and they will have up to date information on local parking and public transport. They may be able to offer discounts on travel or negotiate charges on your behalf with local providers.

3.11 PRIVATISATION AND DISINTERMEDIATION

In recent years much state funding for DMOs has been reduced or cut altogether as governments have had to tighten their belts and prioritise spending. This has resulted in the creation of wholly or partly privatised DMOs. Now in most parts of the world, DMOs are semi-public organisations that partner up with both private sector organisations as well as local or regional authorities (Raj *et al.*, 2013). The key role of these DMOs is unchanged in that they still primarily exist to generate interest in the destination. However, without state funding DMOs have had to explore alternative ways to finance their operations and this has resulted in many organisations adopting a membership framework. This means that the destination stakeholders pay an annual fee to the DMO and in return for their investment they are included in the DMO's promotional activities. Stakeholders who do not pay into the scheme will either not be represented or will not be promoted to the same extent as paying members. This can therefore result in a less comprehensive and less unbiased service to users. In other words, as an event planner you may wish to use the DMO to run a venue finding search in the area but a privatised DMO may only conduct the search across their member venues as opposed to all the viable venues within their area. On the whole, most major DMOs operate fair and robust services as it is important that they demonstrate leadership and cohesion (Rogers and Davidson, 2016) and a collective approach to marketing the destination will be more effective for all destination stakeholders (Naipaul *et al.*, 2009).

Disintermediation is a term which means the reduction of the use of an intermediary and this is a trend that is very much evident in the 21st century (Rogers and Davidson, 2016). For the tourism and events industry, technology now provides us with the means to access destination information and this has led to disintermediation. In other words, as tourists and

Image 3.1 The Las Vegas Strip.

Source: Brian Jones/Las Vegas News Bureau.

as event planners we can search online for accommodation, venues and ideas for things to do in a destination meaning that we no longer need to use an intermediary, such as a TIC or CVB, to help us. We may feel that as it is very easy to conduct an online search we have no need for the services of an intermediary. Furthermore, if, as the event organiser, you engage the services of a DMO to run an accommodation booking service for your attendees, it can be quite challenging to encourage people to use it rather than to look online themselves. The research undertaken by Lee and Fenich (2016) indicates that there are times when attendees are able to secure their accommodation for the event at a better rate online than by using the accommodation booking service and the ramifications of this can be disastrous as it can lead to attendees' mistrust of the event manager.

However, when assessing whether or not to use a DMOs as an intermediary, it is worth remembering that they exist not only to promote the destination but also to facilitate events and support event managers via a 'strong enabling role' (Park et al., 2014, p. 266). This can mean providing free maps and marketing materials as well as organising fam trips and site visits. DMOs can often assist with aspects of event planning where the involvement of the council or government departments is needed. For example, they may be able to offer advice on planning and licensing applications, road closures etc. In some cases, they may also be able to negotiate civic support for your event or provide you with additional funding and as such it is worth talking to the region's DMO to assess the many different ways in which they may be able to support you and contribute to the organisation of the event.

3.12 BIDDING FOR EVENTS

There is now intense global competition between destinations to compete for large scale events that are going to create a significant economic impact in the town or city in which they are held. Not only do these events generate an enormous visitor spend in the area but they also encourage private investment and sponsorship and draw the attention of the media and a global audience. Therefore, the organiser of such a large scale event has the power to choose the destination which will benefit from hosting their event. As such, there can be a bidding process for the event which involves interested destinations submitting a detailed bid document or proposal to the event organisers which demonstrate their vision for hosting the event. The proposal will contain all the data that the event management team requires about the area in order to consider it as the location for a large scale, international event. This may range from specific details of venues and bed stock as well as information about hospitals, police, laws, regulations and visa requirements. Shortlisted destinations may also be required to deliver a presentation to the event manager and discuss their proposal in detail as part of the bidding process and there may be a lengthy visit to the destination during which the event management team will meet all of the destination's key stakeholders. In other words, the destinations CVB or primary DMO will usually lead or coordinate the destination's bid and they will invest a lot of time, effort and money into persuading you to choose their destination. The bidding process for large scale events can take several years to complete but the selection of the right destination is integral to the success of a large scale international event.

3.13 CHOOSING A DESTINATION – THE VENUE MANAGER'S PERSPECTIVE

As there are so many venues now competing for the attention of local, national and international event managers it can be a huge and constant challenge to ensure that your venue is visible to potential clients. For many venue managers, small marketing budgets mean that achieving visibility is very difficult; therefore joining one or several DMOs will open up your marketing options. Firstly this will give you a presence on their website, which may receive more traffic than your own website. You will be included on venue searches and you will have the option to be featured at key trade shows. Many venue managers find that the cost of having a stand at a major national or international trade show is prohibitive, plus taking at least two members of staff off site to attend the show for 3 or 4 days adds to the cost. However, if your DMO is going to have a stand at the exhibition, as one of their members you may be eligible to stand share. This means that the stand will feature the name of the DMO, but you will be able to send one member of staff to work on the stand during the show to promote both the destination and your own venue. If this isn't possible, you should be able to ensure that your venue is promoted to visitors to the stand by way of your brochures, leaflets and business cards.

DMOs often undertake or commission research and will share the results with their members. For the venue manager, this can mean that you are kept up to date with trends that are affecting the area such as fluctuations in visitor numbers and changing **demographics**. DMOs can keep you abreast of intended changes to the area and are often involved in strategic town and city planning. As such they can make useful allies as they will try to represent the interests of their members in all of their undertakings. Furthermore, due to the historical set up of DMOs, many still have strong links with local and national authorities. Therefore they can often advise members on issues connected to legislation, planning applications and other areas of responsibility that lie with the government.

As membership of DMOs generally comes at a cost, as a venue manager you must undertake a cost benefit analysis, particularly if you are located in an area that is represented by more than one DMO. This involves looking at what is included in your annual membership fee and what comes at an extra cost. For example, stand sharing and access to take part in fam trips can incur an extra fee. Also check to see how searches are conducted. For example, some DMOs will sort the results of a venue-finding search in order of who is the most up to date. This means that venues that communicate regularly with the DMO and keep their availability, hire charges and other information up to date are more likely to feature at the top of search lists.

Once you join a DMO, invest in your working relationship. Attend meetings and get to know the DMO staff. Take advantage of all of the member benefits as the training and networking events can be very useful to the venue manager, particularly if you or your venue is fairly new to the events industry.

3.14 SUMMARY

When it comes to choosing a destination for an event, the event manager now has more viable options than ever before. Venues all over the world can offer state of the art facilities in locations that may be new and exciting to event attendees. With so much choice, it can be a long and difficult process of choosing a destination that is going to be suitable for an event. Working with DMOs is a good option for the event manager due the multiple services that they offer and their unparalleled destination expertise. The events industry is highly competitive and very lucrative, partly because of the multiplier effect that is generated by event tourism. As such DMOs will work hard to secure event business and consequently they can offer support, resources and services, often at no cost. DMOs can be a valuable partner when organising events as they help to filter information and offer expert guidance. However, when choosing a destination, the event manager must assess all that the destination has to offer in relation to the event aim and the expectations of both the client and the event attendees.

3.15 FURTHER READING

The following sources are particularly useful for further reading on the subject of understanding destination management and choosing an event location:

Chiappa, G.D. (2012) How Do Meeting Organizers Choose Convention Sites Based on Different Types of Meetings? An Empirical Analysis of the Italian Meetings Industry. *Event Management* 16, (2), 157–170.

Crouch, G.I. (2010) Destination Competitiveness: An Analysis of Determinant Attributes. *Journal of Travel Research* 50, (1), 27–45.

Morgan, N., Pritchard, A. and Pride, R. (2011) *Destination Brands*. Oxford: Elsevier.

Rogers, T. and Davidson, R. (2016) *Marketing Destinations and Venues for Conferences, Conventions and Business Events*. London: Routledge.

Initial venue considerations

LEARNING OUTCOMES

By the end of Chapter 4, you should be able to:

- Identify the key points to consider when beginning to search for a venue
- Understand how to conduct an efficient venue finding search
- Issue a request for a proposal to a venue

4.1 INTRODUCTION

Once a destination has been selected for an event, the event manager may have a huge number of potentially suitable venues to choose from within that location. Therefore evaluating venues can be a very time consuming process as, even for a short and straightforward event, the role of the venue is going to be significant. There is a lot to consider when choosing an appropriate space including the precise location of the venue, room capacities, hire charges, facilities on site, access and catering options to name a few.

When beginning the search for a suitable venue it helps if the event manager has some basic information about the event. The search can then begin either by using online resources, trade publications, industry contacts or the services of an intermediary.

Ultimately visiting potential venues is essential in order to fully appreciate what the venue can offer but also to understand how the building or site presents the event manager with particular challenges. However, the venue selection process begins with gathering and analysing information and this chapter will guide you through this activity highlighting factors to consider and providing you with a checklist of information to collect.

4.2 GATHERING INFORMATION

In order to start looking for a venue it helps if the event manager can estimate the time of year that the event will take place (season or month), an estimation of the number of attendees, the rough outline of the event programme and the budget available as this information will immediately help to narrow down the list of potential venues.

Much of the initial search for a venue can be done online. Venue websites can be hugely informative and it is often possible to download a brochure as well as take part in a virtual

Table 4.1 A basic technical specification

	Main room	Syndicate 1	Syndicate 2	Dining hall
Seating capacity	Theatre 1,500 Classroom 750 Banquet 800	Theatre 300 Classroom 150 Banquet 200	Theatre 300 Classroom 150 Banquet 200	Theatre 900 Classroom 400 Banquet 780
Stage size	13m × 10m	Portable staging provided up to 7.3m × 3.65m	Portable staging provided up to 7.3m × 3.65m	10m × 7m
Sound provision	Full auditorium coverage Infra-red system for the hearing impaired	Mobile equipment provided	Mobile equipment provided	Full auditorium coverage Loop system for the hearing impaired
Lighting provision	Extensive rig provided	Dimmable room lighting provided	Dimmable room lighting provided	Extensive rig provided
Blackout provision	Yes	Yes	Yes	Yes
Exhibition floor space	995m²	250m²	268m²	850m²
Power	200A TPN Powerlock 125 TPN Ceeform 63 TPN Ceeform 32 TPN Ceeform 63 TPN Ceeform	Various 13A sockets around walls	Various 13A sockets in ceiling and around walls	125 TPN Ceeform 63 TPN Ceeform 32 TPN Ceeform 63 TPN Ceeform 32 TPN Ceeform 16 TP Ceeform
Ceiling height	3m rising to 15m	3m	2.6m	3m rising to 10m
Get-in	Trailer height up ramp	Ground level rear of venue	Ground level rear of venue	Ground level
Floor loading	Unlimited if spread	105lb/sq.ft.	105lb/sq.ft.	105lb/sq.ft.

walk around the site. Venue websites are repositories for information such as a technical specification which gives details about available facilities as well as photographs of previous events and testimonials from past clients. Technical specifications (often abbreviated to tech specs) can be quite challenging to understand, even for the most experienced event manager. Therefore, don't worry if you cannot understand everything that's noted on the spec, but take note of obvious information such as the room capacities, blackout facilities and whether **AV** equipment is available at the venue.

There are a number of trade directories which serve the events industry. These are electronic or paper catalogues which list venues and other suppliers. These directories usually include specifications for each venue and these are often grouped geographically. Using a directory can therefore be quicker than an internet search in order to compare and contrast venues against a set of criteria such as the number and capacity of rooms available to hire.

Many venue managers will exhibit at industry trade shows. This is a key marketing tool which enables them to showcase their facilities to a wide range of visiting event organisers. As such, attending trade shows can be a useful way to meet venue managers and gather information on a range of international venues and facilities. Such industry events are also a great way to network and meet your contemporaries. Word of mouth is a powerful marketing tool in any industry and it can be useful to talk to other event managers and find out which venues they have used successfully in the past. However, as trade shows take place occasionally, you may need to gather venue information more speedily and therefore a trade directory or internet search might be quicker.

4.3 LOCATION

Even though the destination of the event will have been determined by this point, you will probably have a large number of viable venues to choose from and therefore the shortlisting process can begin by assessing their locations in relation to on site and local amenities. In particular look at drop off and parking facilities at or near the venue as well as local transport provision and the availability of taxis. Many venues are located in areas that are well served by local transport and road networks. Sometimes this is a result of urban development, around historical venues for example. And sometimes this is by design, as is the case with a number of purpose built venues that have been located in areas that already have such infrastructure in place. A number of large, international exhibition centres for example have been purposely built on sites that are near to motorways, principal railway stations and even international airports.

CASE STUDY 4.1 THE MILANO CONGRESSI, MILAN, ITALY

The Milano Congressi (MiCo) is one of the largest purpose built event venues in Europe. It has more than 70 rooms, an overall capacity of up to 18,000 people, and 54,000 square metres of exhibition space. As such it is an ideal space for large-scale performances as well as international conferences and exhibitions.

The MiCo is located in the heart of the city and is easily accessible by public transport or by car. There are three metro stations and a train station within a 5 minute walk of the venue. The Milano Nord Domodossola train station is served by urban and regional lines

Image 4.1 The Milano Congressi.

Source: https://www.fieramilanocongressi.it

as well as the Malpensa Express line which connects to Malpensa international airport. Milan has a further two international airports, Linate City Airport and Bergamo Orio al Serio, and both have direct bus links to the city. Many of these transport links were in place before the MiCo was designed in 2001 and the existing infrastructure contributed to the decision to locate the venue in this part of the city. Since the venue opened, additional metro stations and stops have been created to increase access to the venue. Plus the nearest motorway was extended in the direction of the MiCo which means that driving from the venue to the nearest motorway takes just a few minutes. This is part of the venue and the municipality's long term strategic plan to ensure the venue remains easily accessible. Additionally the venue owns 1500 parking spaces and these are supplemented by a further 2000 nearby spaces which are owned by the municipality.

Milan is a compact city and like many of its European counterparts, it has new and old districts. The MiCo straddles the two halves of the city and it has several entrances on sides facing both the modern and historical districts. This means that users of the venue can walk to some of the most beautiful and historic sites in Milan, such as the Arco della Pace (Arch of Peace) and the Sforza Castle, in under 15 minutes. The modern part of the city continues to evolve and the main entrance to the MiCo is located within an ongoing development of residential accommodation, shops, parks and other amenities.

Public transport in Milan is efficient and relatively cheap compared to many other European cities. This, alongside the city centre location of the MiCo and its varied transport links, provide the venue with its key competitive advantages and are crucial to its success. Milan lacks a strong destination brand identity compared to other Italian cities such as Rome, Venice or Florence. Therefore the combination of modern facilities located in a part contemporary and part historical setting with excellent transport links make the MiCo a leading twenty-first century event venue.

www.micomilano.it

Few venues have, by modern standards, adequate parking spaces. Although some venues have their own car parks, these are not necessarily going to be reserved for (or even made available to) event attendees. If car parking is going to be essential to your attendees, the number, location and availability of private and public car parks should be assessed when investigating potential venues and as Shone and Parry (2010, p. 129) suggest, consider your audience's preferred modes of transport.

Amenities in the vicinity of the venue are important too and the event manager may wish to assess the number and variety of restaurants, hotels, shops, visitor attractions and places of interest. Naturally this will need to be done in relation to the purpose of the event as, for example, a rural venue away from other distractions might be ideal for an intense corporate training day, but far from suitable for an all day, drop in community event.

4.4 RESIDENTIAL VENUES AND LEISURE FACILITIES

Many venues are residential, which means that as well as having function rooms they also offer bedrooms which may be made available to event attendees. Hotels are the obvious example of a residential venue, but a good number of academic, unusual and sporting venues also have accommodation on site. The event manager may require a residential venue in particular for an event that is going to last for longer than one day. This is common with conferences and other corporate events but it is also a feature of festivals and celebrations. Venues that have the potential to accommodate attendees the night before or after the event may also be desirable, particularly if the event is likely to attract visitors from afar. As such the event manager may decide to purely look for residential venues. However it is a good idea to also consider venues that are located in areas with a good number of hotels nearby. It is also worth comparing the quality of the event space with the quality of the bed stock. For example a number of universities have state of the art classrooms that make excellent event spaces, but by comparison the student accommodation block will not offer the same facilities as a hotel and this may fall short of what some event attendees will be expecting. And as Fenich (2012, p. 60) illustrates, it is important to match attendee expectation with the level of service offered by the accommodation provider as 'the availability of specific amenities often drives the delegates' expectations of the facility'.

As well as the availability of bedrooms, it is worth considering additional leisure facilities that the venue has to offer. For example a restaurant, bar, swimming pool, spa or even a golf course might make for appealing additions to the event experience and serve to attract more attendees. The event manager will need to assess whether such facilities present added event value or will serve to distract attendees away from the purpose of the event!

ACTIVITY 4.1

Make a list of types of events. Against each event identify some of the key venue facilities that are either essential to the event or could enhance the attendee experience. For example, landscaped gardens can enhance a wedding venue as they make a beautiful backdrop to the wedding photos. Against each event identify venue facilities that could detract from the event such as the examples given above.

4.5 CAPACITY

Having a rough idea of how many people will attend the event is helpful at the start of the search as the venue's capacity is always going to be key to its suitability to the event. Therefore when undertaking an initial search note the venue's overall size as well as the breakdown of the various room capacities. Most venue websites and brochures will give a full breakdown of these capacities as they will vary according to the nature of the room usage and the furniture, equipment and staging being used. For example, an empty room of around 350 square metres may hold 400 people for a reception during which everyone will be mainly standing and chatting. However, if the same room were to be set up with tables and chairs for dinner (known as banquet style), the capacity of the room will be significantly reduced to, perhaps, around 250 people. Naturally, room set ups that require a lot of chairs and tabling will have smaller capacities than rooms used for dancing, standing or looking at exhibition panels. Table 4.2 describes the principal room set ups used in events and image 4.2 illustrates the most popular room set ups.

Matthews (2016) advocates an early chat with the venue manager if it is likely that you are going to need unusual room set ups. Furthermore, it is particularly important to assess the

Table 4.2 Room set ups

Theatre style	Rows of chairs facing towards the front of the room
Classroom style	Rows of chairs against tables facing towards the front of the room
Boardroom style	Chairs around a large table or chairs around a rectangle created with several tables
U-shape or horseshoe	Chairs around a u-shaped set of tables
Banquet style	Chairs around circular tables
Cabaret style	Chairs around two thirds of a table, facing towards the front of the room
Reception style	Few tables placed informally around a room upon which guests can place food/drink
Herringbone style	Rows of chairs against tables angled towards the centre of the room

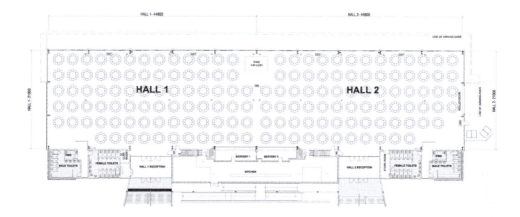

GALA DINNER
SEATING - 1570 PAX

Image 4.2 A sample floorplan.

ACTIVITY 4.1

Using Image 4.2 (a sample floorplan), identify which of the dinner tables you would designate as your five VIP tables for the most important guests at a banquet. The VIPs need to be served before the other diners, the five tables need to be reasonably close to each other but they should not be near entrances, exits or toilets.

number, size and location of rooms within the venue. If several rooms are needed for the event it is worth looking at the venue's **floorplan** and noting whether or not these rooms are close to each other or even on the same floor. Most venues can provide you with floorplans for rooms that you are going to be using and how they might be set up. These are also useful for judging the proximity of tables and chairs to the stage, to the toilets and main entrance etc. An example is shown in Image 4.2.

If rooms are near to each other, attendees should be able to navigate their way around the event quite easily. If rooms are not adjacent to each other you will need to consider the distance between them, the availability of lifts, the route attendees will take and the time this will add to the event programme. One of the great benefits of using some academic or sporting venues is that they can often be comprised of a great number of rooms, often linked or in close proximity to each other.

CASE STUDY 4.2 A VENUE WITH INTERCONNECTING ROOMS: CROKE PARK

In 1864 Maurice Butterly began leasing a 21-acre area of land in the parish of Saint George in Dublin. The area became known as 'Butterly's Field' and between 1891 and 1984 it became a well-used location for athletics meetings. In 1894 Butterly sold his sports field to the City and Suburban Racecourse and Amusements Ground Ltd who continued to use the land for athletics meetings and other sporting events. The field was also hired out from time to time to the Gaelic Athletic Association (GAA). The GAA was founded by a group of Irishmen who were determined to establish a national organisation aimed at making athletics more accessible to the masses and to reintroduce traditional Irish sports. They were hugely successful and led the launch of more than 2,200 GAA clubs all over the country and generated huge interest in the games of hurling and Gaelic football. In 1913 the GAA took ownership of the field and developed it into the largest stadium in Ireland which is now called Croke Park. Croke Park has a match day capacity of 82,000 people and every year it hosts the finals of the inter-county All-Ireland Championships in both hurling and Gaelic football.

The venue has become one of the largest sporting arenas in Europe and it is now used for a variety of events every year including major sporting competitions, concerts, meetings and exhibitions. Take That, One Direction, Pharrell and Ed Sheeran are among the high profile acts that have performed sell-out shows at the stadium. It is also a busy visitor attraction featuring the GAA museum and public tours of the venue to include the dressing rooms, media centre, players' tunnel and VIP seating area. The venue benefits from its central location which is only 5 minutes from the city centre and within easy reach

Image 4.3 Croke Park.

Source: ©www.irelandscontentpool.com/Sinead McCarthy.

of Dublin Airport and Dublin Port. Additionally there is a four star hotel adjacent to the stadium and there are 600 free parking spaces on site.

As an events space, as well as the pitch and arena seating, there are 100 meeting rooms and eight suites available for hire and these can be used for various small to large events. As Croke Park has been refurbished and developed over the years, these spaces have been specifically designed to act as a versatile, blank canvas with lots of natural daylight and up-to-date technology. In total there is over 5000 square metres of space which can accommodate up to 100,000 people at an exhibition or 5,000 guests at a private party all on one level of the building. Ninety three of the meeting rooms are located on the same level of the stadium. The interconnecting rooms offer great flexibility as an event space. This means that when rooms are combined a range of layout options become possible and panoramic views across the pitch are created. All in all, the available rooms suit a variety of events from small board meetings to large scale galas and have made Croke Park one of the most popular event venues in Ireland.

Source: https://crokepark.ie

It may be possible to reuse rooms several times within one event and with a different set up each time. In such cases the time required to set up, dismantle and reset rooms will need to be discussed with the venue but this is worth pursuing as reusing rooms may cut down on the overall hire charges. At most events, it can be very useful for the event staff, and the event manager in particular, to have access to a private room. A separate space in which to answer calls, coordinate the event from behind the scenes and store valuable items can be invaluable. As such it is particularly useful if this room is located close to the heart of the event and is lockable.

It's also important to remember that events that will require a fluid movement of a high number of attendees, from room to room for example, will need to be monitored for bottle necks and overcrowding and this will need to be discussed with the venue manager as part of the event preparation (see Chapter 11). Overcrowding obviously poses a danger to safety and must be controlled, but using a room well below its capacity can also negatively impact an event. The atmosphere of an event can be greatly shaped and influenced by the capacity and set up of the room and if a room is not full this can be detrimental to the ambience. However, at this early planning stage of an event it may be prudent to look for venues that are close to the anticipated maximum attendance number and focus on these and other venues that are slightly too small or too large.

4.6 THE DESIGN OF THE VENUE

As well as noting the overall size of the venue and individual room capacities, it is important to assess the design and layout of the building as much as you can from the venue website or brochure. In terms of appearance, the age and nature of the property will generally be evident in the architecture and older buildings may have quirky, attractive and distinct features on the interior and exterior walls, on the ceilings and also in terms of the size and shape of rooms. The Sensoji Temple in Japan is one such example as it was completed in 645, making it Tokyo's oldest temple and a distinctive venue.

Modern day and purpose-built venues are typically less adorned and more likely to have well-proportioned and regular shaped internal rooms. The absence or presence of these features can be both useful and detrimental to the event manager and should be considered in the early stages of venue shortlisting.

Unless the event that you are organising is going to make full use of all available rooms on site, it is unlikely that you will have exclusive use of the venue. There may be several other events taking place in parallel to yours and of course the venue may also be in use in relation to its primary function. As such it is important to look at the entrance to the venue and the internal layout of rooms. If the venue has one main entrance, you will probably have to share

Image 4.4 The Sensoji Temple.
Source: ©Yasufumi Nishi/©JNTO.

this space with other users. Therefore there may be restrictions on the number or size of welcome notices or signage that you can place at the entrance, on exterior walls or in the communal areas of the venue. As you assess room capacities and layout, you should also note whether access to the rooms is direct or via other rooms, on which level of the venue they are located and whether they are near any busy, and therefore potentially noisy, areas such as catering points, lifts or stairwells. Ultimately a visit to the venue and a conversation with the venue manager will address any concerns that you may have but if total privacy is key to the success of your event then these considerations must be made early on.

4.7 FACILITIES

It is important to assess what other facilities the venue has and can make available to an event and its attendees. As well as tables for dinners and other refreshment areas, the event manager will need to know how many tables are required for other purposes such as an information or registration point, office or work space or table top exhibitions. It's worth asking the venue whether or not they have partition boards. These can be very useful for designating specific zones within an event and can help to maximise the usage of a large space, or reduce the size of an overly big room. Similarly, some venues will have their own portable staging which can be moved from room to room as required and can provide a low level platform useful for elevating speakers, comperes or drawing attention to specific props or marketing materials. Chapter 8 discusses audio visual equipment at venues in more detail, however it is also worth noting that many venues have their own **lectern**, **dais** and other small items of portable staging equipment. Typically, venues that have their own stock of furniture and equipment are likely to have ladders, **cherry pickers** and other tools that can be used to move and set up equipment during the **get in** and **get out** periods of an event.

4.8 CATERING

Although the catering elements of the event may be discussed and finalised some time after the venue has been booked, it is a good idea to weigh up the catering options at each venue as part of the initial assessment. This can be a surprisingly complex process and it is discussed in detail in Chapter 7. However at this stage it is worth investigating whether the venue has its own catering team. This is standard practice at many venues such as hospitality providers and common at a good number of academic, sporting and unusual venues. Usually, if the venue has a catering team on site, the event manager is going to be obliged to use them for the provision of all refreshments at the event. Although there is usually room to negotiate with the team on catering charges, this is going to be restricted by the fact that once the venue has been chosen, the choice of caterer is nil.

Where venues do not have their own on-site team of caterers, they may have a list of recommended local catering companies that they are happy to allow to operate on their premises. There will typically be a variety of names on a preferred supplier list, and although the event manager can usually only appoint a caterer from the list, they will have some choice and therefore scope to negotiate.

On rare occasions the venue will have neither on-site caterers nor a list of preferred suppliers and thus allow the event manager to choose the caterer of their choice, or provide refreshments themselves. Although this may initially seem like a cost saving option the opposite

CASE STUDY 4.3 CALLOW EVENT MANAGEMENT

Callow Event Management is a Belfast-based event management company with experience of organising events throughout the UK and further afield. They offer full event production services and can supply world-class entertainment or simple event styling.

Ruth Ellis is the Events and Special Occasions Manager at Callow Event Management. At any one time she can be working on a variety of events and juggling 20 projects or more, all at different stages in planning. Without doubt the more challenging events are the ones that involve the team learning something new. When Ruth joined the company, her job focused largely on gala dinners for the corporate and charity sector. Over the last 3 years the business has developed very quickly and clients' expectations have grown to encourage different styles of events, in different venues, for a wider range of audiences. Ruth's favourite events are sporting ones such as a golf tournament, because it's a sport she knows nothing about, so they are a particular challenge especially if they require careful and detailed planning. 'I'm a logistics super-fan', says Ruth, 'and there's always an edge of high-end quality with a golf event, which allows me to fool myself that being an event manager is glamorous. It's not!'

One of Ruth's favourite venues is a white room style venue, with the potential to bring in whatever you want in terms of décor and production. 'I always aim to "wow" clients and their guests, thinking outside the box to make a venue look as different, new and fresh for their event as possible, because of course, everyone wants to host their event somewhere that their guests have never been before', says Ruth.

However, especially in a small country like Northern Ireland, it's not easy to find a new venue, and it never stays new for long, so a white canvas venue that allows you to design its atmosphere and look from scratch is ideal. Unfortunately, hotel venues aren't on Ruth's favourites list, as they can tend to be rather traditional with limited fun and originality. Another downside to using many venues is that you are limited as to which third party suppliers you can use. For example, you might only be allowed to use their in-house caterers, whose menu and/or budget don't necessarily work for your client. The bar can also be an issue, where the client might want to bring their own wines, or the hotel has a business arrangement with a specific décor company who aren't quite up to scratch. All that said, it's the staff working at a venue that make it or break it. Ruth says that 'if you have helpful staff who understand your client's needs, recognize your position as the event manager and appreciate the business, you'll usually make a good event a GREAT event'.

http://callowevents.co.uk

is often true. Many venues who offer this option have limited kitchen space or equipment. Hiring in the required cooking and refrigeration units as well as cutlery and crockery will prove very expensive.

4.9 AVAILABILITY

The primary function of a venue should be considered as part of the assessment of their availability. For example, while purpose built centres are generally available to hire all year round, the same cannot be said for most other types of venues. Academic venues that are primarily being used for educational purposes may be unavailable for event use during the academic year which typically runs from September to July. It may, however, be possible to hire rooms during the Christmas and Easter breaks, half term or reading week. Similarly, sporting venues may have heavy restrictions on their availability during the period of relevant sporting competition or training. Unusual venues can also have restricted times of use for private events. Typically central areas of museums and visitor attractions can only be hired in the evening while theatres and cinemas may only be available during the day. Although hotels and other hospitality providers are generally available for event use all year round, they may be particularly busy with day to day operations during the summer and at national holiday times and notable celebrations such as Valentine's Day, Christmas and New Year. Although it may still be possible to hire these venues at these times, it may be particularly difficult to do so at short notice and it is always likely to be expensive at peak times.

4.10 STAFF

It is becoming far more common today to find a specialist event team working at a venue. These personnel are usually highly trained event specialists, responsible for working closely with event organisers to ensure the successful planning and delivery of the event within their venue. A number of venues will have a designated wedding co-ordinator, to work alongside couples planning to hold all or part of their wedding celebrations at the venue. Other venues may have a designated business events co-ordinator to take responsibility for overseeing meetings, conferences and other corporate events to be held in their premises. The benefits of working with designated venue staff are many as they will have excellent venue knowledge, experience of what works and what doesn't and access to a range of additional suppliers. The offer of being provided with a specific venue-based event co-ordinator to work with can be very valuable to the event manager and in the long run may save a lot of time and money. Some venues will also offer the event manager the services of a technician or stage manager as part of their booking. This is particularly common at venues with much of their own AV equipment. Again, this can save the event manager time and money in sourcing a production team. As such, the availability of staff should be considered from the offset. It is also worth noting that although new venues or venues without an events team may offer attractive discounts to entice event organisers, this must be evaluated against working with an experienced and knowledgeable venue team.

4.11 PRICES AND RFPS

The cost of hiring a venue can vary enormously – this is discussed in detail in Chapter 9. Charges may be dependent upon the number of rooms required, the length of the hire period, the nature of the event, the catering requirements and the time of year to name a few. Many venues will advertise their day delegate rate on their website or in their brochure. As this is usually a straightforward per capita charge (based on the use of one meeting room, stationery, AV equipment and refreshments) it will only apply to simple one day events such as a short conference or training session. For the majority of events, a DDR isn't applicable. This means that for a venue to provide an event manager with a comprehensive list of applicable hire charges, they will require a certain amount of event information first. This is done via a process of writing and submitting a request for a proposal (**RFP**).

The process of submitting and receiving an RFP begins with the event manager writing up key information about the event to give to prospective venues. The information can be based around the client's brief with details of any notable requirements. Table 4.3 provides you with a checklist for writing an RFP.

Generally the more information you can include in the RFP, the more likely you are to get an accurate response from venues. You may wish to omit information about your client at this stage in the process unless you feel that this could positively impact the response from the venue. For example, if the client works for a registered charity the venue may have a reduced set of hire charges (see Chapter 9). The RFP can usually be emailed directly to the venue and you can expect a quick response. Typically the venue will reply by providing you with a quotation (prices) and a proposal (written explanation of charges). The proposal should outline how the venue can accommodate the event, which rooms the venue are proposing that you hire and details of the venue's availability. In most cases the prices on the quotation can be negotiated. At this stage in the process, the charges are based on a rough outline of the event, which may change and there are a number of ways that you can negotiate on charges which are discussed in Chapter 9. Once you have gathered the proposals you can begin to evaluate the responses by assessing which venues can accommodate your event and how closely they can meet your requirements. Figure 4.1 illustrates the RFP process.

It is worth noting that if you want to avoid entering into the RFP process with hundreds of venues you can assess probable charges based on what you already know about the venue. The DDR gives an indication of cost and, for example, a five star hotel will obviously be more expensive than a three star establishment. Large, purpose built venues may be expensive (but cost effective in the long run) and popular unique venues are likely to be pricey in comparison to academic or sporting venues if they are hired out of season. However, if you are going to

Table 4.3 A checklist for writing an RFP

Event information	
Date	Preferred day/date/time of year and duration of event (to include get in/get out)
Audience	Approximate number of event attendees
Programme	A basic outline of the purpose of the event and key programme features
Rooms	Approximate number of rooms required for the event with an indication of purpose or set up per room
Accommodation	Approximate number of bedrooms required (if applicable)
Catering	Outline of main catering requirements
Contact information	
You	Your name, title, email address and phone number
Your client	Appropriate information about your client (only)

Figure 4.1 The RFP process.

send an RFP to every possible venue in a particular area then it is worth considering using an intermediary, such as a DMO or venue finding agency, to take care of much of this leg work. In this case you will provide them with the RFP and they will take responsibility for sending it to venues and collating the responses and this is discussed in more detail later in this chapter.

4.12 ACCESS

Access to the venue should also be considered as part of the initial search. Access in terms of location has been discussed earlier in this chapter but this broad term also refers to access for event attendees with disabilities as well as access to set up the event.

In the UK the Disability Discrimination Act of 1995 sets out the legislation that is in place to protect and promote the rights of people with disabilities, and similar laws exist in most countries. Since the Act was introduced, many UK venues have modified their buildings to provide greater ease of access for people with limited mobility and greater provision for people with hearing impairments. However some historic venues, including some hotels, visitor attractions and theatres for example, are unable to alter the infrastructure of the building which means that there may be restricted access for people with impaired mobility. Rogers and Davidson (2016, p. 222) suggest that an increasing number of event managers are conscious of their legal obligations and will now only consider using fully accessible venues with adapted toilet facilities and suitable entrances and corridors. But at a minimum, you should plan for an inclusive event when investigating potential venues.

Similarly access to the building in terms of how equipment can be delivered and installed should also be considered. The get in and get out periods of events can be particularly busy and complex and if your event will require moving a substantial amount of furniture, equipment and staging into the venue, access to the building in order to do this should be considered from the offset. The event manager may need to investigate the width and height of entrances to the building and the location of these access points in relation to the rooms being used for the event. Floor loading limits will need to be observed and there may be date and time restrictions on when deliveries can take place prior to the event. Therefore, the event manager should study the venue's **technical specification** and be sure to include an estimate of the amount of time required for both the get in and get out in the RFP, as typically the venue hire charges will apply to these timings.

As we have seen so far in this chapter, there is a lot to consider when shortlisting venues and gathering information is time consuming and laborious. Fortunately there is a free and effective way to speed this up by using an intermediary such as a venue finding service or a DMO. However, if you are going to conduct the initial search yourself, Table 4.4 provides you with a checklist of the key venue considerations to include.

4.13 VENUE FINDING AGENCIES AND DMOS

Venue finding agencies are typically private companies set up to do all of the necessary research and legwork for event managers and they just need the event brief or the RFP to get started. Once this is provided to the venue finding agency they will conduct a search and present the event manager with their findings and recommendations. Generally this service is provided to the event manager free of charge. Agencies will usually take a commission from the venue that is ultimately booked for the event. The commission is usually a small percentage of the

Table 4.4 A checklist of key initial venue considerations

Consideration	Notes	Tick or comment
Parking		
Nearest car park	For cars and/or coaches	
Nearest drop off point		
Nearest taxi rank		
Nearest bus stop	Main line or regional	
Nearest train station		
Nearest airport	National or international	
Nearest motorway		
Amenities		
Restaurants	As appropriate to attendees' (tastes/budget)	
Shops		
Attractions/places of interest		
Accommodation		
Number of bedrooms at venue		
Quality of bedrooms at venue		
Number of bedrooms near venue		
Range of accommodation near venue	As appropriate to attendees' (tastes/budget)	
Number of additional bedrooms within walking distance of venue		
Capacity		
Capacity of main room		
Capacity of additional rooms		
Capacity for key event requirements, e.g. exhibition, dinner etc.		
Location of rooms/internal layout	Are rooms close to each other? On the same floor? Near to busy communal areas?	
Availability of lifts		
Design		
Age/style of building		
Notable exterior design features		
Notable interior design features		

Table 4.4 *continued*

Consideration	Notes	Tick or comment
Facilities		
Furniture	Free or chargeable?	
Partition boards		
Portable staging		
Lecterns/daises etc.		
Catering		
In house/preferred supplier/own choice		
Availability		
Days/times/seasons	Are there obvious hire period restrictions?	
Staff		
In house team/designated coordinator		
Technician		
Other	Are the venue offering event staff (stewards/marshals) etc.?	

overall value of the booking to the venue which Rogers (2013, p. 65) suggests is around 8 to 10 per cent.

While such services can save the event manager a lot of time and effort, and can appear to be excellent value as a free service, the event manager should take care when entering into search agreements with agencies. Depending on their size and level of expertise, agencies may not have the relevant wide ranging destination expertise needed to undertake a full and rigorous search. Furthermore, some agencies may be keen to secure business with venues that offer them an above average commission and this may influence the recommendations that they make. Therefore it may also be worth considering the use of a DMO.

DMOs can undertake a venue finding search within their specific destination and this service is usually provided to the event manager free of charge. If the DMO is state funded, this can often mean that the service they provide must be fair and transparent. As such they will conduct an impartial search of all suitable local venues and provide the event manager with a full set of results which gives details of all available and suitable venues. However, privatised DMOs, operating as profit making businesses, may only conduct searches (for venues or accommodation) among their fee paying members. This means that some viable venues may be omitted from the search. Furthermore, privately operated DMOs may also be influenced by commission rates. Even so, it is worth considering the use of an intermediary particularly if you can find one that can show evidence of their experience or one that other event managers are willing to recommend. Rogers and Davidson (2016) suggest that DMOs generally provide a more comprehensive service than a venue finding agency and the best intermediaries will take on much of the legwork for you. They have unrivalled destination knowledge and will only send the RFP to venues which they know are capable of and suited to hosting the event. They also have great bargaining power with their members and as such they may provide you with a fast, efficient and money saving service. Figure 4.2 illustrates the process of using a DMO.

Figure 4.2 The process of using a DMO to conduct a venue finding search.

4.14 EVALUATING PROPOSALS

Whether you use a DMO or another intermediary to conduct the venue finding search, or you decide to do this yourself, you are likely to receive several proposals and you will therefore face the challenge of evaluating the results. Once you have received all of the proposals, or the intermediary has provided you with a summary of the results, you will need to compare them. There are a number of ways in which to do this. The most obvious way is to compare the hire charges of the venue. However, hire charges will not necessarily be comprehensive so it is unwise to base your decision purely according to the cheapest quotation. Review each proposal to make sure that the venue is offering you the use of enough rooms to cover all of your requirements. Check to see if they have mentioned dates, particularly if there are specific days, dates or times of the year that they cannot offer you. If you have only searched residential venues, check that they can offer you enough bedrooms to accommodate all of your attendees. Finally you should appraise the tone of the proposal because as Rogers and Davidson explain (2016, p. 166) the proposal is more than just information, it's also an opportunity for the venue manager to sell the space by highlighting why you should choose it. Therefore look for clues as to the venue's interest in you and your event, their level of expertise and their willingness to negotiate their offer.

Taking into account all of the information that the venue has provided, you can compare offers and formulate a shortlist according to the best fit. However, remember that you are doing this as a paper exercise and you are basing the shortlist on some but not all of your venue requirements. Therefore it is prudent to draw up a final shortlist of a handful of potential venues that seem to be suitable. But before making your final decision it's vital that you conduct a site visit and view the venue in person.

4.15 INITIAL VENUE CONSIDERATIONS – THE VENUE MANAGER'S PERSPECTIVE

As a venue manager it is essential that you keep the venue's website up to date as most event managers will refer to it as part of the process of considering you for their event. It is also worth investing time, and usually a little money, in making sure that your venue is featured in key trade directories and that the information about the venue that is recorded there is current. Most trade directories are updated annually and you will be sent a reminder to check your entry. Even though the venue's website will be your main marketing tool, it is important to produce a paper brochure too. Many event managers, DMOs and venue finding agencies like to have a print out of all key venue information and having a professionally formatted and printed brochure is another important marketing tool that you can take to trade shows and networking events.

Maintaining a strong relationship with DMOs and venue finding agencies should ensure that you are included in relevant venue searches, providing your venue meets the minimum event requirements such as the capacity of your rooms and the venue's availability. It is essential that you reply to an RFP quickly, as in many cases the expected industry standard is that the client will receive the results within 24 hours of starting the search. Upon receiving an RFP, read it through carefully, making a note of any obvious reasons as to why the event is not suited to your venue. Whether or not to submit a proposal is an important and strategic decision. It's unethical to submit a proposal if you are not genuinely able and interested in hosting the event and doing so will damage the venue's reputation as well as your relationship with the DMO or client. However, there are times when you must make an assessment of the RFP which may result in you choosing not to submit a proposal. For example, you may wish to decline a relatively small event with a long **lead time** if such a booking would make it difficult for you to bid for a larger event later on. As there are a number of factors to consider when submitting or declining a RFP, it takes an experienced venue manager to assess the risk and make a decision.

When putting together a quotation and a proposal it is important that your documentation is comprehensive, covering all key requirements, so that it is clear to the client how your venue could accommodate their event. However, it's also important to indicate that you are open to negotiating the offer. This could mean reducing the hire charges or adding extra value to the booking, such as offering the use of AV equipment, staff etc. This can be discussed face to face during a site visit at a time when you will also be able to get more information from the client about the planned event. If there are certain dates that the venue is not available or certain requirements that you cannot meet, you should stipulate these in the proposal with your suggested alternatives. Unless you have a specific arrangement with the intermediary, you should also indicate how long you are prepared to hold any provisional dates or prices that you have put in the proposal. Finally, it's important to personalise the RFP so that the documentation conveys your interest in the event and your hope of working with the event manager.

4.16 SUMMARY

The initial search for a venue can be a time consuming process as there is a lot to consider in order to ultimately make a decision which is going to be right for the event. There are a number of ways in which the process can be speeded up, not least by using a venue finding agency or DMO. However, even with the use of an intermediary the event manager will need to be able to estimate the time of year that the event will take place, a suitable location, the number and type of attendees, the rough outline of the event programme and the budget available. If the event manager is going to search for venues independently, venue location, capacity and price are likely to be significant factors. However the availability of accommodation, leisure and other facilities, catering options, building design, the availability of staff and dates and general access to the venue are also important.

Gathering and analysing information about these factors is an essential part of the initial stage of the shortlisting process but as no venue is ever completely perfect it is useful to prioritise these factors and consider what is essential and where you may be prepared to make compromises. When making these decisions it is important to keep in mind the aim of the event, what your client is hoping to achieve and what the attendees are going to expect. This can help you to shortlist venues based on what is most appropriate to the event rather than according to your personal preferences. Ultimately visiting venues is essential in order to fully appreciate what they can offer but also to understand how the building or site presents the event manager with particular challenges. No venue is ever completely perfect for an event and compromises will have to be made. However much of the required venue information can be collected from the venue's website or brochure and technical specifications and photos or virtual site visits can be particularly useful.

However, before finalising the shortlist of venues, you should give consideration to one of the most important and significant trends affecting the events industry in the twenty-first century; that of sustainable event management. Chapter 5 explores sustainability in event and venue operations and provides a number of useful tips and case studies illustrating the complexities of responsible event planning and delivery.

4.17 FURTHER READING

The following sources are particularly useful for further reading on the subject of initial venue considerations:

Bladen, C., Kennell, J., Abson, E. and Wilde, N. (2012) *Events Management: An Introduction*. London: Routledge.

Bowdin, G., Allen, J., O'Toole, W., Harris, R. and Mcdonnell, I. (2011) *Events Management* (3rd edn). London: Routledge.

Dowson, R. and Bassett, D. (2015) *Event Planning and Management*. London: Kogan Page.

Goldblatt, J. (2007) *Special Events: The Roots and Wings of Celebration* (5th edn). New York: Wiley.

Whova publications (available at https://whova.com).

Sustainability in event and venue management

LEARNING OUTCOMES

By the end of Chapter 5, you should be able to:

- Understand the concept of sustainability within the context of event and venue management
- Recognise frameworks for sustainable practices, sustainability standards and venue and event certification
- Identify ways in which to practise responsible event management
- Understand the basis of venue grading schemes

5.1 INTRODUCTION

The topic of **sustainability** and the importance of incorporating sustainable practices in both our home and professional lives has gained much ground in the last few years as we have begun to realise how certain forces have been very damaging to the world. This has led us to develop theories and actions relating to sustainability; a way of trying to protect the world and limit the damage from some of these forces. As such sustainability is an important and emerging trend within event and venue management. The events industry has been actively developing and adopting sustainability principles and practices in recent years and this chapter will provide an overview of key developments, frameworks and guidelines for incorporating sustainable practices into event management, with a particular reference to the use of the venue. In terms of venue management, being green means developing the building into an environmentally friendly site and being sustainable means continuing without damaging the environment (Schwarz *et al.*, 2015). The discourse around the identification and measurement of sustainable venue management practices has led to a renewed discussion of ideas for venue grading and venue certification. This chapter will therefore include a review of some of the current initiatives and discussions around the concept of measuring venue quality and the potential value of such schemes to the event manager.

5.2 SUSTAINABILITY IN EVENT MANAGEMENT

The need for sustainable events has emerged from the effects of **globalisation** and the realisation of how our actions impact the world and put pressure on the environment. Added to this we have seen in recent years an increase in consumer demand for sustainability and mounting pressure from environmental interest groups for businesses of all kinds to introduce sustainable, responsible policies. This has been advanced by government initiatives to bring sustainability practices into every aspect of our lives and Figure 5.1 represents the emergence of the concept of sustainable events management.

The most widely accepted definition of sustainable development, refined by the United Nations, is development that meets the needs of the present without compromising the ability of future generations to meet their own needs. Further attempts to define and explain sustainability have resulted in new terminology – the triple bottom line. What this term suggests is that sustainability concerns three areas; effects on people, the planet and profit margins.

Therefore the sustainability management of events means taking care of all three. Consequently, the modern day event manager has a responsibility to clients and stakeholders that requires the delivery of an event which minimises negative impacts and can endure without the over consumption of resources (Getz, 2012). Sustainable events will have a positive impact on people, the planet and profit margins and thus help to meet the economic, sociocultural and environmental needs of event stakeholders (Ferdinand and Kitchin, 2012).

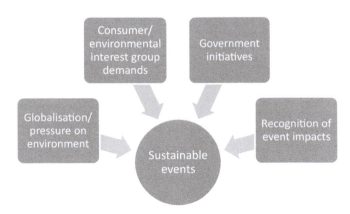

Figure 5.1 The emergence of sustainable event management.

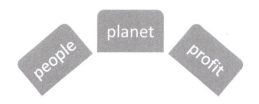

Figure 5.2 The triple bottom line.

Furthermore, professional event planners have an increasing ethical and legal duty to plan and deliver events that are environmentally, socially and culturally responsible (Bladen *et al.*, 2012). Responsible events are sensitive to the economic, sociocultural and environmental needs within a local host community, and are organised in order to create the best output for all involved or affected by the event (Raj and Musgrave, 2009). In reality, for many event professionals, sustainability is now equated with survival (Brown *et al.*, 2015) and this means that placing sustainability at the core of event management practices is not just important but it has become an essential part of the role, and event organisers must adopt increasingly responsible practices in order to stay competitive (Lee and Slocum, 2015).

5.3 FRAMEWORKS FOR SUSTAINABLE EVENTS

In order to understand sustainability in relation to venues and events and to put in place a model for planning and delivering events that are sustainable, several attempts have been made at creating sustainable event frameworks. Perhaps the first attempt at creating such a framework with the involvement of the events industry is the Hannover Principles which is the name given to a set of guidelines for the design of buildings and objects.

> The Hannover Principles aim to provide a platform upon which designers can consider how to adapt their work toward sustainable ends. Designers include all those who change the environment with the inspiration of human creativity. Design implies the conception and realization of human needs and desires.
>
> (William McDonough Architects, 1992)

The guidelines were formulated as part of the planning process for the Expo 2000 world fair which was held in Hannover. The Hannover Principles focused on the elements and thereby included consideration of water (minimising usage), air (minimising pollution), earth (recycling) and spirit (encouraging feelings of belonging) (Ferdinand and Kitchin, 2012).

Another important milestone in the development of sustainable event management practices was the introduction of British Standard 8901. The British Standards Institution produces standards for a range of services and products and it certifies compliance with these standards. BS8901 was developed specifically for the events industry and one of the key drivers of the introduction of the standard was the 2012 Olympic Games and the desire to prove that the Olympics, as a mega event, can be delivered in a sustainable manner. BS8901 covers three key areas of events: environmental responsibility, economic activity and social progress, thereby mirroring the triple bottom line. The standard provides a benchmark for the management system that is used to produce the event, and companies that have been awarded BS8901 have implemented the highest possible sustainability standards (Bladen *et al.*, 2012). The framework

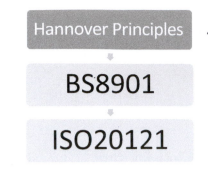

Figure 5.3 Sustainable event frameworks.

helps event managers to ensure that events demonstrate environmental responsibility, for example, by giving guidance on how to reduce carbon emissions and waste. Economic activity is central to the framework and this can be achieved by using local suppliers and ensuring the event is economically viable. Social progress is also part of the framework and can be achieved by involving the community in the planning of the event, ensuring fair employment of people who work on the event.

BS8901 has since developed into a new international standard – ISO20121 which was launched at the time of the London games in 2012. ISO, the International Organisation for Standardisation, is an independent organisation based in Switzerland that publishes standards and specifications for products, services and systems in order to uphold quality, safety and efficiency. International standards are marks of quality assurance and thereby a basis for enhanced client or customer satisfaction (Rogers and Davidson, 2016). As such the international standard will continue to provide confirmation that an event has been planned and implemented in line with sustainability standards and these apply to the event owner, the event manager and suppliers to the event (Case, 2013).

5.4 SUSTAINABILITY GUIDANCE FOR EVENT MANAGERS

There is conflicting evidence of the views and attitudes of event attendees towards sustainability and events. According to Ferdinand and Kitchin (2012) today, people are conscious about 'green' events and part of the process of deciding whether or not to attend an event will involve weighing up how environment-friendly it is and they are becoming more active in contributing to reducing the impacts caused by the event. However, much research points to event guests showing a lack of appreciation towards the sustainability related efforts of the event organiser and this can even go as far as complaints about the inconvenience and poor quality that can result from the implementation of sustainability practices (Teng *et al.*, 2015). Nonetheless, sustainability is certainly growing as an area of concern for event attendees and increasingly the trend set by the LOHAS generation (lifestyle of health and sustainability) indicates a growing demand for organisers to implement an event sustainability policy (Heipel, 2012). Communicating with event guests would seem to be the key to securing the support and engagement of attendees with what you are doing as a responsible event manager (Teng *et al.*, 2015). However, changing the way we plan and manage events and encouraging responsible behaviour at events is challenging and adds another dimension to the role of the event organiser.

Fortunately there are now plenty of sources of information, guidance and support to help event managers design, plan and deliver sustainable events. There are a number of professional associations for event managers to join and one of the benefits of membership is access to this type of practical information and guidance. There are also several books on the topic of sustainable event planning and many free guides that can be downloaded from the internet. Information, guidance and advice can be found on every topic including water usage, carbon emissions, waste management, recycling, transport management, greenhouse gas emissions and tips for offsetting impacts.

CASE STUDY 5.1 MARINA BAY SANDS

The Marina Bay Sands hotel and venue complex comprises of extensive and flexible event spaces, 50 dining options including award-winning restaurants, more than 170 premium brand shops and over 2,500 rooms and suites. It was the first events facility in South East Asia to obtain the ISO 20121 Sustainable Events Management System certification and it is the single largest building in Singapore to secure the Green Mark Platinum Award by the Building and Construction Authority (BCA).

Image 5.1 Marina Bay Sands.
© Shutterstock.

The venue is committed to the long-term protection of the environment through these objectives:

* Reduce energy usage by 1.25 per cent
* Reduce water use by 6 per cent

continued

- Increase staff awareness of sustainability
- Increase client awareness of sustainable meetings
- Increase health and safety throughout property operations
- Increase use of sustainable food on property
- Increase supply chain sustainability
- Increase social impact of environmental issues
- Increase sustainability into development and design of major renovation projects
- Improve their environmental management system
- Decrease waste sent to landfill/incineration by 10 per cent

Marina Bay Sands drives sustainability through their Sands Eco360 Global Sustainability Program, a global strategy with the objective to continuously improve the stewardship of the business, the environment and the community. One of the ways in which this is achieved is by providing event organisers with a 'Green Meeting Concierge'. This person will work closely with organisers to plan and customise a sustainable event. The Green Meeting Concierges are professionals with knowledge and experience in both sustainability and event planning. They will work towards client values and goals and provide guidance in setting event sustainability goals.

Some of the ways in which the venue promotes sustainability includes:

- Offering the 'harvest menu' option which uses only fresh ingredients that have been sourced locally
- Providing a Sands ECO360 Impact Statement which summarises the total energy and water consumption, recycling rate and carbon emission of the event and highlights achievements towards sustainability initiatives
- Customising a corporate social responsibility led event which enables attendees to give back to the community
- Providing the Marina Bay Sands Meetings App which allows event organisers to update event schedules and make new announcements in real-time without creating waste with printed material
- Providing sustainable decoration options which can be reused, recycled or planted after the event
- Designing a zero-waste component which ensures that at least one aspect of the event is completely waste-free

The Green Meeting Concierge will act as a liaison between the event manager and all internal operating departments to ensure successful implementation of sustainability plans and they will work with the event mangers PR team to communicate messages about the event sustainability efforts. The Green Meeting Concierge will create a post event impact statement and post event report which consolidates the event's environmental impact data and achievements.

Source: www.marinabaysands.com

5.5 SUSTAINABLE VENUES

According to Lee and Slocum (2015) event managers have not yet reached the point where the venue's sustainability practices greatly influence choice of venue. This is a view supported by Adongo (2011) and the agreement is that price, location and the quality of the venue still outweigh other factors such as sustainable practices. The notion of 'quality' is discussed later in this chapter but Teng *et al.* (2015) suggest that event attendees may consider venues with environmental credentials to be of higher quality than others. But what is certainly true is that all stakeholders in the events industry have a role to play in promoting sustainability and venues play a central role in the industry (Adongo, 2011). Therefore, as part of the process of venue selection it is important to give some consideration to the actions that venues are taking to deliver more responsible events and to promote appropriate use of their spaces.

The construction of venues alone can be one of the most environmentally damaging acts as this can involve the reduction or disturbance of wildlife, trees, grasses, plant life and other vegetation (Schwarz *et al.*, 2015). Additionally, the creation of infrastructure can have significant negative sociocultural impacts. The displacement of people as a result of new buildings can be detrimental to social, cultural and business relationships (Quinn, 2013); therefore the development of any new venue must be carefully and strategically planned. New buildings as well as established venues can create significant negative environmental and social impacts as they rely heavily on natural resources via the consumption of large quantities of energy, water, and non-renewable resources and thereby they create an increased threat to the environment (Teng *et al.*, 2015). However Heipel (2012) suggests that many venues have invested much time and effort in developing and implementing sustainability policies and as such they are further ahead in this area than event planners. For example, most large hotels have all-encompassing environmental policies (Jakobson, 2015) and many venues now provide sustainably sourced food, are environmentally conscious throughout the property and support projects that involve employees helping out in the community (Hennessy, 2015).

CASE STUDY 5.2 THE UNON *SUSTAINABLE EVENTS GUIDE*

Established in 1996, the United Nations Office in Nairobi is a major events venue and has been leading the way in promoting sustainable event management. At UNON events are regular and often quite large occurrences as they have become standard business practice within the United Nations for the simple reason that they are often the most time efficient and effective way of sharing thinking, identifying solutions and reaching agreements. At the same time, however, they can leave a significant environmental footprint through consuming energy and water, generating waste, polluting the air and water, and contributing to climate change by creating greenhouse gas emissions. As a venue, UNON wanted to combat these impacts and it began doing this by:

- Providing shuttle buses for event participants
- Ensuring that caterers meet waste management standards
- Donating unused publications to Kenyan schools
- Recycling plastic, paper and other solid waste through no-fee contracts with private sector recycling companies

continued

In 2008 UNON decided to collaborate with the United Nations Environment Programme (UNEP) to share some of this good practice and together they produced a guide to green meetings in 2008. In 2011 and with the support of Local Governments for Sustainability this was developed into the *Sustainable Events Guide* which provides much valuable information to help event planners maximise the positive impacts and minimise the potential negative ones in the course of planning and delivering events.

The guide is very comprehensive with six detailed sections:

Section 1: Sustainable events as opportunity for change – an introduction to the concept of sustainable events and the benefits these can bring to event organisers and other stakeholders involved.

Section 2: Managing and communicating sustainable events – guidance on management and communication aspects of sustainable events, with a special focus on the engagement of relevant stakeholders.

Section 3: Implementing sustainable events – a summary of the main conference areas and the actions that can be taken to reduce potential negative impacts and increase benefits (with a special focus on venue selection, marketing and communication, accommodation, transport, exhibiting and catering). This section also covers recommendations on how to embed social criteria throughout event preparation and implementation (small local business support, social integration, food waste, etc.).

Section 4: Climate neutral and climate friendly events – an overview on the topic of carbon offsets and proposals for calculating and offsetting the remaining greenhouse gas emissions generated by an event.

Section 5: Reporting on sustainable events – guidelines on how to report on an event's sustainability measures.

Section 6: Sustainable events checklists – detailed sustainable recommendations for the day-to-day organisation of an event.

The benefits of incorporating sustainability considerations into event planning can be manifold. Sustainability considerations lead to environmental improvements, financial advantages, creating a positive image for the event planners, and social benefits for the local community. They can also trigger secondary positive effects such as innovation in the marketplace, thereby stimulating new product growth; and by raising awareness and inspiring change they can create long-term benefits for the broader community.

Source: © United Nations Environment Programme, 2012.

However, as McKinley (2015) explains, although a venue may be designed and operated in accordance with sustainability standards, it takes the cooperation of the event manager to drive forward change and planners must follow guidelines suggested by the venue manager. For example, research undertaken by Hischier and Hilty (2002) pointed to the negative environmental impacts created at conference venues but many of the impacts are actually attributable to the actions of the event organisers, for example, by using large quantities of printed material at the events. Therefore, venues are often a great source of information and guidance to event managers when it comes to planning and delivering a sustainable event.

CASE STUDY 5.3 THE MELBOURNE CONVENTION AND EXHIBITION CENTRE

Image 5.2 MCEC Convention Centre, Melbourne.

Source: The Melbourne Convention and Exhibition Centre.

As a venue, your commitment to sustainability is admirable. Do you find that the event managers that you work with are equally committed?

For many event professionals sustainability is common practice and expected these days. The majority of event companies have their own sustainability action plans and goals in place, so at Melbourne Convention and Exhibition Centre (MCEC) we work hard to ensure we can help our customers achieve these. Given the current climate and the topical subject, we have found that we are hosting a larger percentage of events which feature sustainable topics and content. This means that, as a host venue, we need to ensure our practices align with the discussion points of the event too. Their commitment to sustainability is also often determined by the origin of the event and the organiser. Melbourne as a city has a strong focus on sustainability and is implementing a range of initiatives to improve in this space, so we find local events have this commitment embedded.

As a venue, how do you encourage event managers to plan and deliver sustainable and responsible events?

MCEC is passionate about sustainability and the preservation of our environment. When planning each event, we work very closely with our customers to ensure they have all the information and advice they need to plan a sustainable event. We provide all our customers with a 'Green Approach' flyer, which outlines a number of ways we can support them and their event in achieving a range of green objectives.

continued

These include:

- *GreenPower:* Our customers can offset their events' environmental impact by purchasing GreenPower. After their event concludes, our GreenPower supplier can offset the total amount of electricity used with energy generated by accredited renewable sources, including solar and wind.
- *Charity partnerships:* MCEC partners with local charities including Launch Housing, SecondBite and OzHarvest. We can arrange introductions between the event and these important charities (or any other charity of their choice) to facilitate a range of sustainable initiatives, including the donation of left-over food and merchandise items.
- *Waste streams:* We can recommend suppliers and contractors that will help events minimise their environmental impact. Our preferred cleaning contractor is IKON, a company that invests heavily in recycling and waste diversion. If the event chooses to work with IKON, we are able to support by developing customised waste streams to reduce landfill and increase recycling.
- *Sharing their plans:* We help events communicate their sustainability goals to both their attendees and exhibitors to help them gain wider support and participation. This is often achieved through simple suggestions, such as asking their speakers to replace flip charts with whiteboards or requesting that attendees bring their own writing materials.
- *Measure and reporting:* Our expert event team is able to track the events' progress and help them develop realistic sustainability KPI's, including waste diversion rates, energy consumption and food origin, which we report back at the conclusion of the event.

What kind of practical support or guidance do you offer event managers to support them in efforts to be sustainable?

All our Event Planners and Operations Managers are trained and well versed in our sustainable practices. They are able to utilise their knowledge to advise our customers on ways they can achieve sustainable practice based on their event requirements. The following are sustainable initiatives already ingrained in our business, which support the green credentials for all events held within our venue:

- *Waste management:* We recycle and compost at every possible opportunity to minimise landfill, and partner with a local business that collects and repurposes wooden delivery pallets into bespoke furniture.
- *Sustainable menus:* Our talented chefs source local produce that's in-season, where possible, decreasing our food miles and allowing for the creation of fresh, sustainable menus. Our cooking oil is cleaned and re-used and surplus food is donated to OzHarvest and SecondBite to support families in need.
- *Charitable donations:* Donation points throughout our venue allow visitors to drop off any unused event items, including drink bottles, notebooks, t-shirts, pens and satchels. We donate these items to our charity partner, Launch Housing, on behalf of our customers.

- *Zero plastic bottles:* We have eliminated bottled water from our catering service, instead opting to provide chilled, filtered water for events and in all meeting rooms. Partnering with Nespresso, we return used coffee pods to be recycled.
- *Battery recycling:* We have a long-standing relationship with the Royal Children's Hospital and donate partially-used batteries to HeartKids and the Starlight Children's Foundation, which are used in children's toys in the hospital's play area.
- *Energy conservation:* Cutting-edge rooftop solar panels provide hot water to all public restrooms, and the Convention Centre's sensor-controlled lighting turns off when rooms are not in use. We use energy efficient radiant slab heating and cooling throughout the Convention Centre, and only use air conditioning when spaces are in use.

What are the main challenges of delivering sustainable events?

We work hard to ensure that outstanding customer service and the protection of our environment go hand-in-hand; however this can sometimes be a complicated balancing act. As a venue, we pride ourselves on our customer-centric approach and flexibility to help our customers achieve their vision for their event. When a customer's event vision doesn't entirely align to best sustainability practices we are often presented with the challenge of finding a way to overcome this. In these situations we are fortunate to have the support of a range of sustainability partners across our business, who work with us to find a solution to overcome this.

What are the key challenges of managing a venue while meeting sustainability goals?

While our Convention Centre is world-leading in regards to sustainability, our Exhibition Centre provides a constant challenge when trying to improve our environmental impact. Due to both its construction age (a 21-year-old building) and the type of common event requirements for exhibitions, it has taken large investment across a range of capital works upgrades to improve its environmental impact. The exhibition market has a reputation for generating high volumes of waste, so we have been challenged with finding ways to minimise the volume and educating our customers in this space. It has taken time, however we are starting to see a positive change in this space.

How important is your accreditation to you and does it help you to stand out as a venue?

We are very proud to share our environmental achievements, both as the first convention centre in the world to be awarded a 6-Star Green Star rating and our recent Gold EarthCheck rating, and we are actively continuing our operational efforts to reduce our environmental footprint.

These accreditations give us an important bench mark to maintain and help us to stand out as an industry world-leader in this space. With an increase in awareness regarding the importance of sustainably, we are finding that these accreditations are putting us in a good position to attract global events to Melbourne.

Source: Leighton Wood, Chief Operating Officer at Melbourne Convention and Exhibition Centre.

ACTIVITY 5.1

Imagine that you are organising a food festival and have chosen to use a local museum as the venue for the event. Create a list of all of the paper documents that you would normally use to promote the event (e.g. leaflets) and all of the paper documents that you might need to give to attendees before event day and on arrival (e.g. ticket, programme, map). Devise alternative and creative ways of sharing information that do not involve generating paper copies.

5.6 SUSTAINABILITY CHALLENGES FOR VENUES

Despite the clear efforts of venues to prioritise sustainability in event operations, there are a number of challenges faced by venue management teams. For example, there can be a number of high and unexpected costs involved in remodelling and renovating venues in order to conform to environmental standards and updating buildings to achieve the requirements for environmental recognition is difficult and offers uncertain benefits (Teng *et al.*, 2015). Furthermore, many venue managers have experienced challenges in implementing and executing sustainability policies at an operational level across a large organisation and small venue managers have had to prioritise on one aspect of sustainable management (Jakobson, 2015). Additionally, many venue managers find that there is a limited number of green suppliers for them to work with and a limited number of green products and a scarcity of suitable resources for their needs and this has been identified as a key barrier to the success of some suitability initiatives in certain venues (ibid.).

One area of that has been particularly challenging for venues, and also where there has been much success, is with catering operations. Chapter 7 discusses the types of catering operations at venues and the relationship between the venue and the catering team can greatly influence event design and delivery. However, a number of venues that provide refreshments can find it a challenge to build an effective partnership with food and beverage suppliers particularly if they are attempting to source produce locally (Lee and Slocum, 2015). There are a number of benefits of working with local suppliers including supporting the local community, cutting down on food transport costs and being able to confirm to event organisers and attendees how food has been processed and where it has come from. Plus there are indications that event attendees are willing to pay a price premium for locally sourced food items (ibid.).

5.7 MEETING THE EXPECTATIONS OF ATTENDEES

A key part of event planning will therefore involve meeting the expectations of the attendees and the client, in terms of their attitudes towards sustainability. As discussed in Chapter 2, the characteristics of the intended target audience may have a significant influence over the choice of venue and as part of the process of selecting a venue you should consider the audience's attitude towards sustainability and the level of importance of working with a venue that has a similar position.

As part of the discussion that you will have with venues, and as part of the process of gathering information about venues, identify the ways in which venues provide information to users about their environmental/sustainability policy. Check to see if they have a sustainability action plan in place and are taking steps towards areas such as energy reduction and conservation, recycling and responsible waste management. If, as Lee and Slocum (2015) suggest, event attendees are increasingly concerned about sustainability in the provision of food and beverages, seek a venue that supports the use of recyclable products, donating leftovers to a food bank and buying food from local vendors. And check to see how the venue will support you in communicating to attendees what is being done at the venue to promote sustainability and how they can participate in such initiatives during the event.

5.8 CORPORATE SOCIAL RESPONSIBILITY AND BRANDING

Alongside the emergence of sustainability as a key issue in business management, there has been an increase in the recognition of and demand to adopt **corporate social responsibility** (CSR) principles. The concept of CSR is that it requires companies to 'integrate the interests and needs of customers, employees, suppliers, shareholders, communities and the planet into corporate strategies. In short, businesses need to be good corporate citizens' (Sloan *et al.*, 2013, p. 242). Subscription to the notion and ideals of CSR has been described as a combination of the dedication of businesses to environmental altruism as well as a need for market competitiveness and this has a significant impact on the management of events. Event organisers are now under increasing pressure to incorporate sustainability as well as corporate social responsibility practices into the organisation of events in order to meet the standards of their client's organisation as well as to enhance their client's reputation and image (Lee and Slocum, 2015).

THE INDUSTRY EXPERT'S VIEW 5.1

CORPORATE SOCIAL RESPONSIBILITY IS AN ESSENTIAL PART OF CREATING EVENT ENGAGEMENT

Chris Lee, partner and CEO of ACCESS Destination Services, www.specialevents.com

As event planners, we have the opportunity to be so much more than simply organizers of buses, boats, ballrooms and badges. Events are meant to be shared experiences. Increasingly, event participants and guests (especially millennials) expect more than just things from us – they want experiences. They want shared experiences that inspire them. In my 28 years in the industry, I've been a part of some pretty amazing events, but it's difficult for me to think of shared experiences more meaningful, more powerful and more universally inspiring than those focused on giving back.

Most of us today are familiar with the term CSR. The World Business Council for Sustainable Development defines CSR as 'the continuing commitment by businesses to contribute to economic development while improving the quality of life of the workforce and their families as well as of the community and society at large.' I like that this definition acknowledges how many people are affected by CSR – employees, families, communities! The positive impact of CSR on local communities and causes is undeniable,

continued

but the experience can be just as significant for those individuals and groups who are giving their time and resources to a meaningful cause.

As planners, we're always looking to get the best from each destination, so isn't it time we give back to those destinations and local communities? Planning a successful CSR campaign is similar to designing any successful program. First, identify your company's existing charitable giving causes and integrate them into your meetings. If your company has not identified a charity or cause, you have an opportunity to pioneer CSR in your organization through your events. Incorporating CSR activities into events is a great way to enhance the experience and reinforce your company's values. Get everyone involved across all departments; perhaps your HR executives have ideas for integrating CSR into your events. After all, they are stakeholders in improving morale and employee retention.

Successful, inspiring CSR programs combine the camaraderie and interaction of traditional team-building events with social consciousness and community benefits. CSR campaigns should feel unique to your company and be aligned with your corporate values. Inspiration doesn't have to end when the program does. Following a particularly meaningful CSR and team-building event ACCESS produced for a long-term client, the participants were personally moved to do even more. At dinner that evening, a small group decided that each person would donate $10 to the charity they had benefitted at that day's CSR event. This spontaneous act spread to the table next to them and so on until virtually every one of the 1,000 participants had contributed. We suddenly had a massive cash donation that was in addition to the care packages our client just delivered. The vice president of the company then took the microphone, thanked everyone, and announced that the company would match the donations they had made that night! 'The sense of pride and camaraderie in that room was bigger than we could ever have expected,' he said afterwards.

Giving is inspirational, and generosity is contagious. As leaders in the events industry, let's remember that Corporate Social Responsibility is not only a responsibility, but also an opportunity. We give not because we should, but because we can.

Source: http://www.specialevents.com/corporate-events/corporate-social-responsibility-essential-part-creating-event-engagement

This impacts the choice of venue, as frequently event organisers must seek out venues that have a brand and image that aligns with their client. As Rogers and Davidson (2016, p. 214) explain, the event manager must try to assess potential venues in terms of their ability to reinforce their client's brand:

For example, a planner choosing a venue for a meeting of a bank's shareholders may opt to hold it in a castle, to reflect and reinforce the bank's brand, if that includes values such as tradition, strength and the unassailable protection of their customers' assets. By way of contrast, a young video games start-up company, whose values are more closely associated with modernity, informality, creativity and fun may find it appropriate to hold their meetings in an amusement park.

However, one of the challenges of identifying suitable venues is the lack of any standardised grading criteria for venues. Any venue can market itself as a space that can be used for events and in most countries, there is no regulatory or quality control framework in place for event venues. This therefore presents the event manager with the challenge of how to select the best quality venue for their event and matching venue brand with client brand.

5.9 VENUE GRADING SCHEMES

There is a strong argument for the introduction of venue grading schemes as a mechanism to support the decision making process undertaken by the event manager. Furthermore, as Adongo (2011) suggests, given the high number of venues in operation, a grading scheme could not only assist event managers with choosing a venue, but by creating an expectation of quality we could see increased competition among event venues. There are also suggestions that governments should be responsible for regulating venue performance as this is the only way that environmental policies and regulations will be properly enforced (Teng *et al.*, 2015).

Although as discussed in Chapter 3, in many parts of the world it is commonplace for the national or local DMO to inspect and grade accommodation according to specific criteria. This thereby provides both event organisers and guests with standardised benchmarks to use in order to book appropriate accommodation. There have been a number of attempts to introduce a similar inspection and grading system for other types of venues however one of the challenges of such a system is identifying what constitutes a quality service within a venue and how this could be measured (Adongo, 2011). Consequently, event organisers can seek to assess the quality of a venue and brand appropriateness through various measures and indicators. For example, the accommodation grading criteria used in hotels is also a good indication of the quality of their event facilities and the general level of service at their facility. Other types of venues may have received certification such as BS8901 or ISO20121 or accreditation from an industry association such as The Association of Event Venues (AEV). Furthermore, there are a number of international standards that apply to elements of venue management. ISO 9001 is a management system that demonstrates quality in all areas of a business to include facilities, training, people, services and equipment. It is being adopted by many venues as a means of providing quality assurance to clients as well as motivating staff and demonstrating a commitment to ongoing development (Rogers and Davidson, 2016). Additionally ISO 14000 applies to environmentally sustainable operations and aims to reduce an organisation's environmental footprint particularly through reducing waste and pollution. This standard is also being adopted by venues who use it not only through operational management of the building but also as a marketing tool to promote a positive image of the business (Schwarz *et al.*, 2015).

CASE STUDY 5.4 GL EVENTS VENUES AND ISO 14001 CERTIFICATION

GL Events Venues is based in France but represents 40 venues across 23 cities including Paris, Barcelona, Brussels, Budapest, Rio de Janeiro and Sao Paolo. The venues include concert halls, arenas and convention centres that host a variety of events for up to 10,000 people.

In 2012 GL Events Venues secured ISO 14001 certification which is a standard confirming the use of an environmental management system within the organisation.

continued

The standard covers improvement in three areas – energy management, water management and waste management. The core principal of the ISO standard is continuous improvement and consequently each organisation that is awarded certification is audited each year and re-certified every three years to ensure that continual progress is being achieved.

GL Events Venues have continued to successfully renew their ISO 14001 certification because they consider it to be an important part of their venue operations and they have focused on protecting the environment by limiting the environmental impacts related to the organisation of their events. They have also experienced growing expectations from their customers and other stakeholders to integrate sustainability into their operations. They feel that there has been a noticeable trend towards sustainability criteria being used by clients in their search and selection of suitable event venues and for GL Events their certification gives them a competitive advantage.

They have also noticed that there are growing legal and regulatory pressures to take environmental concerns seriously. Plus, the control of their energy performance is now directly linked to their economic performance, in that by optimising their consumption of water and energy they have seen a positive impact on their operational costs.

The ISO 14001 certification helps GL Events Venues to meet the environmental commitment of some of the event organisers and public authorities that they work with. Some of GL Events Venues achievements have directly benefited event managers, for example the improvement of waste management systems and the addition of recycling bins ensures a more comfortable and clean event experience for attendees.

The certification also provides a quality assurance to the event organiser as, from a technical and regulatory point of view, the commitment to maintain the ISO 140001 accreditation requires a high-level of facility control by the venue. It also helps GL Events Venues with their commitment to their corporate social responsibility policy which is based around the three pillars of sustainable development (the triple bottom line) which are:

- Think Green (environment)
- Think People (employment and workplace conditions)
- Think Local (social progress)

The CSR policy has two key priorities; to offer employees a professional environment in which they can grow and find fulfilment and to support customers in achieving their own commitments and objectives. GL Events Venues currently employ over 4000 people in 140 different professions and they consider this to be one of the reasons that they are a leading organisation within the events industry as this broad range of complementary and integrated skilled workers enables them to manage every aspect of the event chain. As a market leader, GL Events Venues feel that they have a certain responsibility towards the sector and the ISO 14001 certification is a key measure of their environmental program and commitment to suitability.

Source: http://www.gl-events-venues.com/gl-events-venues-renewed-the-iso-
14001-certification-for-the-event-venues-in-france

Table 5.1 summarises some of the ways in which the event manager can identify a suitable event venue in terms of sustainability and commitment to corporate social responsibility. These are broken down into the three key areas of accreditation, policies and practices.

Table 5.1 *Ways to identify a venue's commitment to sustainability and CSR*

Accreditation and awards
Does the venue have certification (e.g. ISO20121)?
Has the venue received any recognisable sustainability awards?

Policies
Does the venue have a sustainability policy?
Does the venue have a CSR policy?
Does the venue state their commitment to the welfare of their staff?
How does the venue demonstrate a commitment to the local community?
What information does the venue have about their supply chain/responsible purchasing?

Practices
Does the venue have an energy saving programme?
Does the venue have solar panels?
Is the venue using water saving devices?
How much and what kind of recycling is the venue using and promoting?
Does the venue have a carbon emissions offsetting initiative?
Does the venue/in-house caterer use locally sourced foods?
Does the venue have an environmentally conscious waste management system in place?

5.10 EVENT CERTIFICATION

If you are going to invest much time and effort in identifying and working with responsible stakeholders, including the venue, and delivering a sustainable event, then it is worth considering the process of event certification. As Lee and Slocum (2015) explain, there are now a number of schemes and initiatives available to event planners to demonstrate how their event is meeting sustainability standards. Securing green certification of the event shows attendees that you and your client's organisation have a commitment to responsible event management and it presents you with the opportunity to share good news about the event.

Additionally, the evaluation of events continues to be an important part of the cycle of event management. Event evaluation is discussed in Chapter 11 but essentially this involves measuring the effects and impacts that events have had on the environment as well as the attendee experienced. This can involve measuring the sustainability of the event as well as the social, cultural and environmental benefits created by the event. Increasingly evaluation is related to certification in that event evaluation demonstrates what has been achieved as well as how organisations need to improve and as such evaluation is at the centre of true sustainability (Brown *et al.*, 2015, p. 136). Therefore securing accreditation for your organisation or for the event may be something that you wish to secure as part of the process of delivering a responsible event.

5.11 SUSTAINABILITY AND QUALITY – THE VENUE MANAGER'S PERSPECTIVE

As a key stakeholder group within the event management industry it has been important for venues to demonstrate a commitment to business ethics and sustainable practices. And on the whole, venues have embraced this challenge and have been leading the way in terms of attaining green accreditation and encouraging the responsible planning and delivery of events.

Venue managers may find that there is much research to suggest that implementing green measures may not be as costly as envisaged however the benefits are incremental rather than immediate and investments will be realised in the long term which needs to be factored in to budgeting and financial planning (Jakobson, 2015). However, there is much to be gained from implementing sustainability initiatives as it can be a mechanism for increasing business and improving the reputation of the venue. Taking part in optional grading schemes has similar benefits too for the venue, as not only does this act as quality assurance for the event manager but it can give a venue a competitive edge and it can be a useful tool in venue marketing. However, in terms of emerging trends in event management, it is evident that there is an increasing expectation for venues to meet sustainability standards and to be able to demonstrate how this is being achieved. Therefore, where venue managers have historically been quite active in encouraging sustainability in event planning, event managers are taking an increasingly proactive approach to selecting and working with suppliers that meet specific ethical standards.

5.12 SUMMARY

The growing awareness of the negative environmental impacts created by individuals and businesses has led organisations to rethink their management processes and integrate environmental initiatives into their strategic planning (Whitfield et al., 2014, p. 300). In the context of industries such as tourism and events, environmental initiatives are being used to reduce or eliminate the negative impacts associated with the production and consumption of goods and services (Jakobson, 2015). Venues have been great advocates for encouraging change towards making sustainable choices and they have been proactive in educating event planners on sustainability issues (McKinley, 2015). Event managers are increasingly focusing on adopting principles of reducing, reusing and recycling and taking advantage of the growing body of advice and guidance on planning and delivering responsible events. In particular much more consideration is now given to minimising waste and using recyclable products as well as a notable effort to move to electronic event promotion. The benefits of applying sustainable principles to venue and event management practices are gaining more attention, for example sourcing food from local farmers provides healthier, more sustainable menu options and also stimulates rural economies and local culinary culture (Lee and Slocum, 2015).

The quest for quality standards in an ever developing events industry has resulted in the call for more ways of ensuring that stakeholders provide the highest standards of service and facilities possible and this is particularly true of venues (Adongo, 2011). However the widespread lack of governmental regulation or industry mandate, alongside under developed green supply chains, also serves to limit the adoption of environmental initiatives in the events industry (Jakobson, 2015). However, the quality of the venue has an enormous influence on the choice of venue and destination made by the event manager and increasingly, quality is overlapping with attitudes towards sustainability and the adoption of corporate social responsibility practices. The crucial factor most likely to determine the extent to which venues adopt sustainability practices will be the level of demand of such features and how much venues can use green measures as selling point (Davidson and Hyde, 2014, p. 182). The evolving role and responsibilities of the event manager now involves investigating the green credentials of all potential suppliers. Increasingly, we will see the sustainability policy and practices of venues being scrutinised as part of the process of shortlisting potential venues. Only once the event manager has limited the number of possible venues for an event, can the arrangements for site visits be made and then the process for selecting a venue can continue.

5.13 FURTHER READING

The following sources are particularly useful for further reading on the subject of sustainability in an event and venue management context:

Case, R. (2013) *Events and The Environment*. London: Routledge.

Holmes, K. (2013) *Events and Sustainability*. London: Routledge.

Raj, R. and Musgrave, J. (Eds) (2009) *Event Management and Sustainability*. Oxford: CABI.

Sloan, P., Legrand, W. and Chen, J.S. (2013) *Sustainability in the Hospitality Industry* (2nd edn). London: Routledge.

BSI publications (available at www.bsigroup.com)

* *Sustainable Events Management*

Event Scotland publications (available at www.eventscotland.org)

* *Sustainable Events*

VisitWales publications (available at https://businesswales.gov.wales)

* *Sustainable Events and Festivals*

Organising a site visit

LEARNING OUTCOMES

By the end of Chapter 6, you should be able to:

- Understand the key purposes of site visits
- Confidently organise a site visit
- Identify all the things that you need to inspect during a site visit
- Appreciate the role of the site visit in the process of negotiating with a venue

6.1 INTRODUCTION

Once the event manager has shortlisted potential venues to a handful of viable options, then the arrangements for site visits can be made. A site visit or inspection is a tour of the venue in person and it is undeniably the best method for fully exploring the space available and absorbing the feel of the venue. A site visit provides the event manager with the means to test out the space and assess its full potential, and ultimately negotiate the charges and terms with the venue manager. Site visits therefore have a significant and strategic role to play in the organisation of events and they should be carefully planned in advance. There is a lot to take in when visiting a venue for the first time and this chapter contains lots of checklists that you can take with you to ensure that you don't miss anything. The chapter also provides insight and guidance as to what to expect from a site visit and what to make sure is included in a trip to each potential venue.

6.2 THE PURPOSE OF THE SITE VISIT

The site visit is an important stage of the event planning process that occurs after the RFP process is complete and before you book the venue, as illustrated in Figure 6.1. You may visit the venue a number of times during the event planning process, but the first site visit is particularly important.

Figure 6.1 The role of the site visit in event planning.

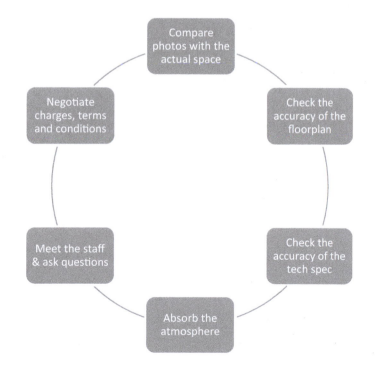

Figure 6.2 The key purposes of a site visit.

There are many purposes of attending a site visit, but spending time in the venue and thoroughly exploring the space in person is the best way to evaluate the suitability of the venue for your event. Both Lloyd (2013) and Bowdin *et al.* (2011) agree that the visit will enable you to check to see if the venue matches up with how it has been described to you so far and is as it appears in photos or on websites. Bowdin *et al.* (2011) go on to suggest that the primary purpose of the site visit is to confirm the accuracy of the floorplan and technical specification, however, it can be a far more valuable use of your time. A visit in person will allow you to fully absorb the ambience of the venue, and as Matthews (2016, p. 171) explains, familiarity with the venue is essential in order to effectively produce your event. The site visit can present you with a chance to explore, ask questions, take photographs, meet staff and discuss with them how your event can work within the space available. Figure 6.2 illustrates the key purposes of attending a site visit.

The site visit is an essential component of event planning and as both Sekula (2013) and Egan (2013) confirm, planning an event without first visiting the venue could lead to a range of avoidable issues such as unexpected costs and changes to rooms and layouts.

THE INDUSTRY EXPERT'S VIEW 6.1

AN INSIDER'S GUIDE TO HOW TO CONDUCT A VENUE SITE VISIT

Chris Powell, Event Director, www.theeventexpert.co.uk

The right venue, and the way it is laid out, really does set the tone and sense of occasion of your event. Picking the perfect venue for your event does, however, require extensive research and a thorough and well thought out site visit.

How do you ensure your site visit really does deliver?

Once you have a shortlist of 2–4 venues that really do fit your venue search criteria, it's time to pay them a visit. While you can do a lot online, you must remember an event venue is effectively trying to 'sell' itself to you. As life sometimes shows you . . . everything is not always as it seems. The way to find out if your venue is indeed everything you have read is to arrange a site visit.

A site visit is a scheduled meeting with, ideally, the venue manager. I recommend trying to arrange your meeting when the venue is being prepared for an event and to take a colleague along, as you will be amazed what somebody else sees, that you do not.

An important point to note here is that a venue site visit doesn't start when you walk through the front doors. It starts on the drive or journey to it – what sort of location is it in? How easy is it to get to and find? What's the parking and immediate environs like? I also recommend using the mode of transport your guests are going to have to use on event day – just so you can see whether their journey is going to be pleasant, easy or really not something you would want to do during rush hour!

I use the following simple 3-stage system when conducting a venue site visit.

Stop

- Give the venue your full concentration. Turn off your phone.
- Create a venue evaluation checklist to help guide the conversation.
- Take as long as you feel you need. If you are not sure, go back again. It is an important decision and not one to take lightly.

Look

- With an aesthetic eye, what's your overall impression, and then with a critical eye, give it a real good looking at!
- Is it attractive and well looked after (inside and outside)? Does it reach a good standard of cleanliness?
- Try to visualise your event taking place there and remember to take some photographs for future reference.
- Look everywhere inside and outside that is relevant to your event, to minimise any nasty event day surprises.
- Think about the logistical ease of your event set-up and break-down. Will it work there?
- Check the accuracy of the floor plans and other technical packages. Do you really know what you are getting?

Listen

- Are the venue's staff polite and courteous?
- Are all your questions being answered to your satisfaction?
- Do you get the impression that they are genuinely interested in helping you deliver a great event?
- What sort of event experience does the event day team have? They will be the team that helps you set up and run your event. You need to know how well you work with them.

The key is to be prepared. This is not some sort of informal wander around, but an important meeting which has serious ramifications if you get it wrong. Nobody blames the venue when it is not up to scratch – they blame the event manager. So, it's worth taking these meetings seriously!

6.3 SPATIAL AWARENESS

One of the most valuable benefits of undertaking a site visit in person is that you can walk through the event in the space that you are potentially going to use. This allows you to start to get a feel for how the event will work and also how you may need to adapt the event programme to make full use of the space at your disposal. It is a good idea to walk around the venue as if you are an attendee. This not only allows you to fully assess the event rooms but also the communal areas. Consider the direction attendees will take from the moment they arrive, as they move between rooms, as they use toilets and lifts, and as they leave the building.

The venue manager will be able to advise you on flow and pinch points. For example, they will tell you if you need to stagger entry or egress, or provide multiple entry points to ensure that people can walk around your event safely and comfortably. In addition to this, consider what attendees will see, hear, smell or touch as they move around the site. Their sensory experience within the building will be connected to your event and the impression they have of the venue will be entirely bound up with their memory of the event. You may only be able to control some of what they will experience in the venue, so during the visit assess what you can alter and what you cannot.

6.4 THE ITINERARY

A site visit can usually be arranged quite quickly with the venue staff. It may have been offered in the proposal, as venues will usually be quite keen to invite you to view the space in order to complete the booking. Often the venue will have a number of personnel who you will come into contact with at different stages in the event planning process. A large or busy venue may have several staff whose role is to work with event managers. They may have a sales team who are responsible for promoting and marketing the venue and in this case, they will have replied to your RFP. The sales manager may organise the site visit and be the person that you talk to in order to negotiate the hire charges and terms and conditions. Some venues will have a separate operations team. These staff will work with event managers who have made a booking with the venue and you may find that a particular person is appointed to work with you once you have confirmed that you are going to use the venue. Typically, the operations team will have experience of overseeing events and they will work closely with you in order to provide you with venue-specific advice and support as you develop the programme for your event. They may also attend the site visit in order to answer some of your operational questions.

Shone and Parry (2010) suggest that if you have used a venue finding agency to help with the RFP process it can be worthwhile hiring one of the agency staff to accompany you on the site visit. If this isn't appropriate, it can be useful to take a colleague with you on site visits, particularly if you have never visited the venue before or have never organised the type of event that you plan to hold there. A second set of eyes can be useful for providing a different perspective on what the venue has to offer and where it may constrain the event. A colleague can also take notes or photographs during the visit while you concentrate on asking questions and absorbing information. Bowdin et al. (2011, p. 497) suggest that an unannounced visit to the venue can be useful to check the ambience of the space and also the quality of the customer service from venue staff. If it's possible and practical for you to drop in to the venue without an appointment, you may certainly get a more authentic experience of the venue than you will on a planned visit. However, you will still need to arrange a site visit in order to view all areas of the venue and to discuss your event with the venue's staff.

A good venue team will put together a structured itinerary for the inspection that gives details of the parts of the venue that you will be visiting and the staff you will be meeting. Table 6.1 is a sample itinerary. If you are not provided with one it's a good idea to let them know in advance all the areas that you would like to see during the visit and the topics that you would like to discuss. This might include viewing all potential rooms as well as the communal and external areas of the building and reviewing the hire charges, facilities and availability of the venue. Depending on the size of the venue and the complexity of the event that you are planning, this may mean that the inspection will last for several hours and you should set aside ample time for this. If possible, arrange to visit the venue at roughly the same

Table 6.1 A sample site visit itinerary

10.00	On arrival at the venue, please report to reception
10.00 – 10.30	Coffee in the boardroom with the sales manager and a review of the proposal and quotation
10.30 – 11.30	An inspection of the ground floor rooms, to be joined by the operations manager
11.30 – 12.00	An inspection of the outside areas of the venue, to be joined by the site manager
12.00 – 12.30	An inspection of the first floor rooms, to be joined by the technical manager
12.30 – 13.15	Lunch in the restaurant with the venue team to include the catering manager and a review of the catering options at the venue
13.15 – 14.00	Meeting in the boardroom with the sales manager and the operations manager to go over final questions

time of the week and on the same day as the event so that you get a real sense of how the space will work. For example, you may want to assess how much natural daylight various rooms receive and how noisy they are at lunchtimes.

ACTIVITY 6.1

Imagine that you are about to organise a private party in a well-known visitor attraction. Create a detailed itinerary for a site visit to the venue which lists all of the facilities that you would want to inspect during the visit.

6.5 ASSESSING THE EXTERIOR OF THE BUILDING

The inspection should begin, or at least include, a detailed look at the exterior of the building. The main entrance to the venue will provide your attendees with their first taste of the event so consider what impression it gives. Is it clean and well maintained? How about the paths and walkways? Is the outside of the venue well lit? How close is the venue to the road? Questions to ask the venue staff include whether or not a welcome banner or signage can be used on the front of the building or near to the main entrance. Ask whether or not there will be other people using the venue's entrance on event day. If so, it will be essential that it is clear to your event attendees that they have arrived at the right place. Consider how you will be able to convey this, including checking for nearby prominent buildings or landmarks. Is it clear where the car park, drop-off points and main entrance are located? If you aren't sure of the answers then it's unlikely that your event guests will be either. As you walk around the outside of the building make a note of whether the ground is level or there are steps or steep inclines. Is there a smoking area or any notable eyesores? Are there gardens or seating areas outside? Is there space for a temporary structure such as a marquee? Is there nearby residential housing at the front and/or back of the venue? If so, this could determine acceptable noise levels and finish time of events.

Although most of your attendees are likely to use the venue's main entrance, during the site visit look at all of the potential entrances, including any at the rear of the building. You may wish to provide your high-profile performers or VIPs with a separate, more private, entry point. You may also prefer to have a route in and around the venue for staff which is separate to the one that your attendees will be using. You must also assess the loading options at the venue. This is going to be a significant consideration if you are likely to be using a lot of additional furniture or equipment that will need to be installed in various rooms. If there is a service road and rear entrances to the venue ask to see them and check whether the venue has a **service lift** so that you can fully assess the ease of access for equipment and staging.

Use the checklist provided in Table 6.2 as you inspect the exterior of the building and ask questions that relate to what sort of pre-event information you will need to share with attendees to ensure their smooth arrival at the venue.

ACTIVITY 6.2

Go and visit a nearby public venue that is available for hire as an event space. Using the checklist provided in Table 6.2, appraise the front of the building and inspect any areas at the back of the building that are open to the public. Make detailed notes of any pertinent features of the building, the grounds and the local area. Write up your notes so that they could go into a welcome pack for attendees to ensure their smooth arrival at the venue.

6.6 ASSESSING COMMUNAL AREAS

Once you step into the venue, assess the space around you. Is the hall or reception area well maintained? Is there room for you to put a welcome desk or registration point? Will you be able to have your own event staff stationed here to great attendees? Can you theme this space in any way to identify the event to guests as they enter? The venue manager should be able to answer all of these questions and give you examples of what other organisers have done in the past. Many venues can provide welcome signage, will personalise welcome boards and provide furniture for registration or information points, but it's a good idea to find out exactly what can be provided free of charge to you.

Most venues will have a plethora of communal areas that your event attendees may share with venue staff as well as other users of the building. Typically, this includes foyers, restaurants, toilets, lifts and outside space such as gardens and smoking zones. If you are going to be able to secure exclusive use of the venue you are more likely to be able to dress these areas. Dressing areas may include putting up decorations, advertisements or marketing materials and adding props or lighting. However, in most cases, exclusive venue usage is unlikely and you will be sharing these spaces with other people. In this case you may be very restricted as to what you can do in the communal areas. It is important to clarify this during the site visit. Venues are usually very careful to ensure communal areas are clean and presentable at all times and you may have to accept that you cannot personalise these spaces for your event. Nevertheless, make sure that you inspect all of the communal areas of the venue that your guests might use and check to see if they are clean and tidy and can be decorated or personalised for your event.

As you walk around, make a note of the appearance and demeanour of any of the venue staff that you pass by, as it is likely that they will come into contact with your event attendees.

Table 6.2 A checklist for the exterior of the building

Name of venue:	Tick or comment
Is the main entrance obvious, clean and well maintained?	
Are the paths and walkways well maintained?	
Is the outside of the venue well lit?	
How close is the venue to the road?	
Can signage be hung at the main entrance?	
Any nearby landmarks?	
Location of car park:	
Location of drop off points:	
Is the ground level?	
Is there a visible smoking area?	
Notable eyesores?	
Outside gardens?	
Seating areas?	
Room for a marquee, etc.?	
Residential location?	
Any rear entrances?	
Service road?	
Additional observations:	

Table 6.3 A checklist for interior communal areas

Name of venue:	Tick or comment
Is the hall/reception area well maintained?	
Is there room for you to put a welcome desk or registration point here?	
Will you be able to have your own event staff stationed here?	
Can you dress the entrance hall/reception area?	
Is the restaurant well maintained?	
Can you dress the restaurant?	
Are the toilets well maintained?	
Can you dress the toilets?	
Are the lifts well maintained?	
Can you dress the lifts?	
Are the outside areas well maintained?	
Can you dress the outside areas?	
Are staff well-presented?	
Are staff attentive?	
Is there a cashpoint?	
Is there a shop?	
Is there a cloakroom?	
Additional observations:	

Are they well-presented and attentive? Are they providing the same level of care to guests who are not obviously taking part in a site visit with the venue manager?

Finally, make a note of all of the facilities in the venue that your guests might use such as cashpoints, shops and cloakrooms, but check with the venue manager that these will be open or available at your event. Table 6.3 is a checklist that can be used when inspecting the communal areas of the venue including the entrance hall, reception area, corridors, toilets and lifts.

6.7 ASSESSING EACH ROOM

As you begin

As you begin to visit each room that is available for you to hire there are lots of things to consider, starting with their location within the venue. This includes the following:

* How close is each room to toilets, stairs and lifts?
* Are the rooms clustered or spread out?
* If event attendees will be moving between rooms during the event, how long will they need for this and will it be obvious to them as to which direction to go in?
* Do rooms have names or numbers?
* Are the rooms near to communal areas and, if so, will you be disturbed by lots of noise?

As with the reception area, it is important to check on signage around the venue and enquire as to whether or not you can put up your own directional signage in halls and corridors. And, although you may be planning on using different rooms within the venue for different purposes, take comprehensive notes on each room so that as you develop the event programme you can evaluate the potential of each room for each element of the event.

Questions to ask in each room

In each room consider the following points:

* How wide is the entrance and is it level or is there a step up or down into the room?
* How does this compare to any other entrances into the room?

You need to consider whether the venue, as well as specific rooms, are wheelchair accessible and also how any equipment will be delivered into specific rooms.

* Is the door lockable?

This may be important if you are going to leave the room unattended at any time.

* Is the room clean and well maintained or in need of updating?
* Is it old fashioned?
* Is the décor neutral?
* What is the colour scheme?
* What colour is the carpet or what type of flooring is there?
* Is it uniform in shape or is it irregular?
* Can you put decorations up on the walls?
* Can you put down temporary carpeting?
* Can you hear noise from other parts of the venue?

If you can hear noise, note whether this is coming from other rooms or communal areas of the venue. The venue manager may be able to control what type of events are taking place in rooms adjacent to your room, but they are less likely to be able to alter activities taking place in communal areas.

- What does the room smell of and why?

If the room has a particular smell, is this coming from something fixed such as wooden furniture or is it coming from something temporary such as food being prepared?

- What is the ceiling height?
- Is the room well-lit and is the lighting adjustable?
- Are there windows and blackout facilities?
- What is the view like?

The answers to all of these questions contribute to the ambience of the room and it's important to use the site visit to get a real sense of the atmosphere in each room and how what you do in the room might alter it.

- Does the room feel hot or cold and is the temperature adjustable?

Compare this to when your event is going to take place so that you can take into account seasonal variations. But check with the venue manager to see if the heating or air conditioning can be altered in each room.

Visualise the event

Next, begin to visualise the event taking place in the space and think about how you might set up the room.

- Does the room have an obvious focal point?

If it doesn't, you will need to think carefully about where could you put staging, demonstrations or activities.

- What furniture is already in the room and what condition is it in?
- Will you need to hire tablecloths and chair covers, or can the venue provide these?
- Are there any fixed items of furniture or décor that will have to stay in the room?

This might include heavy items like pianos, so check with the venue manager as to what has to stay and what can be moved into another room.

Furniture

Most venues will have an ample stock of tables and chairs but never take this for granted. Always check with the venue manager and be sure to ask whether or not there is a charge to use the venue's furniture. It's beneficial to have a clear idea of how many activities will be taking place throughout the event as even the most well-stocked buildings may struggle to fill every room with a complete set of tables and chairs at the same time. The venue will usually be able to help with arranging for extra furniture items to be hired for the duration of the event but this cost will usually be passed on to the event manager (see Chapters 7 and 9 for further details).

It is also worth noting that many venues have limited space for storing furniture which can result in an unsightly stack of chairs and tables at the back of rooms. Usually venues are quite careful not to place unwanted furniture in rooms that are being used, but sometimes they have no choice but to do this, so it may be prudent to double check this with the venue manager. If the venue has a lot of furniture on site it may be possible to choose the type of chairs and tables that you wish to use. If so, ask to see a sample of each style available and consider whether or not you will need to hire chair covers or tablecloths to alter their appearance as appropriate to your event.

Electricity, equipment, Wi-Fi and backstage areas

Further questions to ask include:

- Where are the power sockets and how many are there?

There may be a number of obvious as well as hidden power sockets, but if you are organising an event that will draw heavily on electricity, such as an exhibition, pay careful attention to how many sockets there are and where they are located.

- Is there an emergency exit?

If there is, the pathway to this will need to be kept clear.

- Is there an obvious curtained off or backstage area?

If not, is there a room nearby that you could use as a **green room** or event office?

- What fixed AV equipment is in the room and is there a **lighting rig**?
- What else does the venue own in terms of portable equipment, including lecterns and staging, and can these be reserved for your event?

Even events that are not going to feature performances often make good use of a little bit of staging which can help to elevate a speaker or draw attention to a noticeboard or similar feature. While assessing what's available, check to see if the venue can provide any AV equipment and also whether or not the venue has a **PA system**. This is discussed in detail in Chapter 8, but during the site visit it is a good idea to gather information about what equipment the venue has and whether this will be available for you to use and if so, at what cost.

Today most of us assume that venues will have a strong mobile phone signal and good access to fast Wi-Fi. However, it is always unwise to make assumptions about what is available. Remote venues may not have the same level of provision as those in urban locations. Similarly, some historic buildings may not have complete Wi-Fi coverage. Therefore, always check this with the venue manager, particularly if you are planning to incorporate the use of the internet, particularly social media sites, into the event programme.

Room set ups

Finally, within each room that you visit consider how you may wish to have the room set up. For example, will theatre style seating be appropriate, or is cabaret style going to suit the activities taking place? Providing the rooms are not in use, a good venue manager will normally have arranged for rooms to be set up in the style that you have indicated on your brief. If this has not been done ask the venue manager to explain how the rooms are usually set up. For example:

- Which way do the seats normally face?
- How many chairs in a row of theatre style seating, or how many chairs fit comfortably around a table?

These are important questions to ask so that you can begin to visualise the room being used and also so that you can assess sightlines as well as **acoustics**.

Sightlines are the path of vision that attendees will have towards the stage or front of the room. Poor sightlines are often the result of pillars or similar obstructions, or a room set up beyond a comfortable capacity. An attendee with restricted sightlines will ultimately have a poor event experience and thus, during the site visit it is a good idea to assess how likely this is to happen in each room. Similarly, the acoustics in each room in a venue will vary because they are affected by the shape and size of the room as well as the material of the building and the objects within it. The capacities of each room will vary according to the style of set up and the amount of additional furniture or equipment brought into the room, so discuss your ideas with the venue manager during the site visit.

6.8 INSPECTING ANCILLARY ROOMS

Rooms for speakers, suppliers and performers

During the site visit it is important to discuss with the venue manager the potential requirements of your speakers, suppliers, performers and staff. These can sometimes be extensive and will often vary from the venue requirements that your attendees will have. In due course, you will need to check the contractual agreements that you make with your suppliers to ensure that their venue requirements can be met and this is discussed in Chapter 7. At the time of the site visit it will be unlikely that you will have hired any event suppliers, nonetheless speakers and performers may have a long list of venue requirements and the venue manager will be able to offer advice on how to accommodate likely requests. Typically, speakers will have specific stage requirements including microphones and use of computer equipment, a projector and screen. They may request a personal dressing room with a shower, towels and a clothes rail as well as refreshments and overnight accommodation.

During the site visit check to see if there are dressing rooms or changing room facilities at the venue or an area that could be used as a green room. A green room is a lounge provided to performers to use before and after their performance. Ideally the designated green room should be close to the performance area but segregated from event attendees. As the event organiser, you may wish to provide similar facilities for event VIPs such as the client, speakers and key personnel by designating an area similar to a green room which is located behind the scenes and gives these people somewhere to relax away from the pressures of the event.

Rooms for staff

You may wish to use or hire venue staff to support event day operations and this is discussed in Chapter 7. But, in any case, you will probably have at least a small team of your own event staff working with you at the venue on event day and potentially you could have a large team of stewards. Therefore, as part of the site visit you should investigate the venue's facilities for

Table 6.4 A checklist per room

Name of room:	Tick or comment
Width of largest entrance:	
Any steps into the room?	
Lockable door?	
Is the room clean and well maintained?	
Shape of room (uniform or irregular)?	
Colour scheme/décor?	
Carpet/floor colour?	
Approximate ceiling height?	
Lighting (good, natural, adjustable)?	
Blackout facilities?	
Is there a view?	
Is the temperature adjustable?	
Is there a focal point?	
List of furniture:	
List of fixed items:	
Number and location of power sockets:	
Location of emergency exit:	
Audible noises? Where from?	
Does the room smell? What of/why?	
Is there a backstage area?	
List of fixed and portable AV equipment/lecterns/staging/etc.:	
Is there a lighting rig?	
Does the room have Wi-Fi?	
Is the mobile signal strong?	
Additional observations:	

you and your team. You will need to ensure that your staff can leave their personal belongings in a safe place which may be either a lockable room or one that is going to be manned at all times. You may wish to provide staff with a common room where they can relax during their breaks. You may also need a space in which you can brief your staff before the event starts and possibly throughout the event as well. The venue may be able to provide one room that meets all of these requirements which would be preferable in order to keep costs down. You must also consider your own venue needs as the primary event organiser. For example, will you need some sort of office space at the event; a place where you can charge your phone and plug in a laptop? You may need somewhere to store key items such as gifts for speakers, uniforms for staff, stationery etc. If the event is particularly complex you may need a control room from which you can monitor activities or direct operations. It can be useful to have a room for all of these purposes which is fairly near to the event but which is also private, so that occasionally you can escape from the hustle and bustle of the event and gather your thoughts!

6.9 CATERING OPERATIONS

Catering is an integral part of most events. Discussing catering arrangements during the site visit is a wise idea. It is common to be required to work with a specific caterer provided or recommended by the venue and this will usually be indicated to you by the venue prior to your visit (see Chapter 7). Many venues will provide refreshments during your visit and this is an opportunity to taste the food and meet with the catering or banqueting manager. A recent study undertaken by Lee and Slocum (2015) suggests that the quality of the food at the event is more important to attendees than the range of food items available. Therefore, although the initial site visit may be too early on in the planning process to discuss menus, it is still advisable to start to get an idea of what is available and how catering operations are carried out at the venue. For example, is there a restaurant or dining area? Is this a public space or can it be used by event attendees only? Is it possible to have catering laid out in all of the rooms that you might hire? If not, how far will everyone have to walk to collect refreshments during breaks? Can food and drink be served to your VIPs in the green room? If you are planning on incorporating a formal dinner in the event, it is worth asking specific questions about capacities for banquets and any menu restrictions.

6.10 ACCESS FOR ALL GUESTS

An important aspect of the site visit is evaluating the accessibility of the venue for everyone who might attend your event. Rogers and Davidson (2016, p. 222) note that event managers are now far more aware of their legal responsibility to create a fully accessible event and this is easily achievable in most venues. Generally modern venues have excellent access for guests with physical disabilities including wide doorways for wheelchair entry, lifts, disabled toilets and ramps. However, a number of unique venues in particular, may be very old and, although they will have been refurbished over the years, they may not have the same level of provision as newer buildings. Similarly, most venues have excellent facilities for the hearing impaired such as an **infra-red system**, but older buildings may use portable **induction loops** which operate in a slightly different way (see Chapter 8). As part of the site visit it is important to evaluate the building and facilities in terms of access for all guests and Case study 6.1 provides a checklist.

CASE STUDY 6.1 INCLUSIVE DESIGN

Proudlock Associates is a UK-based award-winning disability and inclusive design consultancy. They work with a range of clients across the private, public and voluntary sectors, and they provide planning and design assistance. They have worked with a number of venues including academic institutions, hotels and listed and heritage buildings, and they audit venues and provide recommendations on improving the design of buildings. They are leading the way in approaching building design that improves disabled access. However, rather than use terms like 'disabled access', Proudlock Associates prefer to use the term 'inclusive design' instead. A building that has an inclusive design is a venue that is accessible to everyone through a single provision which includes physical, visual, auditory and intellectual accessibility.

Examples of venues that they have worked with include Accor Hotels, The British Library, Battersea Arts Centre and Hoxton Hall. Hoxton Hall is a multipurpose arts venue but it was originally a music hall and dates back to 1863. During its recent refurbishment, Proudlock Associates worked with the architect and the venue management team on updating the design of the building.

Tracey Proudlock is the founder of Proudlock Associates, and she has put together a checklist for event planners which includes lots of advice on things to look out for during the site visit:

1. Check to see if the venue has an access statement or plan which gives details of how they accommodate disabilities.
2. Check the number and location of Blue Badge parking spaces at or near the venue.
3. Check that local taxi firms have accessible vehicles.
4. Check that wheelchair users can be allocated appropriate spaces in each room.
5. Check that guests with ambulant disabilities are allocated appropriate seats.
6. Check that the venue maintains their facilities (e.g. a loop system and **evacuation chairs**) and that staff will be on hand during the event to help.
7. Check that the **PA system** is connected to hearing enhancement equipment.
8. Check that microphones are appropriate to everyone using them.
9. Check that wheelchair users can sit comfortably at the venue's tables.
10. Check that there will be assistance provided at any self-service catering points.

Sources: Conference News (2015d), http://proudlockassociates.com/.

6.11 RESIDENTIAL VENUES

If the venue you are inspecting is residential make sure that you have a look at the on-site bedrooms and ask to have this included in the itinerary for the site visit. This is a good idea, even if you are not yet planning on making any accommodation reservations. Make a note of where the bedrooms are located in relation to the rest of the rooms that you are thinking of using. If you are using a hotel, the star rating of the bedrooms will indicate the quality of accommodation, but it is always worth inspecting the rooms and looking at the different options available from single rooms to suites. If a number of your attendees will need overnight accommodation, either before, during or after the event, try to have a look at a range of local options and discuss setting up an accommodation booking service with the local DMO. If you haven't yet worked with them, the venue manager can usually introduce you and arrange for you to meet with a representative as part of your site visit.

When you are arranging the site visit, ask the venue if you can stay overnight in one of the bedrooms. This will enable you to experience the accommodation exactly as your guests will, and you can sample the breakfast as well as any leisure facilities on site such as a pool, spa or gym. Some venues will be happy to provide you with a one night complimentary stay, but if not, most venue managers will usually be able to arrange a generous discount on your booking.

Table 6.5 provides you with a checklist to use when inspecting the bedrooms either at a residential venue or in nearby hotels and accommodation providers.

If the venue is not residential then it is worth inspecting the bedrooms available in nearby hotels and other accommodation providers. This will be an important investment of your time if some or all of your attendees are going to require overnight accommodation, particularly if you are going to have to organise a headquarter hotel. However, even if you do not expect many of your attendees to stay in the destination, it's worthwhile visiting one or two hotels on the same day as the site visit as, in the long run, this may save you time as frequently clients, speakers, performers or staff will ask you to make arrangements for them to stay overnight before or after the event.

Not only is the site visit an opportunity to explore the venue but it is also a chance to get to know the destination. Even if you have taken part in a fam trip or already know the area

Table 6.5 A checklist for accommodation

Name of accommodation provider:	Tick or comment
Rack rate (breakfast included?)	
Proximity to event venue	
Proximity to station, airport, etc.	
Parking (on site? Free?)	
Number and type of rooms (e.g. single, twin, double, balcony, standard, suite)	
Amenities in room: • Towels • Tea and coffee making facilities • Mini bar • Hairdryer • Ironing board • Docking station • In-room safe • Toiletries	
Laundry service	
Observations (e.g. is the room clean and well maintained?)	

quite well, extend your site visit to allow time to view a selection of restaurants and attractions as well as checking out the proximity of the train station and car parks. Look to see if there have been any major developments or changes since you were last in the area. Even if the event you are organising is going to be quite short you can still use the destination's image and facilities to help promote event attendance. Therefore, it is useful if you have a sound knowledge of what is available in the destination and experience of using these facilities first hand.

6.12 VENUE STAFF

One of the most important aspects of the site visit is meeting and getting to know the venue staff. Venue staff will have an unparalleled knowledge of their building's facilities and will be able to offer a range of tips and advice on how best to use the space for your event. They will be able to offer an insight into how other organisers have used the venue for similar events and they are best placed to help you to use the facilities effectively. Venue managers can provide support, advice and resources throughout the planning process and they can make excellent allies on event day. It is worth investing time and effort in developing a strong relationship with the venue team (see Chapters 7 and 11).

If it is possible to meet other staff at the venue this is also worth doing. Talk to the porters who set up the rooms and the duty manager who takes full and final responsibility for venue operations. It can be both reassuring and encouraging to get to know the people that are going to be present at your event and will play a key role in ensuring it is successful. Figure 6.3 illustrates the various venue staff that you and your guests may encounter during the event.

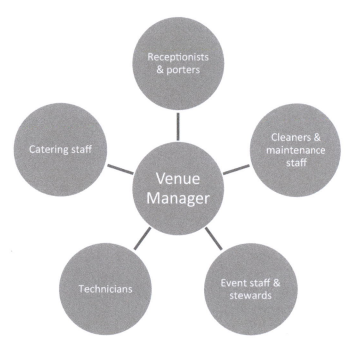

Figure 6.3 Venue staff.

6.13 STARTING NEGOTIATIONS

Until the point at which you confirm with the venue that you would like to book their facilities, all hire charges and terms and conditions are negotiable. Therefore, the site visit is an ideal opportunity to discuss these face-to-face with the venue manager. Negotiating charges is commonplace in the events industry and it isn't something that you should be afraid of or shy away from doing. Successfully negotiating a deal with a venue is discussed in Chapter 9 but it is a good idea to start this during the site visit. For example, ask the venue manager to explain all of the hire charges, room by room. If there is normally a charge for using AV equipment, furniture or electricity, make a note of this during the inspection as you may be able to have the charges reduced or dismissed as part of the negotiation process.

The terms and conditions of hire refer to the things that you will be allowed to do on site and the things that are prohibited or require special permission. The full terms and conditions are usually set out in a contract that you will sign to confirm the booking. Much like the hire charges, the terms and conditions may be negotiable, but any changes you want to make are best done before you sign the contract. Chapter 10 provides more advice and guidance on contracts but during the site visit ask the venue manager to go over the main rules and regulations at the venue. Typically, these might include what time events must finish in the evening and how loud they can be. What licences are in place and what permits or licences will need to be sought by the event manager (e.g. for alcohol, gambling etc.). Also, check to see what the venue's policy is on decoration, signage and the use of items such as confetti and candles. Ask about any special procedures for the get in and get out and whether or not the venue will accept deliveries in advance of the event.

6.14 SITE VISIT EVALUATIONS

Once you have completed all of your site inspections you should be in a position to evaluate the venues and come to a decision as to which one best fits your event requirements. It is important to take some time to digest the information that you gathered during the site visits and reflect on the benefits and drawbacks of using each venue. Generally, you will need to make some compromises when using any venue and it is important to know which aspects of the event plan are flexible and can be tailored to work within a specific space and which are not. If you have any additional questions about the venue or need any of your notes verified then you should contact the venue manager to discuss them. It can be useful to discuss the results with some of your key stakeholders such as the client and sponsors and take into account their views on the appropriateness of the venues you have seen. Once you are happy with your decision you should communicate this to the venue manager and you may be asked to put your decision in writing via email. Remember, that once you enter into a verbal or written agreement with the venue it becomes more difficult to negotiate the charges or terms of the agreement. Therefore, you should read the rest of this book before confirming your intentions to them.

6.15 ORGANISING A SITE VISIT – THE VENUE MANAGER'S PERSPECTIVE

Site visits are a crucial stage in negotiating a booking with a client, particularly if they are new to the venue, therefore as the venue manager it's important to carefully plan for each inspection. There are a number of benefits to inviting a client to visit on a busy day when they will be able to see events taking place at the venue. Seeing the venue in use is the best demonstration of how the space works. However, this may restrict which parts of the building the client will be able to inspect so it may be easier to arrange a site visit for when the venue is relatively quiet. Set aside plenty of time for the visit so that the client doesn't feel rushed and there is ample time to see as much of the venue as possible. Setting an itinerary for the visit is useful because as the venue expert you know how long it will take to adequately view the relevant parts of the building and grounds. Build in refreshment breaks and time for questions and discussions. If possible, arrange for the rooms that you will be viewing to be set up (as closely to the details in the RFP as possible) as this can help the client to understand how you think the room should be (or must be) laid out for their event. Walk around the venue an hour before the client is due to arrive and check to make sure that areas you will be visiting are as tidy as possible and any rubbish has been removed from the room. Research the client and their event as much as possible before the visit. Use appropriate sources, such as LinkedIn, to look at a photo of the client as it helps if you recognise them when they arrive at the venue (particularly if you don't have a reception area where they will check in on arrival). Check with them to see if they would like to attend alone or with a colleague, if they have any dietary requirements and if they need any help booking overnight accommodation.

Before the day of the visit re-read the proposal and the quotation that you submitted in response to the RFP. Be prepared and be ready to answer questions about hire charges and terms and conditions. The experienced venue manager will know what discounts and extras can be offered to a client. They will also be able to make a judgement as to how much to offer during the site visit in order to secure the booking (see Chapter 8 for further insight).

Remember that every minute of the visit contributes to the client's view of the venue. Therefore, brief all of the venue staff in advance of the visit. Invite relevant staff members to some or all of the visit so that they can answer questions relating to their area of responsibility. Arrange for a light, but impressive, lunch to be served during the visit. Answer all of the client's questions as accurately as possible. For example, if some of the venue is looking a little tired and you are asked if it will be refurbished before the event, be honest about whether this is likely to happen as its unwise to make any promises that won't be kept. Similarly, if the venue has a strict policy on what signage and decoration can and cannot be used then be clear about this from the start. If you are asked questions that you can't answer, explain to the client that you will check and get back to them. Put together a pack of information for the client to take away with them at the end of the visit. This could include the venue's brochure, your business card and sample menus. Make it clear to the client that you are available to discuss the booking after the visit if they have further questions but also be clear about your expectations. If you can only hold provisional dates for a limited time then explain this to the client and ask them when they expect to make a final decision about the venue.

6.16 SUMMARY

Egan (2013) warns that although the site visit can turn out to be quite a lengthy and complex process, it is going to be essential to inspect all potential venues in order to make the right choice and deliver a successful event. Venue inspections are an integral part of the event planning process and a personal visit to the venue and the destination is the best way to assess all of the facilities available. Not only that, but a structured and well organised site inspection will provide you with the opportunity to meet the venue team, explore the space, get a feel for the venue and begin the process of negotiating the hire charges and terms and conditions. A personal visit to each venue is the best way to make a final judgement about its suitability but there is usually a lot to take in during a visit. Therefore, allow plenty of time to walk around the building, use the checklists to verify information or to prompt you to ask questions. Use the site visit as an opportunity to walk through the event, discuss options with the staff and start to understand how you will use the venue to shape the attendee experience. The next step in the event planning process usually involves confirming and booking the venue and Chapter 10 explores the complexities of entering into a contractual agreement. However, it is important to make sure that before you sign a contract you have an understanding of venue hire charges (see Chapter 9) and what you can expect from the venue in terms of working with them and their suppliers, which is explained in the next chapter.

ACTIVITY 6.3

The key learning outcomes from this chapter are:

- Site visits have a very important part to play in the organisation of an event and they should be carefully planned.
- You should ensure that you have plenty of time for the site visit and be prepared with a list of things that you want to inspect. Take checklists with you and it can be useful to bring a colleague too.
- The site visit is an opportunity to negotiate with the venue so be ready to ask questions about how the venue can support you with the delivery of your event.

Based on what you have learnt from this chapter:

Visualise yourself organising a 1-day conference for 100 bankers at a well-known London hotel. The key purpose of the conference is to discuss sensitive information about the future of the bank and delegates will be travelling from all over the country to attend. You must now plan the site visit of the hotel to ensure that it is a suitable venue for the event. You are keen to keep all hire charges as low as possible.

Task 1 – Identify your objectives for the site visit (e.g., what do you want to achieve by the end of the visit?).

Task 2 – Put together an itinerary for the site visit, ensuring that you have time to inspect all the important parts of the venue and to discuss your event plan with the venue manager.

Task 3 – Draft key questions that you intend to put to the venue manager as part of the negotiation to secure the best deal possible with the venue.

6.17 FURTHER READING

The following sources are particularly useful for further reading on the subject of site visits:

Conway, D. (2006) *The Event Manager's Bible: How to Plan and Deliver an Event* (2nd edn). Oxford: How To Books.

Davidson, R. and Hyde, A. (2014) *Winning Meetings and Events for Your Venue.* Oxford: Goodfellows.

Powell, C. (2013) *How to Deliver Outstanding Corporate Events.* Publisher: Author.

Rogers, T. and Davidson, R. (2016) *Marketing Destinations and Venues for Conferences, Conventions and Business Events* (2nd edn) London: Routledge.

Tum, J. (2006) *Management of Event Operations,* London: Butterworth-Heinemann.

CVENT publications (available at www.cvent.com):

•   Making the most of your site visit

HSE publications (available at www.hse.gov.uk):

•   Assessing venue/site suitability

IAPCO publications (available at www.iapco.org):

•   Planning an ICC

Working with venue suppliers

LEARNING OUTCOMES

By the end of Chapter 7, you should be able to:

- Identify some of the ways in which the venue can support you as you develop the event programme
- Understand how to draw upon the venue manager's contacts and local expertise
- Appreciate the nature of the relationship that will develop between your suppliers and the venue
- Recognise the different types of catering operations at venues

7.1 INTRODUCTION

Having completed site visits of all of your shortlisted venues you should be in a position to identify the most appropriate venue to your event needs. This is usually based on a variety of factors including the price, what is included in the venue hire charge and your personal opinion of the venue, having experienced it first-hand. The next step in the event planning process would normally be to contact the venue to confirm the booking and enter into a contractual agreement (discussed in Chapter 10). However the next three chapters of the book are devoted to exploring key topics that the event manager should be aware of before agreeing to the venue's price, terms and conditions. This includes how venues formulate their hire charges and what you can expect from the venue in terms of working with them and their suppliers. The venue is not only the backdrop to the event but one of the most important stakeholders in the event planning process. The venue will have a lot of power and influence over the event and this can extend to controlling some of the suppliers that you work with and the content of your event programme. As Kirk confirms (2015) the venue manager will often take as much responsibility for the event as you will. Therefore, before entering into a legally binding contract with the venue, ensure that you are aware of their authority over key elements of the management of your event. This chapter will cover some of the ways in which the venue manager can be a useful resource during the event planning stage and we take a close look at the types of catering operations within venues.

7.2 VENUE SUPPORT IN EVENT PLANNING

As you progress from the event design phase into event production you will begin to bring the event to life. This will involve developing the event programme, securing suppliers and marketing the event to the target audience. Matthews (2016, p. 176) suggests that effective event production relies on becoming completely familiar with the venue's limitations in order to 'prepare for additional support or to change the production accordingly'. Thus working closely with the venue manager is essential. The venue manager can provide you with a lot of help, advice and suggestions throughout the project management of the event. They should be seen as a useful resource and should be involved in event production. A number of venues will assign a specific contact at the venue to each event manager. This can streamline the process for contacting the venue for support during the planning process. It ensures that you work with someone who becomes very familiar with your event, well in advance of event day, and have continuity of communication. Figure 7.1 illustrates the type and hierarchy of venue staff that you may encounter.

Your contact at the venue will be able to check your event plans to ensure that the activities that you are planning are all viable within the venue. They will be able to offer tips on how to use the space you are hiring and advice on what has worked well, and what hasn't, in the past.

Figure 7.1 Hierarchy of venue staff.

The venue will usually be able to provide you with scaled floorplans for each room that you are using as well as good quality photographs of the rooms and the exterior of the building. Some examples are shown in the images.

These can be useful both as an aide memoire but also for reproduction in your event marketing materials and attendee information packs. The venue will normally have a good relationship with a DMO and therefore they may be able to secure photos of the destination for similar purposes. The venue may also provide you with a summary of how the rooms are decorated and furnished as illustrated in Table 7.1.

Image 7.1 Highland Resort Hotel and Spa, Fujiyoshida City, Japan.

Source: ©JNTO.

Image 7.2 The Gainsborough Bath Spa.

Source: ©VisitEngland/The Gainsborough Bath Spa.

Image 7.3 The Petronas Twin Towers, Kuala Lumpur, Malaysia.

Source: ©Tourism Malaysia.

Table 7.1 A sample summary of furnishings

East Room	
Flooring	Dark grey carpet
Décor	Pale pink walls and dusky pink curtains
Standard furniture	50 × Dark blue upholstered chairs
	10 × Glass topped coffee tables
West Room	
Flooring	Blue and gold carpet with specks of red
Décor	Pale cream walls and cream curtains
Standard furniture	100 × gold gilt frame chairs with blue velvet upholstery
North Room	
Flooring	Light cream floor tiles
Décor	Pale blue walls and dark blue blinds
Standard furniture	200 × black metal framed chairs

Standard furniture will be provided with room hire, and it will be set up as per your requirements.

7.3 DISCUSSING YOUR VENUE REQUIREMENTS

Although you should have investigated what is available at the venue as part of the site visit, once you begin to work on the event go through your requirements step by step with the venue manager. For example if you plan on using rooms for several different activities it is important to check with the venue how long it will take them to change the set-up of the room (in terms of the layout of the furniture), whether they have enough furniture and equipment for everything you are planning to do in each room and whether or not there will be a charge for the staff required to reset the rooms. Important questions to ask about furniture are what types of chairs and tables will be used at your event (e.g. round tables or **sprigs**) and whether or not tables will be clothed or left bare. If you are going to have allocated seating at the event or a formal dinner that will require a seating plan, the venue should be able to advise you on precisely how the rooms will be laid out and provide you with a detailed seating plan of the room that you can use in your event planning. If you are going to feature an exhibition at the event and will be using a **shell scheme**, or indeed if you plan on having a large structure built inside the venue, then you will need to discuss this with the venue manager. You can expect to be required to provide plans for such work several weeks before the event and these may need to be forwarded to the local authority for their approval.

On arrival at the venue, all the rooms that you have hired will have been cleaned in preparation for your event. However, check with the venue manager as to when and how often the rooms that you will be using will be cleaned during the event. Typically the venue will check rubbish bins periodically throughout the event, but the room will only be cleaned after the event has finished and the get out completed unless it will last more than one day. In the case of longer events the venue will normally have the room cleaned again late in the evening or early morning and cleaning will take place around any equipment or exhibits that are staying in situ overnight. If you believe that a lot of rubbish will be generated during the event then the venue manager will be able to arrange for additional cleaning to take place but usually this cost will be passed on to you.

Your contact at the venue will also be able to give you information about the other members of staff that will be working on the day of the event. These people may play a small or a significant role on event day (see Chapter 11). Figure 7.2 highlights some of these roles.

Figure 7.2 Event day venue staff.

The venue manager will be able to confirm whether or not there are cloakroom facilities available at the venue. There may be a communal room where bags and coats can be left (at the risk of the owner) or the option of having a private, staffed cloakroom facility, although this may well come at an extra cost. Similarly the venue may have rooms which have been inspected and approved by the local authority for use as a crèche. This may be worth pursuing if having childcare facilities at the event is desirable. Alternatively the venue should be able to provide you with details of local nurseries and organisers who are available to make temporary arrangements. If you plan on having children attending or taking part in the event then discuss this very early on with the venue manager as you may find that there are regulations that apply in these circumstances that the venue will be obliged to enforce.

For all your other event requirements it is worth remembering that the venue will normally have an excellent network of contacts and should therefore be able to recommend suppliers to you. These will typically be suppliers that they have worked with before and who therefore know the venue well. It is worth asking the venue for advice and recommendations on all aspects of your event plan.

7.4 SITE PLANNING

Crowd management is an important element of event planning and it refers to the process of facilitating the safe movement of attendees around the event site or venue. Although 'it is true that the majority of crowd-related disasters happen at rock concerts and sporting events' (Bladen *et al.*, 2012, p. 211) careful crowd management must feature in the plans for any medium to large scale event. The more people there are attending an event, the more chance there is of an incident occurring and one of the most important ways to prevent this from happening is by having established crowd management procedures in place before event day (Schwartz *et al.*, 2015). As part of the process of planning for a safe event, a safety advisory group may be created to bring together key stakeholders to discuss such plans.

A good venue manager will be proactive in helping you to develop these procedures and in particular your event risk assessment. They will confirm room capacities and how these are calculated, which is usually done based on fire and safety regulations as well as ensuring the

CASE STUDY 7.1 SAFETY ADVISORY GROUPS

A safety advisory group (SAG) is a panel of people formed to give safety advice and guidance to event organisers. It is typically led by local authorities with input from the emergency services and should have clear terms of reference. A typical SAG would consist of the police, fire authority and NHS as well as licensing officers, food safety officers, noise enforcement officers and highways officers from the local authority. Additional specialist agencies such as the coastguard or mountain rescue may also be needed for certain events.

They are important as they provide a mechanism to ensure that safety plans are appropriate to the event and the event managers are competent in their role. They also ensure that all relevant agencies and authorities are fully aware of the event and the emergency plans in place and have contact details for key people running the event.

Although the importance and value of a properly run SAG is undeniable, they are not without their problems and often lose sight of the original intention of giving advice. They frequently take the place of planning meetings which should take place between the agencies or they become a process of signing off the event as safe (or not safe) to go ahead (or not go ahead). It should not do this. Nor should the meeting be used by agencies such as the police to make demands on organisers about their policies and procedures and even get conditions imposed on a premises licence. Sadly, this happens regularly and can make it a challenging experience for event organisers.

All members of the SAG should be competent to be there and to give advice but there are fewer and fewer people within local authorities with events experience and it can happen that the organiser has more experience and is more competent than the officer giving advice. Even the emergency services assess the situation from their own perspective and give advice based on the training they have had or the guidance that they have read without understanding the impact that can have on the wider event and the specifics of the site.

There is also a huge lack of consistency between one authority and another and for organisers that do events around the country they can frequently face having to change plans form one authority to another as they expect and demand different things.

Things I have encountered include seeing an ambulance driving with blue lights where it shouldn't have been – only meters from a live firework display, finding a fire engine that I didn't know was on site, trying to leave site under blue light conditions through a gate that wasn't big enough as the public were trying to get through and finding the police giving instructions to stewards that go against the event plan as well as driving their vehicles in crowded places where vehicle movements were not permitted and moving barriers to go through closed off areas to get a burger!

Source: Andy Grove, HighGrove Events, www.highgroveevents.com

optimum attendee experience (Parent and Smith-Swan, 2012, p. 141). The venue will offer you advice on directing and managing the movement of attendees around the building. This could include suggesting where to position event staff so that they monitor crowds, how long to allow for refreshment breaks or movement between rooms (in order to reduce rushing) and pointing out notable **pinch points** to avoid or to manage carefully (e.g. passageways and corridors that are likely to get particularly busy).

7.5 TRANSPORT PLANNING

For large events it will be essential to put a traffic and transport plan into operation throughout the event and you will need the input of the venue manager, and potentially the local authorities (highways, police etc.) to devise a workable and effective plan. The plan will take into consideration the needs as well as the preferences of event attendees and suppliers. Based firstly on what is going to be essential and secondly what is desirable, the plan will detail the arrangements that you will put in place to facilitate parking, unloading and dropping off at the venue. Table 7.2 lists some of the specific considerations that you may need to include in your plan.

The venue manager's knowledge and expertise will contribute significantly to the traffic and transport plan. They will be able to confirm to you what is available at the venue and any special arrangements that you will need to make or any regulations that you will need to adhere to. For example, you may have access to all or some of the car park, service road and drop off

Table 7.2 A sample traffic and transport plan

General information
Type and date of event
Timings (get in, event, get out)

Attendee information
Approximate number of attendees
Profile of attendees (e.g. age etc.)
Approximate no. of attendees arriving by public transport
Existing public transport provision
Number and proximity of bus stops, stations etc. to venue
Number and proximity of drop off/pick up points at venue
Suggestions for increasing public transport provision
Approximate % of attendees arriving by car
Existing number of car park spaces
Suggestions for increasing car park spaces/park and ride scheme etc.
Requirement for parking suspensions
Requirement for road closures, diversions etc.
Suggestions for managing congestion (e.g. traffic marshals)
Existing signage and suggestions for additional signage into and around area

Supplier information
Number and type of suppliers, supplier vehicles etc. (e.g. no. of articulated lorries)
Anticipated arrival times of suppliers
Anticipated number of vehicles for others (staff, performers etc.)
Space available for vehicles to load/unload
Space available for vehicles to park (at venue, and in destination)
Requirement for one way system/timed loading and unloading
Plan for ensuring access for emergency vehicles

points providing you meet certain rules. This could include putting in place a system which rotates access, giving suppliers a designated time slot for dropping off and setting up their equipment. You may have to provide event day staff to manage the system, marshal the traffic, ensure the safety of pedestrians and maintain a clear access route for emergency vehicles and venue staff.

Signage in and around the area should feature in the traffic and transport plan. Check with the venue manager as to whether or not there is directional signage to the venue. A number of venues will be well signposted at key entry points into the destination, but ask for confirmation of what is on the signs. For example, the name of some venues are abbreviated and occasionally the more familiar, local name of the venue is used on signage rather than the venue's full and official title.

As part of your traffic and transport plan ask the venue manager to confirm the rules regarding deliveries. For example, will the venue accept deliveries of equipment etc. before event day? If so what address should be given to the sender and where will deliveries be stored and collected from?

7.6 CIVIC SUPPORT

At some events the involvement of local dignitaries can add to the sense of occasion and occasionally draw press coverage of the event. For example the local mayor could officially open the event and address the event audience, welcoming them to the destination. The local authorities may even be keen to play an active role in the event, particularly if it is generating a substantial income to the town or city via the multiplier effect. They may wish to contribute towards the event in exchange for this economic impact and this could take the form of the provision of a reception for all of the event attendees. In such cases the venue may liaise with the local civic offices in order to make the arrangements for the reception to take place at the venue and to be hosted by a suitable dignitary. Civic support for events is sometimes referred to as subvention and this is particularly common within the management of association conferences (see Chapter 9 for further details).

In some cases you may find that the venue is wholly or partly owned by the local council which can facilitate civic support for the event. This can extend beyond the provision of a reception to the council, facilitating several aspects of the management of the event including assisting with marketing, the traffic and transport plan and licensing. However, if the venue is privately owned then the venue manager should be able to help you contact the relevant local council should you wish to pursue civic involvement in the event, or indeed if you need to talk to the council regarding issues such as road closures or licence applications.

7.7 SUPPLIERS' VENUE REQUIREMENTS

To ensure that your suppliers provide you with a seamless service on event day, work closely with them during the planning to ensure that the venue will meet their needs and expectations. This means that you will need to ask your suppliers for information regarding their venue requirements. Sometimes these will be detailed in the contract that they issue you or, as with performers, in their **rider**. Typical venue requirements are listed in Table 7.3 and technical venue requirements are discussed in more detail in Chapter 8.

Table 7.3 Supplier venue requirements

Specific access to unload (e.g. ground floor, ramp, wide door etc.)
Use of a lift, cherry picker, ladder etc.
Access to power (during get in and/or during the event)
A changing room with mirror, shower, towels, clothes rail etc.
A lockable storage area
Access to running water
Refreshments
Table, chairs, other furniture items.

In your negotiations with suppliers discuss payment for items such as refreshments as otherwise you may find that the supplier is not just expecting you to make sure that they can buy food and drink at the event, but that they presume you will organise and pay for their refreshments. Go over their list of requirements with the venue, even if you are aware of what is generally available at the venue, having visited it. For example, the venue may provide you with changing rooms for your performers but they may not be able to provide towels or they may make an extra charge for certain items. Similarly, be sure to check what is going to be available for suppliers during the get in and get out. For example, some venues will have few staff on site and little else going on during the get in, particularly if the venue is not open to the public at this time. This could mean that it's not possible to get a bite to eat or a hot drink at the venue at certain times.

As well as carefully checking your suppliers' venue requirements, you should also provide them with detailed information about the venue well in advance of event day. Table 7.4 provides you wish a checklist of information to share with your suppliers.

Table 7.4 A checklist of venue information for suppliers

Name of Supplier	Info provided
The full address and postcode of the venue	
The time they should arrive at the venue	
What to do on arrival (e.g. collect a parking permit, check in at reception etc.)	
A site plan showing where to unload	
How long they have to unload	
The time that they must be set up by	
Where to park during the event	
Details of what to do when they are not involved in the event (e.g. stay on site etc.)	
The time when they can start to pack up	
What they must do before they leave the event (e.g. speak to a member of the event team)	

With all of your suppliers, be clear about where and what time they should arrive, and what they should do on arrival. You may need to provide different information to different suppliers. For example, contractors with heavy equipment may need to be directed straight to the rear of the building while speakers may arrive much nearer to the event start time and may need to check in at the front of the building.

Make sure that you share important details from your traffic and transport plan with suppliers such as the postcode of the venue, the arrangements for loading and unloading during the get in and get out, and parking arrangements during the event. Ask them to let you know if they foresee any problems with the amount of time you are allowing them to drop off equipment and set up in the venue or with the size of the doors or floor loading capacities. Provide them with an annotated site plan showing them exactly where they need to be throughout the event. Also be clear about what they should do if they are not directly involved in event day activities. For example, if a supplier needs to stay on site during the event in case they are needed, where should they (or where can they) go? Similarly, at the end of the event once they have packed up and are ready to leave should they talk to you before leaving the venue?

As you are likely to be very busy throughout the get in, event and get out, you may wish to designate the role of venue liaison to a member of your event team. This person can be responsible for taking care of suppliers while they are on site, directing them and taking care of their specific venue requirements. This person can also conduct a quick inspection of the venue before a supplier leaves, to make sure that they haven't damaged the building or left anything behind for you to clear up. Similarly you may wish to designate a member of your event team to look after VIPs at the venue. This role could involve meeting VIPs on arrival and taking care of their venue requirements such as showing them to their dressing room or green room area and making sure that they have complimentary refreshments.

7.8 TYPES OF CATERING OPERATION

There are three principal ways in which the catering operations are provided and managed at venues. These are when the catering is in-house or provided by an appointed caterer, when the venue does not have its own team but provides a list of preferred suppliers and when the event manager can hire any company to cater the event, or provide the catering themselves.

In-house catering

If the venue has a catering team based permanently at the building this will either be an in-house department or an appointed company. An in-house department refers to when the

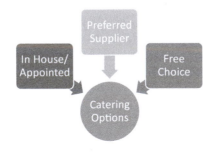

Figure 7.3 Types of catering operation.

venue employs its own catering staff and has a fully equipped kitchen within the building. The catering team may include chefs and waiting staff and be led by a banqueting co-ordinator or a food and beverage manager (often abbreviated to F&B manager). Hotels and other venues whose primary function is to offer hospitality will naturally have an in-house catering team as providing regular food service will be central to their day to day operations.

Appointed caterer

If a venue does not have an in-house team, but needs a regular catering service, they may appoint a caterer. This refers to the process of forming a contractual agreement with an outside catering company. The contract will normally require the catering company to have a certain number of their staff working permanently at the venue to manage the kitchens and meet all of the venue's catering needs. Typically the catering company will enter into a financial agreement with the venue in order to take sole control of the catering provision at the venue. The agreement may include an annual payment to the venue and an additional payment of a percentage of their annual takings at the venue. This payment is in exchange for exclusive rights to provide catering at the venue. Event managers and other users of the venue will be obliged to work with the venue's appointed caterer or in-house team.

There are certain benefits and drawbacks to working with in-house or appointed caterers. The benefits are that these catering staff will be very familiar with the venue and experience of what works particularly well. They are likely to have strong relationships with local suppliers. This commitment to corporate social responsibility and sustainability is evident through supporting local businesses to provide quality and authentic local produce and keeping food transport costs at a minimum. Lee and Slocum (2015) suggest that event attendees may be willing to pay a higher price for locally sourced items so this is worth weighing up against the key drawback of using the in-house or appointed team which is that because you are obliged to use them, you have less room to negotiate costs or terms. Therefore it can be argued that this type of catering operation can lead to high prices and unwillingness to compromise on menus or prices.

Preferred suppliers

Venues that are keen to work with event managers, but who don't have an in-house or appointed caterer, will frequently provide hirers with a list of preferred suppliers. Preferred suppliers are catering companies that are known to the venue, usually because they have worked with them in the past. The venue manager is content to let them use the kitchens on site or to bring in equipment in order to provide a catering service. Usually there will be several companies listed as preferred suppliers. However, it is commonplace for the event manager to have to select a caterer from the list provided. Nonetheless this gives the event manager some choice and therefore room to negotiate. As with an in-house or appointed caterer, a preferred supplier will usually be reasonably familiar with the venue and will liaise directly with the venue manager in order to arrange to access the building and set up equipment for the event.

Occasionally the venue will allow the event manager free choice of caterer. This means that you would be able to hire the caterer of your choice to provide all of the meals and refreshments at the event. Obviously this would give you the greatest choice and scope to provide exactly what food and drink you want at the best possible price you can find. However, it can be high risk and can prove to be more costly in the long run. Venues that allow free choice often do so because they have limited kitchen space or equipment which is often attributable to their original design purpose (Whitfield, 2009). This would mean that the caterer would be obliged to bring cooking and refrigeration equipment into the building as well as cutlery, crockery and everything else needed for a professional catering service. This could prove very costly, not only in terms of what would need to be hired, but also in terms of how much extra time would be needed for the get in and get out. Providing the catering yourself may also seem like an attractive option as this gives you complete control of the menu and costs. However, unless you are trained in food preparation this is unwise as the penalties for not adhering to food preparation and storage regulations can be severe.

Bowdin *et al.* (2011) confirm that the catering operation at the venue can frequently determine why you might choose one venue over another. This is an indication of how significant the role of the caterer is in the success of the event. Therefore before booking a venue, make sure that you fully understand your obligations or options when it comes to providing catering at the event. As Lloyd (2013) warns the quality and service of the catering will leave a lasting impression in the minds of all your guests, regardless of the type of event so it's very important to get it right.

7.9 TYPES OF CATERING SERVICE

Both the catering manager and the venue manager will be able to advise you on the types of catering service that you can have at the event. There are essentially three types of food service – table, counter and buffet and these are illustrated in Figure 7.4.

Table service is the premier level of food service at an event as this occurs when guests are seated and food is brought to them. This is the level of service usually required for formal dinners and banquets. Silver service is the highest form of table service as this is when guests are served individually by waiting staff who will offer food from platters. A plated service is when the meal for each guest is prepared in the kitchen and then brought to them at their table. Finally, family service is when the main dish is plated in the kitchen and brought to the table where guests will then help themselves to vegetables etc. which will be on the table.

Counter service is more informal, and as it sounds, is when guests collect their food from a counter before sitting down to eat. There are three types: carvery, self-service and single point. A carvery is when meat is carved from a joint for guests as they order and usually guests then help themselves to vegetables and other accompaniments. Self-service is commonly found in canteens and cafes – customers walk along a service area helping themselves to items of food and drink. Finally single point service is when the customer collects all of their refreshments from one collection point, commonly found in fast food outlets.

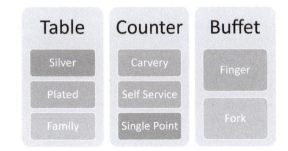

Figure 7.4 Types of service.

The third and final type of food service is buffet service and this is also usually quite informal. During service, guests will usually stand to eat and they may be served or may help themselves to food items which have been laid out on platters. There are two types of buffet service; finger and fork. A finger buffet is usually a selection of cold foods while a fork buffet may have hot and cold food items.

The ratio of catering staff to guests will vary according to the type of service, the size of party, the setup of the room and the time available for the refreshment break. There will be a greater number of staff during table service than the more informal options and the catering or venue manager will be able to advise on ratios for food as well as bar service.

ACTIVITY 7.1

Imagine that you have been tasked with organising a 2-day conference for a large number of delegates. Consider what type of catering service (e.g. silver service, self-service etc.) will be most appropriate to the following conference activities:

- A networking lunch for all guests on Day 1
- A formal dinner at the end of Day 1
- A light lunch for delegates on Day 2
- A private lunch for speakers and VIPs on Day 2

7.10 PAYMENT FOR CATERING

Food

Payment for catering can be dealt with in two separate ways and there are advantages and disadvantages to both. The catering can be paid for entirely by the event manager, thus ensuring that event attendees do not have to pay for their food and drink during the event. This is called payment on account and as the event manager you will normally be required to pay at least a deposit for the food and drinks bill in advance of the event and the balance after event day. If all the refreshments are going to go on an account then you must set aside a lot of time to work with the caterer on all of your event requirements. Things to include are any refreshments to be served during the get in or get out period, water for speakers and refreshments for suppliers and staff. Organising the catering well in advance takes some of the pressure off during the event itself. However, you will need to ensure that the price of all of the refreshments is carefully factored in to your event budget and you have considered all (or all potential) dietary requirements of everyone at the event.

The alternative to catering on account is to have a pay as you go (PAYG) system in operation at the event. This is when all your event attendees pay for what they consume as and when they buy items of food and drink. The obvious advantage to this system is that you will not have to get bogged down in all the catering requirements of your event guests. However, you will still need to work closely with the caterer to ensure that appropriate food and drinks items are available at key times during the event programmes and that there will be enough time to ensure that everyone has time to be served. If you are going to operate a PAYG service for event attendees, you may want to provide a more personalised service for the event VIPs.

Therefore you may wish to arrange to have refreshments, lunches or dinners on account for the client, the speakers etc. This will usually involve them being served in a separate or private part of the venue and therefore you will need to discuss these arrangements with both the catering and venue managers.

Alcohol

It is important to remember that the caterer you work with will often have the right to provide all of the food and drink at the event and this extends to alcohol. Whether you opt for a PAYG or on-account catering operation, you may wish to make specific arrangements regarding bar service and this is quite common. In conjunction with the venue manager, you may be able to choose whether or not you wish to have a bar in operation in all or some parts of the event. Many venues have small bar counters in several of their rooms or portable stations that can be moved from room to room thus providing event attendees with a private bar facility. Where this is possible, you can usually determine whether or not this is a cash bar or on account. A cash bar is the same as a PAYG service whereby your guests will pay for their own drinks. In some cases you may wish to provide a free bar to your guests and therefore a till will operate at the bar and although your guests will not be charged, all drinks ordered at the bar will be recorded and you will be presented with the bill after the event. You may wish to provide your guests with just their first drink at the bar or set a limit on how much can be spent at the bar (this is often advisable to avoid a very big bill!). The limit is referred to as a ceiling and you can determine the ceiling in advance of the event and agree this with the catering manager. During the event, once the ceiling has been reached a cash bar service will resume. It is important to put together a comprehensive plan for bar service with the catering manager and this will help you to avoid paying corkage. Corkage is a fee that you may be obliged to pay if you or your attendees open and consume any bottles of wine or other alcohol that hasn't been purchased from the caterer. This is a common practice at venues with an in-house or appointed caterer and corkage can be significant so it is best to minimise the chance of this charge being applied.

ACTIVITY 7.2

Consider when it would be appropriate to offer PAYG catering or catering on account at various events such as at a wedding or at a business meeting. Would you treat everyone at the event in the same way? Also reflect on whether or not it would be appropriate to offer a cash bar or how you might judge where to set the ceiling.

Considerations

Potentially there is a huge financial advantage to the event manager of having the majority of the event catering provided on account. Particularly if the catering staff are part of an appointed or in-house team. This is explained in Chapter 9 in detail but essentially, if the catering income is going to go straight to the venue (or at least part of it will) then this can be used to offset some or all of the venue hire charges. Finally, whether the majority of the catering is going to be on account of via a PAYG service then check carefully to see what is and what isn't included in the service. For example there may be charges for tablecloths and linen, table decorations, menu cards and a displayed seating plan. It is usually easier to have these items included in the on-account charge but this becomes more difficult with a PAYG service as the caterers are not guaranteed a certain income at your event.

7.11 VENUE TECHNICAL SUPPORT

As with catering, a number of venues will have their own in-house team of technicians to manage all of their AV equipment and oversee technical productions and operations at the venue. Often the services of a technician and the use of in-house equipment is included in the hire charge or can be negotiated as part of the booking (see Chapter 10). This can be a great bonus to event managers as it is commonplace to need to hire a production team to look after the stage management elements of the event. If this is provided by the venue, it is one less expense and one less supplier to source and manage. An in-house technician will be very familiar with what works well in the venue and will usually be available to offer advice and support to you as you develop your event plans.

Venues that do not have an in-house technical team, may provide event managers with a list of preferred suppliers. As with caterers, these will usually be companies that are familiar with the venue and have experience of working within the building. Some venues will provide you with an extensive list of options and others will insist on you using one specific company. From the venue's perspective, this reduces the risk associated with bringing heavy, bulky and potentially dangerous equipment on site and they will generally only recommend or insist that you use reputable and reliable companies. As Salter (2013) explains, when there is a problem with the AV equipment at an event, your attendees will notice and will usually blame you or the venue and therefore venue managers build strong relationships with AV companies that they trust. However, as with caterers, it is important to understand what your options are regarding technical provision and support, before you book the venue.

7.12 ADDITIONAL SUPPLIERS

As the event manager, you will find that the venue is proactive in terms of providing you with detailed information about your options at the venue particularly in terms of catering and technical support. Most venue managers will be extremely experienced in event operations and as such will be able to make a number of additional supplier recommendations to you. This could include suggesting fairly standard suppliers such as a florist and a photographer to even the more unusual requests for specialised equipment or unique performers. It is always worth asking the venue for their advice and recommendations. They will have a wealth of local connections and may be able to suggest someone that you had never considered using.

Many venue managers will be able to book suppliers and make arrangements on your behalf. This is sometimes provided in exchange for a small charge or commission but it can be worthwhile as the venue may be able to negotiate good rates with suppliers that they contract on a regular basis. Furthermore, if they are making arrangements for you this service will usually extend to fully liaising with the supplier in the run up to the event including putting in place all of their venue requirements and arranging the invoice. Alternatively the venue may be able to suggest suppliers that fit within your budget or suggest ways in which you can negotiate a good deal.

Generally the suppliers that the venue recommends or contracts on your behalf will be reliable and will have had experience of using the venue before. This can be reassuring and ultimately this can save you time that you would otherwise spend discussing and explaining what is and isn't available to them at the venue.

7.13 WORKING WITH VENUE SUPPLIERS – THE VENUE MANAGER'S PERSPECTIVE

Most experienced venue managers would agree that the more information you can get from your clients during the planning of an event, the better. As such encourage them to share their event ideas with you and ask you for advice. In the long run it may be easier to put together a comprehensive information pack to give to hirers of the venue which covers key information about the venue such as a reminder of how rooms can be set up and what is available at the venue and what local suppliers you recommend. Take care with recommendations as event managers will assume that you have first-hand experience of working with these suppliers and will trust your opinion. Some venues have a limited number of preferred suppliers and a rigorous vetting process in order to join the list and this helps to control and predict the level of service that the supplier will provide to your client.

In terms of providing furniture and equipment to clients, you may wish to include such offers in your negotiation of venue hire charges. However, it is essential that you also keep detailed records of what you have agreed to provide for each event. This is particularly important if you have several events taking place at the same time as otherwise it is easy to double book the same resources to parallel events.

In terms of catering options at the venue, you may be in a position to choose what can take place and therefore be able to give the client a choice of caterer. In this situation you will need to balance what is best for the venue with what is going to be attractive to the client. Generally the client will prefer to have some choices when it comes to catering the event. However as the venue manager you will need to balance the preferences of the client with what's best for the venue. Allowing any supplier into the building, particularly one with heavy and, potentially, dangerous equipment, is a risk. You can minimise the risk by working with reputable and responsible suppliers.

As you build up a history of working with specific suppliers and hosting various events, keep detailed records of what works particularly well. These can include diagrams of room set ups, popular menus and photos of events that make particularly good use of the building. These can be very helpful when you are asked for recommendations or are involved in contributing to the design of an event.

7.14 SUMMARY

As you begin to make detailed plans for your event, work closely with the venue manager and take advantage of their experience and expertise of hosting events. The venue can usually provide you with plenty of useful information about everything from how the rooms can be set up to what furniture can be provided. The venue manager can make a significant contribution to your traffic and transport plan and they may be able to negotiate civic involvement in your event. Remember that the venue may control some elements of your event such as specifying which AV company you must use and who provides all your event catering. Before entering into a contractual booking with the venue, check to see how much influence the venue will have over your key suppliers. In particular investigate the catering provision at the venue and start to work on your ideas for PAYG or on account hospitality taking into account the likely needs and preferences of your audience and VIPs.

Robertson (2013) advises that it is essential to keep in regular contact with your suppliers and this will entail asking them about their on-site requirements and providing them with detailed information about the venue. If this is done well in advance of event day this should ensure that they provide you with a smooth service during the get in, the event and the get out. Above all, communicate with the venue manager at all times, ask for recommendations and get their input into your event plans. At times the venue manager may try to steer you towards using a particular supplier and when this happens consider why they are doing this. It could be because they are going to make a commission from the arrangement. However, most venue managers will want to ensure that you work with trustworthy contractors and will only endorse dependable suppliers.

7.15 FURTHER READING

The following sources are particularly useful for further reading on the subject of suppliers and event operations within venues:

Fenich, G. (2012) *Meetings, Expositions, Events, and Conferences: An Introduction to the Industry* (3rd edn). New Jersey: Pearson.

Ferdinand, N. and Kitchin, P. (2012) *Events Management: An International Approach* (2nd edn). London: SAGE.

Parent, M. and Smith-Swan, S. (2012) *Managing Major Sports Events: Theory and Practice*. London: Routledge.

Raj, R., Walters, P. and Rashid, T. (2013) *Events Management: Principles and Practice* (2nd edn). London: SAGE.

Shone, A. and Parry, B. (2010) *Successful Event Management: A Practical Handbook* (3rd edn). Hampshire: CENGAGE Learning.

Technology

LEARNING OUTCOMES

By the end of Chapter 8, you should be able to:

- Differentiate between live, virtual and hybrid events
- Understand basic technical production terminology
- Appreciate how to incorporate technology into your plans for a memorable and accessible event
- Identify emerging trends in event and venue technology

8.1 INTRODUCTION

Matthews (2016, p. 177) confirms that after the site visit, the next important stage in event production is communicating with potential venues about your technical requirements. This is so that you can assess what is available to use at the venue, either as part of the hire agreement or at an extra charge. The technical elements of an event can range from basic items such as staging and microphones to an extensive list of requirements to include dressing rooms, internet access, power, lighting and other equipment. Furthermore, the twenty-first-century event attendee is likely to own a personal mobile device and will expect Wi-Fi at the venue. Consequently, as an event designer you may wish to consider incorporating technology into every aspect of the event plan to ensure that your guests have the opportunity to use it to engage with your event. The use of cloud technology and an ever-developing range of apps designed for such interaction are making this possible and there is an increasing expectation for event managers to be technically competent. And while venues of all sizes are embracing technology in order to meet the needs of their clients (Rogers and Davidson, 2016), event and venue managers alike can often struggle to keep up to date with the latest technological trends and developments. Therefore, this chapter will guide you through the principal technical requirements of events and will outline the important questions to ask the venue manager in the event planning process.

8.2 VIRTUAL EVENTS

Bowdin *et al.* (2011) suggest that an important part of event design is considering whether or not a physical location is indeed needed and the recent, rapid development of technology has provided event managers with the option of creating online or virtual events. However, as Getz (2012, p. 31) suggests, 'planned events are social by nature, and many people will only resort to "virtuality" when the real thing is not available'. This is a viewpoint shared by many academics and event professionals alike who agree that the face-to-face interaction that can only be experienced at a live event is not just important, but it remains the strongest motivation for attending events (Tompkins, 2016). Nonetheless, the impacts of technological advances have created not just the possibility of having virtual events, but the appetite for virtual participation.

Arguably virtual participation at events began with teleconferencing, whereby participants in various locations were able to join a conversation (and therefore take part in the event) via their landline telephone. This developed into video-conferencing in the 1980s. More recently the availability of wireless fidelity (Wi-Fi) has enabled the use of voice over internet protocol (VoIP) which allows calls to be converted into data which can be sent via the internet (without a landline).

Today the term 'virtual event' usually refers to a web-based event. This could be an online version of a meeting or conference (a webinar) or media streaming (webcasting) of a competition, show or other type of spectator event. The increasing capabilities of the internet now means that event participants may be able to take part in the event in real time, on demand or a mixture of the two. Virtual attendance of an event may come with the option of choosing to participate in one or several activities, join in forum discussions and visit shops and exhibitions.

Technology has, and continues to, revolutionise our lives and there are a number of obvious benefits to organising and attending virtual events. They can be considerably cheaper to run and greater participation is possible as you can target a global audience. Incentives to attend include minimal registration costs and no travel time which is also arguably better for the environment. However, there are also many distinct drawbacks to virtual events. Both the organiser and the participant must have the skills and equipment necessary to organise and take part in the event. The technology must be dependable, as unreliable Wi-Fi, for example, is a major risk to event success (Heipel, 2012). Furthermore, participation in a virtual event may mean dipping in and out of the event and therefore not getting the full event experience. Choosing to attend some elements of the event will dilute the event experience for attendees. Plus, one of the primary motivations to attend events is to have a socially enriching experience (Bowdin *et al.*, 2011). This is only fully achievable via a live event and there is no doubt that a virtual event cannot provide the same sensory experience that a live event can – and therefore, it is never going to be as memorable.

As the event manager, you cannot fully engage with your attendees at a virtual event as you may never speak to them or see them. This makes it challenging to thank them for coming or to get their feedback on their event experience. Although you can get virtual guests to provide feedback via an online survey, for instance, this is not the same as the instant feedback you get at a live event by, for example, seeing how people react to a particular performer, monitoring whether or not people are enjoying the food, etc.

Therefore, the general consensus is that live events cannot be replaced by virtual ones and many of us would only choose to attend a virtual event if a live event were not available (Getz, 2012). Nonetheless, technology continues to permeate our everyday life and it continues to offer event managers new and exciting ways to enhance events and the attendee experience and this has led to the development of the hybrid event, which are not only the newest genre of events but the future of the events industry (Sox *et al.*, 2015).

8.3 HYBRID EVENTS

A hybrid event is a live event that also includes elements of a virtual event or has an online component and we are seeing an increasing number of event managers designing a blended event as the efficiency of new and improved technology becomes more apparent. Not only does a hybrid event enable live and virtual participation, the technology enables those attending in person to feel a heightened sense of interaction (Morell, 2010).

Generally, a hybrid event uses technology to enhance rather than replace the live event. This could mean designing and delivering a live event whereby most of the attendees are at the venue, with perhaps some speakers involved via a webcast. Alternatively, the whole event could take place with a live audience but also be simultaneously live streamed which is popular with many sporting events and festivals. For many event managers, a hybrid event provides the opportunity to encourage the audience to participate, particularly via Wi-Fi, apps and cloud technology.

Allowing event guests with enabled devices (e.g. smartphones, tablets and laptops) to connect to the venue's Wi-Fi will provide them with access to online resources, information and social networking sites. Providing the event manager is clear about how and when technology should be used during the event, this can be particularly advantageous, as for example, encouraging live tweeting during an event can help engage the audience while promoting the event to any non-attendees (Fisher, 2012).

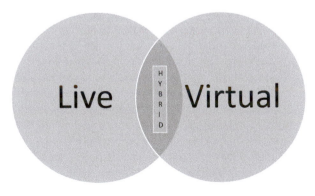

Figure 8.1 Types of events.

CASE STUDY 8.1 MEETING TOMORROW: HYBRID EVENTS

The company Meeting Tomorrow was founded by Mark Aistrope, a travelling sales rep. After struggling to locate and set up AV equipment as he travelled around the country, he decided to set up his own technical logistics company to supply hireable equipment and services to the events industry. Initially he invested in 15 projectors and a small team of dedicated professionals. He developed a website that provided a facility for tracking and shipping equipment and provided help to set up and manage the equipment anywhere in the country.

Today Meeting Tomorrow can provide the latest equipment including iPads, plasma screens and staging. In addition to this the company supports hybrid events via the provision of the technology for live streaming, webcasting, integrated question and answer sessions and private satellite broadcasting. They can provide the facility for a live audio broadcast and connect speakers from up to 500 different locations simultaneously. They can also set up bespoke registration sites that will capture attendee information and they provide the services of a technical director to manage the onsite production at the event venue and remote support for virtual attendees.

Meeting Tomorrow believe that many event professionals are increasingly in favour of hybrid events because of their ability to engage participants and extend the audience. They add that hybrid events help the event organiser to convey the same clear message to all audience members whether they are attending the event in-person or are located elsewhere across the globe. Furthermore, hybrid events increase the return on investment of the live event by extending the availability of the experience and consequently doubling the audience numbers.

Meeting Tomorrow has found that the greatest demand for hybrid events is within conferencing and typically the live event is held in a hotel or purpose-built convention centre. They list the key benefits of hybrid events as:

- On-demand access to live presentations which would otherwise be lost or forgotten
- Increased return on investment via continued on-demand access
- The ability to communicate with remote offices and employees

However, they also note the following challenges of hosting hybrid events

- It is a challenge to create and deliver a great experience for both live and virtual audiences
- Finding a visual production service that has the technical knowledge and a flair for event design is rare

Meeting Tomorrow have attributed much of their success in the field of hybrid events to their flexibility, onsite support and their ability to deliver services nationwide.

Source: https://meetingtomorrow.com/hybrid-events

ACTIVITY 8.1

Imagine that you have organised a product launch for a new car. The event guests include senior management and sales staff from the car company as well as a number of local and national members of the press. What are the various ways that you could encourage your event guests to use their smart phones at the event?

Cloud technology provides even greater access to information and also equips the event manager with the means to communicate in real time with attendees, particularly via apps, which now represent one of the main trends in technological developments (Ball, 2011). Apps can be used pre, during and post event in a multitude of ways including creating personalised agendas and venue maps for attendees, facilitating the sharing of guest and speaker profiles, and taking polls and giving feedback (Clancy, 2015). However, although venues have 'readily embraced the fruits of technological progress in order to enhance their clients' experience while using the facility' (Rogers and Davidson, 2016, p. 217), there still exists a number of challenges when using technology within a venue.

Today, most event attendees expect a reliable and strong internet connection throughout the event and a poor Wi-Fi connection could influence their event experience and reflect poorly on the event planner (McCarthy, 2016). A recent survey of event organisers revealed that fast and reliable Wi-Fi in a venue is a top priority (Dingley, 2016). But despite this, the majority of venues are unaware of their bandwidth capabilities (Ledger, 2013), and a number of venues face ongoing challenges of ensuring their infrastructure is capable of meeting the needs of the twenty-first-century event manager and event attendee. This digital revolution has thereby created an area of continuous conflict between event designers and venues, particularly where free Wi-Fi and reliable bandwidth are not yet available (Heipel, 2012).

8.4 TECHNICAL SPECIFICATIONS

As well as checking the availability and reliability of Wi-Fi at the venue, typically most event organisers will want large screens for projections, changeable lighting, staging and a dedicated AV technician (Dingley, 2016). Most venues will be able to provide you with a detailed list of what is available at the venue, either for free, included in the hire package or at an additional cost. This is usually referred to as a technical specification, which is often abbreviated to tech spec. Table 8.1 is the tech spec for London's famous jazz venue, Ronnie Scott's.

Image 8.1 Ronnie Scott's Jazz Club, London.

Table 8.1 Ronnie Scott's Jazz Club venue tech spec

VENUE TECH SPEC

(LAST UPDATED FEB 2014)

MAIN CLUB

FOH CONSOLE

Yamaha M7CL/48 Digital Mixing Desk
Monitors mixed from FOH.
iPad control via Yamaha StageMix
2 x MY16AT ADAT cards installed

FOH PROCESSORS

2 x Klark Technik DN300 30 band graphics
1 x TubeTech SMC 2B Multi-band Compressor

FOH SYSTEM

d&b audiotechnik
4 x d&b E9 (E902) Mid/High Enclosures (Stereo)
2 x d&b C7 Sub Enclosures (Stereo)
4 x d&b E3 Mono In-Fills (centre & sides)
2 x d&b E3 Mono Delay speakers (rear)
All driven by P1200A & EPAC amps
48 way analogue multicore to stage.
3 x 16 way stage boxes
(see stage plan for positions)

MONITOR SYSTEM

d&b audiotechnik
8 x d&b MAX15 Wedges
1 x d&b E15BX Sub (for drum fill)
6 x Monitor mixes driven by P1200A amps
1 x Porter & Davis BC-2 (drum stool kicker)

RECORDING

Alesis HD24 recorder connected to M7CL via
lightpipe.

STAGE

6m wide (8m with side wings) x 4m deep
Ceiling height on stage is 2.7m There is a
separate stage plan available online showing the
exact stage dimensions to scale.

LIGHTING

6 x bars with a total of 42 static Chauvet
ColorDash Accent RGBW LED mini parcans.
3 x Static LEDJ Parcans (on club logo)
ChamSys MQ40 control desk at FOH

DRESSING ROOMS

Backstage – one small room for two/three artists
with private toilet facilities
Downstairs FOH – one larger room for artists
– toilet facilities shared with public. Access to
stage through audience only.

AV SYSTEM

Panasonic HD video equipment
1 x AG-HPX250 (Handheld HD Camera)
3 x AW-HE120 (Pan & Tilt remote HD Camera)
1 x AW-RP50E (Remote HD Camera Controller)
1 x AW-HS50 (Compact HD Live Switcher)
2 x BT-LH2150J – (21" Monitor)

MICROPHONE STOCK

**RONNIE SCOTT'S is
pleased to be supported
by DPA MICROPHONES**

DPA MICS

1 x d:vote 4099p (Stereo Piano)
1 x d:vote 4099g (Acoustic Guitar)
2 x d:vote 4099b (Acoustic Bass)
1 x 4091 (Omni)
6 x 2011
2 x d:facto II (Vocal)

Other DPA microphones are available upon
request (advanced notice required)

Table 8.1 *continued*

OTHER MICROPHONES:

DYNAMIC MICS

2 x SHURE SM 7b

8 x SHURE SM 58

2 x SHURE SM 58 (with switch)

4 x SHURE SM 57

5 x SHURE BETA 56a

2 x SHURE BETA 52a

1 x ELECTROVOICE RE20

1 x ELECTROVOICE PL10

2 x COLES 4038 ribbon mics (upon request)

CONDENSER MICS

2 x SHURE KSM 9

4 x SHURE KSM 137

1 x SHURE KSM 27

2 x SHURE BETA 87c

3 x SHURE BETA 98a

2 X NEUMANN KM184

2 x ACCUSOUND SC-5 transducers

2 x AKG C414B (upon request)

WIRELESS MICS

1 x SHURE BETA 98h (clip on) UR1

1 x SHURE SM58 (hand held) UR2

1 x SHURE UR4D system on Ch.70

D.I. BOXES

6 x RADIAL J48 (active)

1 x RADIAL JDI (passive)

2 x EMO DUAL (stereo passive)

1 x BSS AR 121 (active)

1 x STAGE LINE (passive)

1 x CANFORD DI (high impedance active)

BACKLINE/INSTRUMENTS

PIANO

Yamaha CF6 Grand Piano (Main Club)

Yamaha Upright Piano (Ronnie's Bar)

KEYS

Fender Rhodes Mk1 – Stage/Suitcase73.

This is a hybrid of a Mk1 Stage top (passive with tone control) and a Mk1 Suitcase bass with sustain pedal.

Yamaha Motif XS 8

DRUMS

Gretsch USA Maple Custom Silver Nitron (18", 20", 22" Bass Drums, 10", 12" Rack Toms, 14", 16" Floor Toms)

BASS

We have a great 3/4 size double bass, (hand built in London, 2012 by Laurence Dixon). It has an adjustable bridge and Realist pickup. Strings are an Innovation braided set – braided core, medium tension, chrome tape wound.

It is a copy of a famous bass owned by Ray Brown, which was made in Cremona, Italy by Nicholas Amati around 1770. It was discovered in Britain in a basement by Ray Brown when he and his then wife Ella Fitzgerald were over doing a show together. The original bass now resides in Canada.

CYMBALS

There is a selection of Sabian cymbals (HHX & Legacy)

Table 8.1 *continued*

PERCUSSION
3 x Meinl Congas with cradle stands

Meinl Bongos with stand

Meinl Timbales with stand

Mark chimes

Various pieces of small hand percussion

GUITAR RIGS
Fender Twin '65 Reissue (Black Face)

Roland JC120

Fender Princeton 1x12" solid state combo

BASS RIGS
SWR 900 Head + 4x10" & 2x10"

Ashdown ABM500 bass head + 4x10"

Trace Acoustic 1x 12" Combo

2 x TC Electronic RH450 Head + 2x10" & 2x12"

Gallien Krueger MB150S (upon request)

All backline and microphone stock is shared between the Main Club and Ronnie's Bar

RONNIE'S BAR
This is a separate smaller venue above the Main Club

FOH SYSTEM
The bar is "T" shaped and has 3 zones to PA
system
NeXO Speakers
Zone 1
4 x PS10 Mid/High Enclosures (Stereo)
2 x LS500 15" Sub Enclosures (Stereo)
Zone 2
2 x PS8 Full Range Enclosures
Zone 3
2 x PS8 Full Range Enclosures

All powered by Nexo amps

Zones controlled by BSS Soundweb wall
controllers

MONITOR SYSTEM
3 x Mackie SRM350 Powered Speakers

CONSOLES
Yamaha LS9/16
Soundcraft EFX8 (in cupboard on bar)

DJ SYSTEM
1 x Pioneer DJM 700 DJ Mixer
2 x Pioneer CDJ850 CD players
2 x Technics 1210 turntables

For further details please contact:
Miles Ashton *Sound & Tech Manager*
Ronnie Scotts | 47 Frith Street | Soho | London W1D 4HT
miles@ronniescotts.co.uk
Skype: miles_ashton

CASE STUDY 8.2 RONNIE SCOTT'S JAZZ CLUB

On 30th October 1959 Ronnie Scott and Pete King opened their jazz club in basement premises at 39 Gerrard Street, in London's Soho. The dream had started taking shape some 12 years earlier when Ronnie, then 20, a promising tenor saxophonist, blew his savings on a trip to New York to see for himself what the jazz scene there was all about. Scott took in most of the New York clubs during his 2-week stay and when it was time to return to London, the seeds of ambition were well and truly sown.

In 1959 Scott and fellow tenor saxophonist and friend, Pete King, started looking round for suitable premises to establish a club and found 39 Gerrard Street, Soho. For a while it had been used as a resting spot for taxi drivers and a tea-bar but it was also a haunt for local musicians. To begin with, the plan was simply to provide a place where British jazz musicians could jam. A loan of £1,000 from Scott's stepfather helped Scott and King sign a lease and advertise in Melody Maker the grand opening performance of the Tubby Hayes Quartet.

The appearance of many jazz giants at the club put it on the map and the fortunes of the enterprise improved to such an extent that Scott and King had to go in search of bigger premises. In the summer of 1965 they found the ideal place at 47 Frith Street, and after raising a further £35,000 they converted and decorated the new hall. In the spring of 1968 it became possible to extend the Frith Street premises by acquiring the building next door. This enabled Scott and King to add an upstairs room for showcasing more acts and a downstairs bar. The new, enlarged club opened in October 1968 with the Buddy Rich Band and an augmented seating capacity of 250.

Then some of the light went out of British jazz on 23rd December 1996 when Scott died unexpectedly at the age of 69. After the death of his friend, King ran the venue successfully for another 9 years, seeing the club reach its landmark 45th anniversary. However, it was never the same for him without Scott and in June 2005 he sold the club to theatre impresario Sally Greene. Introduced to Ronnie Scott's by her father when she was in her teens Greene was a regular in the club for many years. Her reputation for restoring and maintaining the tradition of some of London's oldest theatres persuaded King that she was the right person to take the reins. In June 2006 the club reopened after a 3-month refurbishment and has since hosted some of the biggest names on the world jazz scene.

Today, Ronnie Scott's is one of the world's most famous jazz clubs, attracting full to bursting audiences nearly every night. Since the early days of Sarah Vaughn, Count Basie and Miles Davis, the club continues to present the biggest names in jazz including Wynton Marsalis, Cassandra Wilson and Kurt Elling, all of whom shun the concert halls in favour of the intimate and welcoming environs of the club.

Source: www.ronniescotts.co.uk

The most competent and experienced event manager may struggle to fully comprehend a tech spec, and if your event is going to involve stage production generally you will need to hire the services of a technician to manage this element of the event. However, a basic understanding of common technical provision is helpful if you are a professional event manager.

Sound

As discussed in earlier chapters, the acoustics of each room in any venue may be different. They will vary according to the size of the room (including ceiling height), the material of the building and the type and amount of furniture and equipment in the room. The best way to assess the acoustics are in person during a site visit and this will influence what type of activity is best suited to the space and whether or not sound equipment will be required. As Raj *et al.* (2013, p. 304) explain:

> It is essential to assess the type of venue in relation to overall floor size, internal material finishes, audience capacity, venue proximity to other buildings or adjacent rooms, type of performance and the number of people preforming.

Usually for a large event, sound equipment is essential to ensure that all attendees can clearly hear what is going on. A system of microphones connected to speakers will ensure that human voices as well as music can be suitably amplified. A distributed system of speakers will usually work in small venues, particularly buildings with poor acoustics (e.g., those with hard reflective surfaces such as glass walls) and this involves dotting the speakers around the edge of the event (Matthews, 2016). For complex events and larger venues, a range of types of speakers may be required, and frequently these work best when they are **flown** (ibid.).

The technical specification may give full details of speakers, microphones and rigging at the venue and many venues will keep a selection of microphones in stock, including **lavalier** microphones (ones which usually attach to clothing), handheld or roving microphones (which are wireless) and lead or stand microphones (which are wired). The specification may also make reference to the use of, or suggested position of, a sound desk, which will be used to control the sound equipment during the event. If you are intending on having a band or something similar at the event, it is important to check with the venue if there are any restrictions on noise levels. For example, it is quite common to find that venues located in residential neighbourhoods have noise restrictions in place, particularly for night times.

Lighting

Lighting is an essential part of the event experience as it contributes to the first and overall impression of the event. Once again, the site visit is the best way to assess the venue's natural daylight and artificial lighting options, including any blackout facilities. As Robertson (2013) indicates, there are a number of ways of creating a visual impact including positioning LED uplighters in order to enhance the venue's internal features, colour washes to give impact to the walls, ceilings and stage, and **gobos**, to enliven drab spaces by shining patterns or logos onto them. If the venue has limited equipment available, then you may find that hiring additional lighting equipment will be expensive, however, lighting has the potential to add an extraordinary element to the event and it is one of the key ways to create an emotional impact on guests, providing it is managed by a professional lighting designer (Matthews, 2016).

Equipment

The technical specification will usually give details of the power (electricity) service and distribution set up at the venue, particularly in larger venues. Typically, the power at venues, such as hotels and conference centres, is distributed via either single-phase or three-phase alternating current (AC) and depending on what is available, the equipment provider will determine if this is sufficient (Matthews, 2016, p. 302). Details of available projectors and screens may be listed on the specification including information on whether they can be flown (usually on a truss). If projectors, screens, staging, speakers (or even people) can be flown at the venue, the specification may also include details for **rigging** (reinforced and specially equipped parts of the venue's ceiling). The venue may provide two-way radios, or walkie talkies, that enable the users to communicate across the site via a specific radio frequency. These can be particularly useful if your event is spread across a wide area, as they facilitate the brief communication of important messages to specific users.

Support for disabilities

The technical specification may also make reference to technical support available at the venue to support people with disabilities such as a hearing loop or infrared communication system.

A hearing, or induction, loop system works by reducing background noise in a venue and enabling people with impaired hearing to pick up other sounds more easily. An induction loop is commonly found in separate rooms in venues. The system uses a microphone, an amplifier and a length of cable. The cable is discretely looped around the room such as under the carpet or flooring or in the ceiling and users can access the loop via their own hearing aid. Some venues will have hearing loops in all or some of their rooms, or alternatively they may have portable loops on site. These are portable units that can be carried from room to room by the user and they do not require any installation, although they have a more limited range than an installed loop and are less discreet.

Alternatively, the venue may have an infrared hearing system which operates via different technology. Sounds are fed into an audio source such as a microphone or sound system. These are then processed through a mixer and then move in to an infrared radiator which transmits a signal. Users can access the signal via a receiver such as a hearing aid or a compatible headset. Venues that have infrared systems will also stock a number of compatible headsets. The infrared system is superior to the hearing loop. Unlike the induction loop, the infrared system cannot penetrate walls or ceilings and therefore this ensures privacy of sound within the room which could be extremely important to private events. The infrared system is easier to set up in large venues and is less likely to be affected by the fabric of the building, such as steel, which can impact the signal and frequency response of induction loop systems. Infrared systems can also be multichannel which facilitates multiple use, such as providing audio coverage of a speaker from overseas plus an interpreter's translation of what they are saying.

Staging

If the rooms in the venue that you are using have a purpose-built stage, then the technical specification will usually include details about the stage such as its dimensions, details of the proscenium arch and apron, rigging points and fly bars. Most stages are flat, but a number of theatres have raked stages to enhance the visual effect of scenery or props on the audience. Information about the availability of backdrops and **tabs** (stage curtains) will be useful in helping you to understand how you might be able to use the stage. For example, some stages are very large and can seem unsuitable for certain events as there is such as lot of room to fill and then to use. But carefully positioned curtains, scenery or props will reduce this space to something that is more manageable and create a more intimate space and personable ambience, which might suit a sole speaker or performer, for example.

Venues without a fixed stage, might have portable staging that will be available for you to use at your event. Portable staging comes in different shapes and sizes, but it can be moved from room to room fairly easily and enables you to set up a stage in a variety of different ways.

If the venue has no staging at all, you may wish to consider whether it is appropriate to create one. A stage can be a barrier between performer and audience (which may be desirable), but it also becomes a focal point for the audience and elevates speakers, performers, screens, marketing messages, etc.

Additional information and facilities

The venue should also be able to provide you with details of available auxiliary spaces or rooms, such as the use of dressing rooms or wardrobe (e.g., in a theatre) or office space. The specification may illustrate the availability of a stage door, service road, loading bay and dock door as well as detailing any specific instructions for the get in/get out periods such as ceiling heights, door widths and floor loading capacities. A specific breakdown of the furniture available in each room may be included as well as details of how the room is usually set up. This may include items such as lecterns, daises and music stands.

In addition to what is noted on the technical specification or on the venue's website, there may be other items available for you to use at the venue. Therefore, a discussion with the venue manager about your specific event activities, aims and theme may lead to suggestions of what additional props, equipment or facilities you can use or take advantage of at the venue. Plus, if the venue is providing you with the use of in-house equipment or facilities, this may be on the condition that only the venue staff will move, set up and operate it and there may be extra charges for this.

8.5 RIDERS

When contracting performers and entertainers, they will normally provide the person who has booked them with a rider. This is a type of addition to a contract which details all of the requirements of the artist (see Chapter 10 for details about contracts). This can include their staging and AV needs as well as what they expect in terms of facilities at the destination and the venue such as accommodation, dressing rooms and refreshments. The rider can be used as a method for increasing the overall fee for the performance via the demand for a significant number of extras, particularly hotel rooms and refreshments (Bowdin et al., 2011). Therefore, it must be read carefully and the event manager will need to assess the impact of the rider on the overall event budget.

Additionally, it is important to discuss the rider with the venue to ascertain whether or not the venue can provide the requisite items and services, and if so, at what cost. Many high-profile celebrities have been derided for their lavish and unreasonable rider demands, and indeed, a number of artists' green room requirements can be ridiculous (Matthews, 2016). Nonetheless it is important to check, rather than assume, that the venue can provide items such as towels, drinks and hot meals as well as access to lockable and well-equipped dressing rooms.

8.6 A TECHNICAL SITE VISIT

The best way to investigate all of the available technical equipment and support at a venue is to request a technical site visit. As with a standard site inspection, this can be arranged with the venue manager and it can be helpful if the event manager can provide an agenda or overview of what they would like to see and discuss during the visit. The venue manager can then arrange for a visit that will focus on viewing specific areas of the venue and meeting with certain staff such as the in-house technician or stage manager. If the event manager is planning on hiring their own technician or technical producer, it is important to invite them to the site visit too.

In advance of the technical site visit, it is essential that you have spent time with your production staff in order to go over your event aims and plans. You will probably ask them to write or to contribute to your detailed operational schedule, and ultimately you may employ them to completely stage manage the event. But initially it is important that they understand what you are trying to achieve overall at the event. This will enable them to lend their expertise to the discussions at the technical site visit.

CASE STUDY 8.3 ESSENTIAL QUESTIONS TO ASK YOUR TECHNICAL PROVIDER

A typical event manager is great at multitasking and has exceptional skills in marketing, negotiating and managing projects. However, many organisers, particularly aspiring and novice event managers, have gaps in their knowledge when it comes to the topic of audiovisual technology, even though this is a key element of any and every event. It's easy to feel overwhelmed by the jargon or to completely forget to ask specific questions from your AV provider. But getting the most out of your AV provider can come down to asking the right questions in the first place. Therefore, these five top tips should help you cover some of the most important questions you will need answers to.

1 What's included in the venue contract?

Check your contract with your own technical adviser if possible before signing it and check with the venue as to what they are including in the room hire. Don't take anything for granted; for example, don't assume that power will be provided. Also, be aware that some venues impose restrictions or penalties for using an AV specialist that is not in-house.

2 What does my budget cover?

Be honest about your budget with your venue or AV supplier and also be clear about what you expect and what you need, e.g., do you need it to be sustainable? Will there be live streaming? etc. Make it clear what equipment you will need (e.g. the number of mics, projectors etc.). Also include your plans for any rehearsal time in case this affects the price. Being honest about what you need and what your budget is – it will help to avoid wasting time with a company that cannot accommodate you.

3 Can I arrange a technical site visit?

As all event managers know, a good walk around the venue is very valuable. However, it can be equally important to tour the venue with your AV provider. Having a technical specialist with you will help you to go over any questions that may not have made it onto your own checklist such as the ceiling height and other architectural elements and how these may affect equipment as well as how easy it will be to load and store equipment.

4 What information do I need to give you?

Your AV provider will need information from you about bandwidth and electricity requirements. How much time is needed for the get in and get out? How many presenters/speakers you plan on having and what kind of presentations they will be giving, and what software and hardware will they have or need to use? What types and number of microphones you will need? Ensure that your provider has all of this information so that your event can run smoothly.

5 What staff do you provide?

Not all AV teams are the same, and being clear about what staff come with your AV package will indicate how extensive the service is that you are being offered. For example, knowing in advance whether there is someone to take care of the small details, such as loading up presentations, helps you to make sure that nothing gets missed.

Source: www.eventmanagerblog.com/audiovisual-questions-to-ask

Table 8.2 details what you might want to cover during the technical site visit, with input from the venue team as well as your own production staff.

Table 8.2 Checklist for a technical site visit

Name of venue/room:	Notes
Is there a service road, stage door, rear entrance, dock door, etc.?	
What are the drop off/parking arrangements for technical staff/equipment?	
What AV equipment is available and at what cost? e.g., • Microphones • Two-way radios • Screens • Projectors	
Will front or rear projection work?	
Is there portable staging?	
What furniture is available for use on stage? e.g., • Lectern/dais • Music stands • Microphone stands • Chairs	
Are there any props or scenery available for use on stage?	

continued

Table 8.2 Continued

Are there stage curtains, and how/from where are they controlled?	
How is the lighting controlled and where from?	
Where does a sound desk normally go?	
Is there a backstage area?	
Are there dressing rooms?	
How do performers access the stage?	
Can the audience access the stage?	
Can the event be filmed, and if so where should cameras be positioned?	

As well as discussing the technical specification, the site visit is an opportunity to discuss access to the stage/performance/back of house area of the event. You can seek the views of the technical staff on whether front or rear projection will be used and where the best position for screens will be and how many will be needed. The visit will give you the opportunity to check out the access routes to the stage and back stage areas (for staff, performers and potentially the audience) and see where the sound desk might be positioned. In relation to how the stage may be used, you will be able to start to make decisions about seating. For example, you may wish to give the seats with the best views to your VIPs or reserve specific seats for staff, speakers or award recipients who will need quick access to the stage.

THE INDUSTRY EXPERT'S VIEW 8.1

TECHNICAL PRODUCTION IN CHALLENGING VENUES

Matt Bunday, Managing Director, Matt Bunday Events Ltd, www.mattbundayevents.com

Despite being mainly an outdoor events business, some of my more exciting and interesting events have been in indoor venues. Within the weddings, live music events and specific bespoke events that we do, we have worked in some really interesting, and at times, challenging places. More often than not it turns into a really exciting opportunity. We have been amongst the first to dress a new retro coffee shop, achieve a specific lighting briefing within a venue with fairly unreflective walls or other similar challenges. Memorable examples include when we set up lighting and sound for a wedding in a cave and when we turned a nineteenth-century church (designed by Sir

continued

George Gilbert Scott) into a concert venue (bringing in lighting, sound and cameras for an evening of live music). We have reworked a newly opened nightclub into a James Bond 'Casino Royale' themed evening for a university's graduation ball and we have managed the staging, lighting, sound and AV elements (including a very bright projector!) for a world record attempt in the Live Quarter of the 02 Arena.

Every event is unique to the organisers putting it on, but also every venue is unique to us in terms of what we manage to achieve in it. Based on my experience, particularly in technical production, these are my three top tips for novice event managers:

Find out what else is going on in the venue

Some venues are within buildings that are very multi-purpose. This can mean that you may be restricted as to when you can sound check, or how secure your event is during the load in and build. It can make it harder to safely coordinate a load in that involves working from height or lots of power cabling if the general public are coming through the space. You may also need to coordinate sound check timings carefully.

Ask if the venue is listed or not?

Although a simple check list of 'what can I do' and 'what can't I do' at the venue is highly recommended when meeting the venue management team, one of the first questions to ask is whether the venue is listed or not and at what level. The answer may significantly alter your way of working. You may be in a venue where you cannot even stick tape to the floor or walls. You may need to get creative with how to safely and sensibly run cabling in your venue, but this should be thought about from a holistic point of view rather than at each section of the venue.

Is a venue research evening needed?

I think it's important to remember that quite often how you imagine the event to be and how it is on the day will be different. So, if we are lighting or decorating a venue where we're not quite sure how the lighting will reflect off the walls or how the acoustics will sound, for example, then we may arrange for a follow up meeting at the venue and we will take along equipment with us to test and take photos to then send to the client.

At MBE we always try to be very proactive and these three tips are helpful for avoiding any surprises on site on the day. We know that when time is short or the pressure is on it can be tempting for the client to settle for second best or make rash decisions. We want to avoid this wherever possible so that every decision is precise and thought through in order to make the event as good as it can be.

8.7 CHARGES

At many venues, the use of any in-house technical equipment or facilities comes at a cost which is in addition to the room hire charges. This is usually because of two factors. First, technical equipment can be very expensive to purchase and therefore the venue will want to recoup some of their expenditure. Second, as most venues managers know, hiring AV equipment from a third-party supplier can also be extremely costly, due to the high value and fragility of the kit. Therefore, some venue managers invest in purchasing equipment because they can then offer it to event managers for a slightly lower cost than they would have to pay by ordering it from another supplier. Moreover, as Fenich (2012, p. 174) explains, many venues will not in fact permit event managers to provide their own AV equipment because charging for the use of in-house equipment is a significant income stream for venues. What is perhaps more reasonable is that if the venue is going to give you access to their technical equipment or facilities you may have to pay for their own, trained and trusted, staff to set it up and operate it.

In addition to charges for equipment, facilities and staff, it is important to check with the venue about the arrangements for the get in and get out. For example, usually you will pay room hire charges for the time you will need to set up and break down the event and much of this will be dependent on how long it will take to complete the technical set up and break down. And of course, the actual charge for a performer may be as much as triple their basic fee once you take into account their requirements as set out in the rider (Bowdin et al., 2011). Therefore, in terms of the event budget, you will need to work closely with your production team, contractors, suppliers and venue staff to ensure that you have comprehensive costs for all of your requirements.

8.8 TECHNOLOGICAL DEVELOPMENTS IN EVENTS

Keeping up with the rapid advancements in technology is certainly one of the major challenges for the twenty-first-century event manager. Finding ways in which to not just embrace technology, but to cleverly incorporate it into event design is a key skill. But as we saw with apps, some developments have been particularly driven by, or designed for the events industry.

Geo-location tools, for example, are proving particularly popular and useful to the event organiser as these enable guests to virtually sign in at an event but also to make connections with others doing the same thing. Bluetooth Low Energy (BLE) is a development of wireless network technology. Smartphones are likely to adopt BLE in the future but it is also compatible with the current and widely used version of Bluetooth, which means that future Bluetooth devices could be dual-mode (Gomez et al., 2012). Single-mode chips enable virtual registration and tracking at events whereas BLE-enabled products go a step further and permit attendees to communicate with each other (Bonnerud, 2008). Furthermore, iBeacons, which are small wireless devices, can now be placed in and around the venue in order to track Bluetooth enabled devices. These can be used alongside other scanning technology to provide the event manager with an additional means of capturing data about the attendees at the venue.

Another increasingly popular mechanism for doing this is by using Radio Frequency Identification (RFID) tags. RFID tags are tiny computer chips that act in a way that is similar to a barcode (but more efficiently) in that they provide a means of data collection via an electronic reader device that uses radio frequency waves. Venues that have invested in RFID scanners are now able to offer the event manager the option to include RFID tags in badges which in turn means that the organiser can register and track guests, ensure the right attendees have access to the right areas of the venue and VIPs can be tracked in a way that notifies staff when they are approaching (Rogers and Davidson, 2016).

RFID tags instantly capture large amounts of data and therefore the scanners are being rapidly adopted, particularly in business events where the technology has a lot of potential because of its functionality (Jakobson, 2015), and organisers continue to find new ways of incorporating them into events. Therefore 'it is widely predicted that RFID will also have a

CASE STUDY 8.4 THE LAS VEGAS CONVENTION CENTER'S ANTENNA SYSTEM FOR ENHANCED MOBILE WIRELESS EXPERIENCE

The Las Vegas Convention Center (LVCC), located adjacent to the Las Vegas Strip, encompasses approximately 3.2 million square feet with exhibition space of 2 million square feet and meeting space of nearly 250,000 square feet. The facility is one of the busiest venues in the world as there are nearly 150,000 hotel rooms in Las Vegas alone. In addition to the exhibition and convention space, there are 145 meeting rooms with capacities ranging from 20 to 2,500. A grand lobby and registration area efficiently link exhibition halls and meeting rooms and allow simultaneous set-up, break-down and exhibiting of multiple events. The venue is home to some of the largest conventions and trade shows in the world as it can handle the volume, traffic and grand-scale requirements that make a successful show.

Continuing its commitment to ensuring the facility is the most technologically-advanced convention centre in the United States, the DMO, the Las Vegas Convention and Visitors Authority (LVCVA) has successfully launched one of the nation's largest Neutral-Host Distributed Antenna Systems (DAS) throughout the property. The DAS concept is built on the engineering principle that a linked network of low-powered, spatially separated antennas and repeaters providing overlapping coverage within the confines of an enclosed area improves mobile phone capacity and reception. The system is comprised of common fibre optic, radio, and antenna infrastructure maintained by dedicated technical staff.

Through a partnership with Cox Business/Hospitality Network and InSite Wireless Group, guests visiting the venue will benefit from state-of-the-art wireless voice and data cellular services that are now being transported over the new DAS. This development will provide wireless subscribers a better event experience as they navigate the venue's 3.2 million square feet. It is also a future-proof design; allowing for enhancements in new wireless technologies such as the upcoming 5G mobile phone technology.

'Today's world is a wireless world, and to provide a first rate customer experience, we have to have the infrastructure to ensure visitors have seamless coverage and service', said Hugh Sinnock, LVCVA's vice president of customer experience. 'With the support of our partners at InSite, we've constructed a neutral host DAS infrastructure that will provide reliable, high-speed cellular connectivity within the Las Vegas Convention Center', said Derrick R. Hill, vice president of Cox Business and Hospitality Network in Las Vegas. 'As a result, cell providers will be able to give their customers improved coverage and this will enhance the overall convention center experience for attendees and guests'.

In addition to the centre's existing high-density Wi-Fi network, the capacity of the new cellular DAS is immense. With an ability to deliver service to more than 100,000 guests simultaneously, visitors to the LVCC can expect faster download speeds on their smartphones than typically provided on most corporate networks. Four major U.S. wireless carriers have signed agreements to launch this service. The system can simultaneously accommodate traffic from all of the participating wireless carriers; serving the exploding wireless voice and data demands that are common at today's high attendance, technology-rich trade shows and events.

Source: http://press.lvcva.com/

Image 8.2 Las Vegas Convention Center.

Source: ©LVCVA.

significant impact on the meetings industry in general, and on venues in particular, in the next few years' (Rogers and Davidson, 2016, p. 216).

The future of the events industry could also see wearable technology, implants (e.g. skin chips), and even iris/retina scanning start to feature in event design. Although the latest developments in Virtual Reality (VR) and Augmented Reality (AR) have been slow to penetrate the industry due to the high costs involved, low client interest and issues of unreliability (Fullard, 2016).

8.9 TECHNOLOGY – THE VENUE MANAGER'S PERSPECTIVE

The twenty-first-century venue manager faces the dual challenge of keeping up with event organisers' technological requests and investing time and money in equipping the venue with the latest available technology. The latter can be very expensive and rather daunting, particularly as the terminology alone for each new rapid development can seem very alien. Nonetheless, event organisers are developing new and interesting ways of including technology in event design, particularly to both capture information about attendees and to involve them in the event. Free and reliable Wi-Fi is now a basic request and venues that cannot provide this may find themselves overlooked, particularly as many venues continue to invest in the latest equipment such as HD projectors, LED screens and webcams. Keeping up with the increasing demands for bandwidth will mean continuous investment by the venue but adequate bandwidth capability has become one of the major venue considerations of event managers (Davidson and Hyde, 2014). It can be challenging and expensive to keep up with the latest technological trends and for smaller venues it may be impossible to purchase and store equipment. However, some of the newest technology can aid in venue management and is therefore a wise investment. For example, while RFID technology is proving popular with event organisers, it also offers the venue manager an innovative means of tracking the location of on-site furniture and equipment (Rogers and Davidson, 2016).

Although as Dingley (2016) warns, 'No longer is it acceptable to simply grasp the concept of technology; it's now expected for venues to be as tech savvy as the planners and organizers require it to be to host their events.' This means that there is now more pressure than ever for venue managers to be technologically competent which may require a great deal of training and investment of time and money.

8.10 SUMMARY

Ongoing developments in technology and mass global communication continue to extend event audiences. Virtual and hybrid events are now not just possible but popular extensions of the live events industry. The rapid increase and capability of technology has provided greater scope for engagement and creativity within event production. This in turn provides challenges for both the event and venue manager to keep up! A technical specification is an excellent starting point for understanding what is available to use at the venue, but a dedicated site visit is essential in order to fully explore stage and production possibilities at the venue. Technical support may be available at the venue, free or at a charge, and if your event is going to require any amount of stage management or technical production it is usually best to employ the services of a dedicated professional. Using the venue's in-house equipment may come at a cost in addition to the room hire. The charges are likely to be lower than you would pay to hire in the same kit, although you may find that you are obliged to use the venue's equipment and staff. In addition to these charges, riders may also contain costly requirements and therefore careful budgeting of all of the event's technical elements is essential.

8.11 FURTHER READING

The following sources are particularly useful for further reading on the subject of technology:

Matthews, D. (2015) *Special Event Production: The Resources* (2nd edn). London: Routledge.
Matthews, D. (2016) *Special Event Production: The Process* (2nd edn). London: Routledge.
Conference and Incentive Travel publications (available at www.citmagazine.com)
Conference News publications (available at www.conference-news.co.uk)
EVCOM (Event and Visual Communication Association) publications (available at www.evcom.org.uk)
Event Marketing Blog by Michael Heipel and guests (available at https://michaelheipel.wordpress.com)
Social Media Today publications (available at www.socialmediatoday.com)
Ungerboeck Software International publications (available at https://ungerboeck.com)

Understanding venue charges

LEARNING OUTCOMES

By the end of Chapter 9, you should be able to:

- Identify the factors influencing venue hire charges
- Understand the concepts of REVPAR, yield management and attrition
- Recognise rechargeable costs and penalties
- Negotiate charges with a venue

9.1 INTRODUCTION

Venue hire charges can be surprisingly complex and few venues openly advertise all of their applicable hire charges. Most venue managers use a system of yield management to ensure that they maximise the income derived from room hire but this also means that charges will fluctuate in line with trends and demands. In addition to room hire charges, venues are likely to recharge the event manager for certain services or equipment provided to them during the event. They will also impose penalty charges for failures to meet certain requirements or leaving any damage. Consequently, for the novice event manager this can seem like a minefield that you need to carefully navigate to avoid paying for unnecessary or avoidable costs. Yet most charges are negotiable and even though venues will typically have set charges for rooms, these charges may be flexible. Charges can be affected by a number of variables such as the day, date or time of year that the event is taking place as well as the type of client and type of event. However, most venue managers will also be open to negotiating on certain charges and on occasion the savvy event manager will be able to secure free venue hire. This usually relies on being able to provide the venue with the guarantee of making an income elsewhere from the event. In fact, in certain circumstances, the venue may even offer the event manager a financial incentive in order to encourage them to make a booking. This chapter will therefore guide you through the complexities of room hire and additional charges and it will help you to understand and predict the charges that are going to apply to your event. Tips on how to negotiate with venue managers will provide you with the tools necessary to ensure that you can successfully secure the best deal possible with the venue.

9.2 REVPAR AND YIELD MANAGEMENT

The complexities of venue hire charges are linked to the practices of REVPAR and yield management. REVPAR, which stands for revenue per available room, is a term used to measure the performance or occupancy rate of a venue. Essentially REVPAR is the amount of money that can be generated by selling all of the venue's available rooms and it can be calculated by dividing the sum of the potential room revenue by the number of rooms available (Rogers, 2013, p. 235). One of the key challenges of manging a venue is achieving the maximum REVPAR over the course of a period of time (e.g. one financial year) which can mean raising or lowering charges at different times in the year in line with demand. This is a form of yield management.

Yield management is essentially 'the basic economic theory of supply and demand that dictates that in times of high demand, high prices can be charged, but when demand is low, prices will drop' (Rogers and Davidson, 2016, p. 149). In other words, venues will employ strategies to maximise their income by selling their rooms at the best rates possible to ensure that they are filled as much as possible. This means applying different hire charges based on market demands. Yield management is also built upon understanding, predicting and reacting to consumer behaviour (Berger, 2005). This is a technique that was developed by the airline industry and subsequently adopted by hotels, the first venues that began to vary their accommodation rates on a daily basis depending on actual and anticipated demand (Fenich, 2012, p. 210).

Today this technique has been adopted and adapted by managers of other types of venues besides hotels. Sporting venues, academic and unusual venues are likely to alter both their day delegate rate and hourly room charges according to the level of demand and rates charged by competitors. These venues, like hotels, are also likely to vary their costs due to the seasonality of the primary function. For example, when a sporting complex is not being used for competitions or training purposes, the hire charges for event space is likely to be at its lowest. This is due to a combination of factors. Firstly, the space is not being used for its primary purpose and therefore any income on rooms that would be otherwise left unused is a bonus to the venue. This can mean that the venue manager may offer very low, competitive rates to encourage bookings to fill the space. Secondly, part of the appeal of holding an event at a sporting venue is to take advantage of the adrenaline filled atmosphere that engulfs a stadium or sports ground on a busy match day. However, this will obviously be lacking on a non-match day and therefore the venue manager may offer lower hire charges to offset the lack of atmosphere. Similarly, a number of unusual venues and academic venues will offer lower hire rates during off peak seasons, particularly when the rooms will be completely unused unless they are sold to event managers.

Yield management is also going to be affected by influences such as changing tastes and interests as well as planned future events (e.g. national holidays) and unexpected past events (e.g. terrorist attacks) (Berger, 2005). As such it is important for event managers to keep abreast with industry changes and trends as well as significant influences.

9.3 SIGNIFICANT INFLUENCES AND TRENDS

There are a number of industry and academic organisations that carry out research within the field of event management. The results can be useful for understanding and forecasting industry trends. One such study is the annual UK Conference and Meetings Survey which reported that in 2016, the majority (61 percent) of events in the UK were held in hotels and the next most popular venues were unusual or multi-purpose venues (UKCAMS, 2017). Popularity can lead to inflated hire charges while there is a great demand for these spaces. However, when there is an oversupply this can lead to a fall in prices and a buyers' market emerges (Rogers and Davidson, 2016) and there are certainly more and more venues joining the events industry every year. As such, as an event manager you may want to consider the number of venue types in the location in which you are interested in holding an event. If there are, for example, a glut of visitor attractions this may mean that the hire charges are lower than you might expect to pay for a unique and rather special venue.

Venues that are located in countries or regions that have been affected by severe weather conditions, political instability, negative press coverage or other such factors may struggle to attract event managers. Venues in remote locations, venues that are in need of refurbishment or lack up-to-date technology may also struggle to attract business. Venues who are new to the events industry and lack the experience of their competitors may also struggle to attract business and venues that have limited marketing budgets may struggle to promote their facilities. In all such cases, and many more, the venue manager may offer encouragingly low hire charges. For the event manager, particularly if you have a small budget, these may seem attractive. However it is important to consider whether or not the venue can fulfil your key event requirements and if not how much this will alter the event plan or add to the extra operational costs. Also, if the venue is unpopular or located in an unpopular destination, you must consider what impact this will have on the popularity of your event. On balance, it may be worthwhile spending more on hire charges to secure the right venue for your event and the target audience and part of this decision must take into account all the venue hire information that you can gather.

9.4 DAY DELEGATE RATES

Generally venue hire charges fall into two categories; either a set fee per attendee per day or an hourly charge for each room that is going to be used. A day delegate rate (DDR) is the charge that the venue makes per person attending a specific event, usually a meeting or a one-day conference. The DDR will usually cover the cost of the use of one event room, refreshments (typically lunch and 2 servings of tea and coffee) and a basic AV and stationery package. This charge will usually cover all of the event manager's requirements for a meeting, training event or 1-day conference. For a slightly longer event a 24 hour rate is usually available if the venue is residential. This charge will include everything in the DDR plus an evening meal, overnight accommodation in the venue and breakfast the following morning.

DDRs and 24 hour rates can vary quite a bit, usually depending on the overall quality or location of the venue. However a number of venues charge very competitive rates and these are usually published on their website and in their marketing materials. A published rate, often referred to as the rack rate, can still be negotiated and tips for negotiating with the venue are discussed later in this chapter. Day delegate rates can represent excellent value for money, particularly when the venue will include in the package access to everything that is on site which might extend to use of extensive AV equipment, access to the venue's leisure facilities etc.

For a straightforward 1 or 2-day event, such as a meeting or training event, a DDR or a 24 hour rate is a comprehensive and uncomplicated hire charge. However, for less straightforward events, the hire charges can become rather more complicated.

9.5 STANDARD ROOM HIRE CHARGES

If your event is not a straightforward business event such as a meeting, conference or short training course, then a DDR will not usually cover all your venue requirements and therefore you will need a detailed quotation from the venue which lists all of the room hire charges. Of course this may have been provided to you as part of the RFP process but it may need to be updated as the design of your event progresses and you are able to confirm to the venue your precise requirements.

Typically venues will charge by the hour for the use of each and every room that you intend to use and there is often a minimum hire period of at least 4 hours. The hourly charges may be affected by some or all of the variables shown in Figure 9.1.

Charges are often aligned to the size and therefore the capacity of the room and the bigger the room, the more expensive it will be to hire. Similarly, rooms that are already furnished or equipped with facilities such as staging or AV equipment may come at a premium, and this can sometimes be regardless of whether or not you plan on using the room's equipment and facilities. The time and date of the event can often determine the charges as many venues, in line with their yield management strategies, will charge more for evening use of the venue and for busy times of the week or year, notably weekends and peak seasons such as national holidays and vacation periods.

Many venues will take into account the profile of the event manager or their client when confirming the venue hire charges. As such the hire charges for registered charities may be

Figure 9.1 Factors affecting hire charges.

lower than those that will apply to commercial organisations. Similarly the hire charges may vary depending on the type of event or type of activities that are going to take place at the venue. For example, some venues will apply higher charges to exhibitions if these are going to be highly commercialised trading arenas. The premise being, that the venue is providing a space which will be used to generate spending and therefore the venue expects to benefit from such activity. Also events that are going to be filmed may incur a higher hourly venue charge. Once again this is sometimes linked to the commercial value of the activity but also to ensure that an extra payment can be made to staff working at the venue who may be filmed.

The event manager can expect to pay the same hire charge for the get in and get out periods of any event. Furthermore, the venue may apply hire charges to any rooms that are not in use throughout the event but that cannot be hired to another party. For example, if you were holding a party which included a sit down meal in one room, a casino in another room, and a disco in a third room there may be times during the event when only one room is in use. For example, everyone may sit down to eat together and end up on the dancefloor long after the meal has finished and the gambling has stopped. However, once each of your three rooms is set up for your event, possibly several hours before they will be used, they cannot be hired out to anyone else. Therefore, the venue may charge you for each hour that you are 'occupying' the room as illustrated in Table 9.1.

As well as charging for rooms that are set up but not in use, venues can also make charges for rooms that have been booked for an event but end up not being used at all and this is referred to as attrition.

9.6 ATTRITION

Attrition (also referred to as slippage) is a term referring to unused room bookings and many venues will include an attrition clause in their hire contract. Essentially this means that if the event manager books rooms for their event that they do not use, they will be charged for them anyway. Such clauses 'provide for the payment of damages to the hotel when a meeting organizer fails to fully utilize the room block specified in the contract' (Fenich, 2012, p. 213).

Table 9.1 Hire charges for occupation (not use)

Time	Activity	Room in use?	Hire charge applies?
Room 1: Meal			
16.00 – 18.00	Get in: decorate room etc.	Yes	Yes
18.00 – 21.00	Guests arrive, dinner served	Yes	Yes
21.00 – 23.30	(Guests enjoy casino or disco)	No	Yes
23.30 – 24.00	Get out	Yes	Yes
Room 2: Casino			
16.00 – 18.00	Get in: set up casino tables etc.	Yes	Yes
18.00 – 21.00	(Guests have dinner)	No	Yes
21.00 – 23.30	Casino open	Yes	Yes
23.30 – 24.00	Get out	Yes	Yes
Room 3: Disco			
19.00 – 20.00	Get in: set up disco	Yes	Yes
20.00 – 21.00	(Guests have dinner)	No	Yes
21.00 – 23.30	Disco open	Yes	Yes
23.30 – 24.00	Get out	Yes	Yes

Attrition clauses are common in hotel contracts, particularly when accommodation is included in the overall booking. However they are also used by other types of venues who are adapting similar policies.

Attrition clauses can also be found in contracts that venues have with specific suppliers. For example, some venues will have exclusive providers of certain services (catering, AV, florists etc.) and venues will receive a commission on any income that their exclusive providers make via events taking place at the venue. Therefore, an attrition clause can be imposed if these services are under used by event managers based on the theory that 'the services should be paid for anyway because they were available' (Fenich, 2012, p. 60).

Venues may argue that attrition charges are perfectly fair. If the venue manager reserves rooms for an event and then does not use them it is reasonable to expect payment for these rooms. However, some attrition charges can apply even if the event manager alerts the venue to the fact that they no longer require the rooms. The venue may waive attrition charges if they manage to re-hire the rooms to another organisation for a different event. However, if they fail to do this then they are likely to go ahead and impose the full attrition charge. Occasionally some venues will not actively seek to re-let the rooms to another event manager, as they know that they are guaranteed to receive payment from the original booking.

Attrition clauses are commonly used by hotels and other residential venues and they can apply to the booking of accommodation as well as event spaces. This is the case when the event manager has assumed the responsibility of estimating the number of bedrooms that will be required by people attending the event and staying overnight in the venue and booking this accommodation on behalf of these guests. Event managers will often seek to block book accommodation at the venue if it is available as this can mean securing a reduced rate for the event guests. In turn this is an attractive incentive for attending the event. Additionally, residential venues will often offer generous discounts on the hire of event spaces providing that the event manager also books a certain number of bedrooms. This is particularly true if the event is held out of season and some venues will go as far as offering free event space in exchange for the guarantee of the accommodation booking.

However, attrition clauses are often applicable to the booking of bedrooms as well as event spaces and it can be very difficult to accurately estimate the number of people who will want to stay overnight at the venue. Furthermore, as so many of us now use the internet to book our accommodation, frequently event attendees will find even cheaper rates online for accommodation at the same venue. This can make attendees feel that the event manager is trying to overcharge them for the accommodation and ultimately will lead them to booking their accommodation online and to the attrition clauses being imposed on the event manager.

Therefore, before signing a contract with a venue it's important to look out for all attrition clauses that relate to the hire of the venue, the booking of bedrooms at the venue and the use of specific suppliers at the venue. Attrition can be avoided with careful event planning and careful under estimating of attendance levels and needs. However, even the most experienced event manager can fall foul of stringent attrition clauses and therefore as part of your early negotiation with the venue, it may be wise to ask for all attrition clauses to be lowered or removed entirely from the contract.

9.7 RECHARGES

As well as attrition charges, most venues will recharge event managers for a number of items or services provided to you during the event. These shouldn't come as a surprise as most venues

Table 9.2 Recharges

Rechargeable Item	Examples	Charge
Staffing	Stewards, security, cloakroom etc.	Per person, per hour
Equipment, Furniture, AV and Electricity	Tables, chairs, microphones, power sockets, Wi-Fi etc.	Per item, per day
Office Supplies and Facilities	Photocopying, printing, stationery, telephone calls etc.	Per item
Licences	Alcohol, gambling, music etc.	Contribution to fee
Box Office	Printing/selling tickets	% of sales
Merchandise	Sale of souvenirs (programmes, t-shirts etc.)	% of sales

will provide detailed documentation and explanations about additional charges plus the hire contract will also usually indicate the items, services or situations that may incur additional charges. However, as Fenich warns, 'every square foot of the building has a price attached to it . . . every chair, every table, and every service provided . . . has a price' (2012, p. 63) and Table 9.2 lists some of the notable charges.

Staffing

Providing adequate and suitable staffing at events is essential and different venues will have varying viewpoints on how this may or should work at events held at their premises. Some venue managers will leave the staffing of the event up to the event manager while other venues will provide staff, either included in the hire package or as an extra cost. The role of the venue staff is discussed in detail in Chapter 11 but as part of assessing venue charges it is important to get a clear picture from the venue as to what their policies are on the provision of staff to include stewards, security personnel and cloakroom staff. Stewards will ensure that the event runs smoothly and they can fulfil a number of roles such as checking tickets, directing attendees and answering questions. Some venues will provide stewards and incorporate the fee for this into the overall room hire charge. Other venues will have a bank of staff who can steward the event for an additional charge. It can be worthwhile using the venue's own staff as they will usually be trained, familiar with the venue layout and the venue's policies (e.g. where the smoking areas are located etc.). Moreover the venue manager will usually take on the responsibility of organising the staff rota and managing the staff during the event. If you are going to use the venue's staff it is worth discussing this with the venue manager. For example you may want to train them to carry out specific duties at the event or wear branded clothing or a uniform of your choice.

Other staffing roles that the venue may be able to provide include cloakroom staff and this may be regardless of whether or not the venue has a dedicated cloakroom facility or a makeshift one. If the event is a formal dinner or an evening function, you may want to provide this facility to the event guests and having cloakroom staff ensures a professional, safe and effective means of storing coats and bags.

Most venues will provide security staff if this is deemed necessary by the venue or preferable by the event manager. In many countries it is a legal requirement to have trained and certified security staff at an event, if the event is high risk, likely to be crowded, or will involve the provision of alcohol. As such, most venues will either have a bank of security staff for events or will regularly hire security staff from local organisations. Security staff can fulfil a number of responsibilities beyond the remit of the event stewards such as searching attendees and removing disruptive people from an event. Therefore as well as ensuring the event is legally compliant, they can provide peace of mind for event managers, venue managers and event guests.

Equipment, furniture, AV and electricity

It is quite common to find that venues will charge hirers for the use of equipment and furniture that is already located at the venue. Sometimes this can mean a small charge will apply to every chair or table that is going to be used. More often charges will be applied to the use of any valuable equipment or to heavy items of furniture or equipment that require moving or setting up. This can include items such as pianos, which may require tuning if they have to be moved from one room to another, and this will therefore incur an additional charge for the services of a professional piano tuner.

As discussed in Chapter 8, the use of the venue's AV equipment and the services of a technician may be included in the hire package. Alternatively, the venue may apply charges for all items of AV equipment that are required. If the equipment is in house, and therefore belongs to the venue, the event manager can also expect to pay for the services of a technician as the venue will usually want to control who has access to their own expensive and specialist equipment. In the twenty first century, the free and easy access to reliable and high quality Wi-Fi is something that we have come to expect. However, as we also saw in Chapter 8, this is not always something that venues can readily provide. Some venues will therefore levy a charge for access to a fast connection and this is something that as the event manager, you may wish to discuss early into your conversations with the venue. Particularly if onsite internet access is integral to some of the event activities or something that your attendees will be expecting.

Office supplies and facilities

The organised event manager will ensure that within their event plan they have set aside some office space, or equivalent, at the venue that can be used by themselves, the event staff or attendees as necessary. However, frequently this is overlooked and once onsite you may find that you suddenly need stationery, a photocopier or printer or access to a landline. Most venues managers will usually help out with small requests for printing or paper and dip into their own office supplies. But some venues will make a charge, particularly for things such as a large quantity of colour printing or an international phone call.

Licences

A number of event activities are licensable in most countries. This includes the provision of alcohol, gambling and playing of music and licences can usually be obtained to ensure that the activity can be legally conducted at an event. In some cases the venue will have its own licence which enables the activity to take place on site. But, in lieu of a contribution towards the licence fee, the venue will apply a charge for permitting the licensable activity to go ahead at an event. As with other charges, this should usually be made clear to the event manager well in advance of event day and such charges are usually stated in the venue contract. However, it is worth checking with the venue if any licences are in place for activities that you plan on carrying out during the event and therefore if there are any associated charges.

Box office facilities and merchandise

A number of venues will have their own box office or a similar ticketing facility. This includes theatres, cinemas as well as a number of unusual venues such as visitor attractions. Access to this facility can be very useful to the event manager. Particularly if you are organising an event that will have allocated seating or public or private performances, talks or demonstrations. A chat with the venue manager will determine whether or not you are able to use this facility for all or part of your event. This may result in the venue printing tickets for you to distribute but it could also mean that the venue is able to manage the entire booking system for the event including taking payment for specific activities. There are a number of benefits to using the venue's staff and system to manage the ticketing of an event. It will save you a lot of time and effort and the venue staff will be familiar with the layout and seating plans but in exchange for the box office services of the venue, the event manager can expect to pay either a set fee or a percentage of the ticket sales.

Merchandise usually refers to event souvenirs such as programmes, t-shirts and memorabilia and it is quite common for venues to take a percentage of the sales of merchandise that occur during temporary events such as gigs and shows. Some venues will extend this policy to any merchandise that is sold at the venue as part of any event but particularly if the venue staff have been involved in selling items to the event attendees. But as with other charges, if you plan on selling merchandise at the event it is wise to double check if the venue will be expecting to take a cut of the sales.

9.8 PENALTY CHARGES

As with recharges, venues may apply a number of penalty charges after the event such as an attrition charge. Some of the notable penalties are shown in Figure 9.2.

As you might expect, the venue will charge the event manager for any damage to the venue caused at or by the event. This will include any lasting damage left by decorations, activities or any vandalism carried out by anyone at the event. Most venue contracts include a

Figure 9.2 Penalty charges.

clause which specifically warns about this and therefore the onus is on the venue manager to ensure that no damage is caused to the venue (see Chapter 10 for more information).

The venue will be cleaned prior to the start of the hire period and usually the venue will take some responsibility for emptying waste bins during and at the end of the event. If the event lasts more than a day, the venue will usually clean the rooms that are in use overnight, if this is possible which may well depend on how they have been set up and how much equipment is left in the rooms overnight. However it is usually the responsibility of the event manager to collect and dispose of large quantities of rubbish generated by the event. The venue may allow for a certain amount of rubbish to be placed in their own bins but often the venue will apply a charge for collecting, and particularly, for disposing of lots of rubbish. Charges for this service will usually be available to the event manager and arrangements for rubbish collection can be made with the venue manager. However, the venue may penalise the event manager for the removal of any rubbish that has been left behind once the event and the get out have been completed.

The venue may also apply a penalty charge if they have taken receipt of any deliveries prior to event day unless this has been agreed in advance with the event manager. Most venues that have such charges do not maliciously penalise the event manager for minor inconveniences, but may make a charge if the venue has been unfairly designated as a storage facility for large or numerous quantities of items that they are expected to look after for several days. Similarly, if the venue staff find themselves forced to take on additional responsibilities for the event (e.g. stewarding, stage management, porterage etc.) that were not agreed in advance, the event manager can expect to pay for staff time.

As discussed earlier in this chapter, a number of event activities are licensable and many venues have licences in place which permit these activities to be carried out on their premises. Venues may levy a charge for such activities in lieu of a contribution towards the cost of the licence. If the venue does not have a licence for these activities and the event manager does not secure a licence and goes ahead with the activities, the venue may be fined or charged by the relevant licencing authority. In such cases the venue will pass on the charge to the venue and they may even make an additional charge for the inconvenience or the potential damage caused to the venue's reputation by being fined (see Chapter 10).

As with recharges, penalties shouldn't come as a surprise to the event manager as they are normally reasonable charges that are either being passed on or are being applied because the venue has been inconvenienced. Some venues will provide an indication of their penalty charges in the venue contract. Most venue managers will pass on any charges that they have incurred as a result of hosting an event rather than making a profit out of the situation, however, this is not always the case and event managers should take care to ensure that they do not incur hefty charges (see Chapter 10 for further advice).

9.9 NEGOTIATING AND SECURING THE BEST POSSIBLE HIRE CHARGES

So far this chapter has outlined the various charges that you can expect to pay when hiring a venue but there are a number of ways of securing the best rates possible for your event.

Booking early can secure the best rates possible as venues are generally keen to have the guarantee of confirmed events as early as possible. Conversely, booking at the last minute can sometimes mean that you are able to negotiate a very low hire charge because the chances of the venue securing another late booking are slim. Fenich (2012, p. 210) explains further:

The "yield management" concept may have some negative impact on meeting planners. For example, a planner who books a meeting fifteen to eighteen months in advance may find that, as the meeting nears, total hotel room utilization is lower that the hotel anticipated, so the hotel, hoping to generate additional revenue, will promote special pricing that may turn out to be less than what was offered to the meeting organizer.

However, much of the time the event manager does not have the option of leaving booking the venue to the last minute as this will hold up the entire event planning process. However, if you can be flexible with the time of year and time of the week when the event is to be held, this can be used to negotiate the best possible rates. If you choose dates or days of the week that are likely to be unpopular or dates that coincide with when your preferred venue is likely to be quiet, then the chance of asking for (and being offered) a discount are greater.

Look at the plan of the venue or your notes from the site visit and consider asking for free or discounted use of some of the rooms that you would like to use. Based on the main rooms that you will be using, look to see if nearby rooms are unlikely to be usable by other parties. If the venue will be unable to hire out certain rooms, they may be inclined to agree to a discount. For example, the venue manager is unlikely to hire out any rooms which are beneath or adjacent to rooms that you are going to be using for very loud activities (unless they are sound proofed). Any rooms that cannot be accessed without going through a room that you are using are not going to be hired out to other users either. Plus, if you are hiring most of the rooms in a venue and you are just leaving one or two small rooms empty, then the venue may struggle to find small enough bookings to fill these rooms.

Remember that until the contract is signed, all charges are negotiable, and the venues' sales team should take into account the fact that even after a successful site visit and before the contract is signed, the event manager may be keen to negotiate a good deal (Davidson and Rogers, 2011, p. 189). Therefore enter into a negotiation with a view of what you can offer the venue in exchange for a discount. Most venues are seeking to forge long term relationships with event managers and in particular they want to be associated with suitable events, work with reliable event managers, make a profit, have repeat bookings and host events that generate an income to their partner organisations.

Therefore, when negotiating with venues consider what you have to offer in return for a discount. Figure 9.3 illustrates some of the things that event managers can offer venue managers in exchange for a reduced hire charge.

Figure 9.3 Negotiating with venues.

For example, is your client or the event going to generate media interest and if so could this provide the venue with an opportunity to publicise or showcase their facilities? Can you demonstrate that you are an experienced and reliable event manager and therefore your event is going to be legally compliant, low risk and well organised? If so this indicates that you will not need to take up much of the venue manager's time with lots of questions and this could be worth a discount. Are you likely to rebook the venue in the future or recommend to the client or their organisation, that they use the venue for additional future events? If so, this could be worth a discount on the hire charges on your current event as a goodwill gesture from the venue. And finally, if you can ensure that the venue is going to make an income by hosting your event, and that in addition to this the venue's key partners (local suppliers etc.) are also guaranteed an income from your event, this is often the greatest bargaining chip that you can use to lower the room hire charges.

CASE STUDY 9.1 BROOME CIVIC CENTRE, WESTERN AUSTRALIA

The Broome Civic Centre was designed by architect Norman Rees to reflect the character and charm of Broome with its distinctive Asian influence. The building opened in 1973 and it quickly became a popular venue for concerts and wedding receptions. After a period of closure for a $11 million-dollar refurbishment, it reopened in 2012 to continue to offer residents and visitors to Broome a quality venue for a wide variety of events from conferences to community meetings and parties to performances.

Image 9.1 Broome, Western Australia
© Shutterstock

continued

The venue has rooms that open to the outdoors as well as indoor performance spaces. The main hall seats 450 and has a raised stage for theatrical productions. The stage area offers dressing rooms, toilets and wash facilities. An additional function room can hold 40 people and kitchen and bar facilities are located off the main hall and tables and chairs are included with the hire. Electronic presentation equipment, technical support staff, catering facilities and a fully operational bar are available.

The venue publishes clear hire rates and charges. There is a 4-hour, 8-hour or 8 am to midnight room hire rate which includes the use of chairs, tables, toilets, house lighting, air conditioning, microphones and audio output.

Additional charges apply for technical staff, the use of the bar and bar and security staff. The kitchen can also be hired and event managers have the option to self-cater or work with local catering suppliers although there can be no cooking onsite. The hire of the kitchen does include use of rubbish removal plus use of the dishwasher, steam ovens, cool room, induction hot plates and freezer. Use of crockery is an additional cost.

A basic audio package is included with room hire and additional charges apply for microphone stands, lectern, laptop and drop-down projector screen. Advanced audio packages are also available with additional equipment but when hiring the specialised lighting or audio package, a venue approved technician must be also be paid for and arranged by the event manager.

For events that are open to the public, large events, or events that have alcohol, a member of the venue staff must be present and at the time of booking the venue will estimate the cost of this. It is the responsibility of the hirer to ensure the event will be adequately staffed and there will be additional charges for venue staff if they are needed to help with event operations.

There are recharges for additional cleaning, damage to the property, fixtures of fittings and exceeding the agreed hire period. Additionally, the venue charges $3 commission per ticket sold.

Upon receiving an enquiry or booking form, the venue will provide a quote based upon the requirements of the event. The venue offers a 50 per cent reduction on all charges (excluding deposit) to non-profit organisations, fundraising events or community events. Applications for a discount are subject to venue approval.

Source: http://www.broomeciviccentre.com.au/

9.10 GUARANTEEING THE VENUE AN INCOME

Often the best way to secure a discount on venue hire charges, is by ensuring that the venue is still going to make an income from your event and there are several ways to do this.

If you are going to be using a residential venue, adding accommodation into the booking is a very good way of securing low room hire charges. Lee and Fenich (2016) suggest that a discount could mean securing as much as 40 per cent off of the rack rate. If you are going to book a significant number of bedrooms you may also be able to negotiate free use of the event space and although you will need to be aware of potential attrition charges, overall this could mean a significant saving:

> Conventional wisdom states that the planners do not pay for meeting space in hotels. However, meeting space costs the hotels money . . . staff and materials to clean, maintain,

and operate the meeting rooms and . . . these costs must be funded from somewhere. Most often, these costs are covered by requiring the meeting to commit to using a minimum number of sleeping rooms for a minimum number of nights. The hotel's goal is to fill the rooms that would not be filled by its regular customers.

(Fenich, 2012, p. 59)

The same strategy applies to catering. As discussed in Chapter 7, a number of venues have an in-house or appointed caterer and in both cases the venue will make an income from the food and drink sold at the event. Therefore, by providing the venue with a guarantee that money will be spent on catering, this can be used to offset the room hire charges. Generally, the only way to provide this guarantee is by agreeing to put at least some of the event catering on account. This is when the catering is paid for by the event manager rather than the event attendees. As the event manager, this means that you will have to try to accurately predict the amount of food and drink that will be required at the event and you will pay for the amount of catering that you order, and not the amount that is actually consumed. As with accommodation bookings, this can be a high risk strategy if you are not able to estimate how much food and drink you require. However, the benefit of being able to predict this, with reasonable accuracy, is that you can use this to counteract room hire charges. If you are able to confirm that a lot of catering will be required for the event and that all of it will be on account, and if the venue has an in-house caterer, you should be able to convince the venue manager to waive all room hire charges.

Many venues will have strong relationships with specific suppliers and as we saw in Chapter 7, some of the services or equipment that you want to order for an event may have to come from one of the venue's preferred suppliers. Should this be the case, or if you have the option to use the venue's contacts, this may also give you room to negotiate on venue hire charges. Providing the venue is going to benefit from you using certain suppliers, this can be used to reduce or offset the hire charges. The way that the venue will benefit from this arrangement is that preferred suppliers may pay a fee to advertise in the venue's brochure or on their website. Also, your event will seem lower risk to the venue if your suppliers, particularly contractors for equipment, are well known to the venue and familiar with the venue's layout and policies.

Furthermore, some venues are government owned or subsidised, particularly multipurpose venues that bring much needed economic activity into a specific community (Edwards *et al.*, 2014). Therefore if your event is going to generate significant spend in the area, on transport, accommodation, restaurants etc., then you may be able to secure a generous venue discount which is a form of subvention.

9.11 SUBVENTION

The dictionary definition of subvention is that it is a grant of money, especially from a government, and within the events industry subvention can refer to financial or other kinds of support offered to an event organiser. The offer is usually made by the DMO as part of the bidding process for an event and most offers of subvention are made to the organisers of large, international association conferences. Alternatively, many national DMOs have an application system in place for requesting subvention.

Typically subvention comes in the form of a discount on venue costs, a civic reception, a loan (usually in order to market the event) or a direct subsidy (Rogers, 2013). In order to qualify for subvention, the event will have to meet certain requirements and these will include providing a substantial income to the host destination via delegate spending. If the subvention available in a destination is a discount on the venue hire charges, this may be offered to the event organiser by the DMO or by the venue manager.

Despite a general feeling of dislike towards subvention practices within the events industry (Rogers and Davidson, 2016), the recent report undertaken by the Business Visits and Events Partnership suggests that the number of requests for subvention has increased in recent years (BVEP, 2016).

9.12 PAYMENT

Payment for the venue can be complex and this is usually detailed in the contract that the venue will issue you as part of confirming the booking (see Chapter 10). Frequently the venue will ask the event manager for a deposit in advance of the event, and they will invoice you for the balance of all charges after the event.

The deposit is usually a percentage of the room hire charges but it can also include a percentage of the additional charges of any equipment, services or catering that the venue is going to provide. Occasionally you may be asked to pay the full hire charges in advance of the event. This can apply to a first-time user of the venue, with no credit history with the venue, or if the date of the event is quite near. Deposits are not always refundable and therefore the terms of the contract should be read carefully before committing to a booking.

The event manager will usually receive a final bill after the event, even if the room hire charges have already been paid for in full. This bill will itemise any recharges or additional costs that have been incurred during the event. It is also worth remembering that most venues increase their room hire charges annually, typically in line with inflation. This can mean that there is a difference in price between the charges listed on the quotation provided by the venue at the time the RFP was conducted, and the charges that apply at the time of the event. Once again, this should be made clear to the event manager via the contract but if your event has a long lead time it is worth checking to see how much the room hire charges will increase by between booking the venue and staging the event.

If the event manager has booked the venue via an agency, the agent will receive a commission in exchange for making the arrangement and this is typically between 8 and 10 per cent of the value of the booking (Rogers, 2013, p. 65). This will be paid to the agency by the venue and does not alter the costs and agreement made between the venue and the event manager.

ACTIVITY 9.1

You have been tasked with organising a party at a hotel which will involve a dinner for 50 people, a disco and a late-night buffet. A number of the guests will be travelling a long distance to attend the event. You have yet to book any suppliers and are looking to hold the event on a Monday in November. List the elements of your event that make it attractive to the venue and consider how you can use this to negotiate the room hire charge.

CASE STUDY 9.2 TIPS FOR NEGOTIATING WITH VENUES

Many of us can find that negotiating is not an easy skill so here are some tips on how to negotiate with your event venue.

- Prioritise: make sure that you have a list of your venue requirements that starts with the must haves and finishes with the things that would make nice added extras. Be aware that the venue might offer you some freebies but if they aren't a priority for you then don't let the venue use this as a bargaining tool.
- Don't be hurried into making decisions. It's more important to be sure that you have picked the right venue and that you are going to get everything that you need from them. Usually a provisional booking will be held for some time, particularly if you are hiring the venue out of season. If the venue thinks that you are looking at other options, they might offer you discounts in order to secure your booking.
- Remember that residential venues make a profit from any bedrooms that you are going to book so use this to leverage a better deal on other parts of your venue booking such as the event room or the catering. The more bedrooms you book the better the deal will be, possibly even waived charges.
- Venues have a high and low season. For example, a venue in a resort will be busier in the summer and the same goes for winter resorts. By choosing to hold the event off season you can discuss a cheaper rate because the venue is far more likely to need your booking.
- Although most venues make an income on the event catering you can still negotiate these costs too. Aim to arrange the catering per capita as this means that you won't be paying for refreshments that your attendees won't consume. Make sure that breakfast and lunch gets included in the day delegate rate rather than pay for this separately and ask for a discount on the overall catering bill. Ensure that staffing charges are included in the costs and work closely with the catering team to put together a menu that fits with your budget.
- If your event guests will be staying at the venue and are likely to make use of the leisure facilities, ask for a discount on the use of the spa etc. Out of season, these are likely to be underused anyway meaning that you can negotiate a discount.
- If you are going to use the venue again, providing them with repeat business is the easiest way to negotiate as it is only fair that you get the best deal possible as you should be considered a valued customer. But, it can be worth letting the venue know that you are looking around as healthy competition between suppliers will ultimately mean you will get a competitive rate.
- If you are a novice event manager, it can be worth using a good venue finding service or event agency as they can help with negotiating the best deals with venues and suppliers. Make sure that this is a free service as the agency will make a commission on all bookings. Then once you are more confident at managing events you can remind the venue that you are working with them directly and therefore you are saving them the agency commission fee – so they can pass on this saving to you instead!

Source: http://www.practicallyperfectpa.com/2012/how-to-negotiate-when-planning-an-event/09/14/

THE INDUSTRY EXPERT'S VIEW 9.1

NEGOTIATING WITH VENUES

Ruth Ellis, Events and Special Occasions Manager, Callow Event Management, www.callowevents.co.uk

Working in Northern Ireland is quite different to working in mainland UK, and elsewhere in the world because business works in a very local way here. The industry is condensed, everyone knows everyone, so we can always make an attempt to meet any client's expectations (even the wacky) using a bit of Irish charm with colleagues in venues. Hire charges can vary and depend on the type of venue. By and large venue charges are difficult to get to grips with, because every single venue has a different internal structure, so we need to get our heads around lots of different cost breakdowns which lends itself to fuzzy-eye syndrome, and I'm no maths genius at the best of times! The venues that we work with regularly are great, because we're used to their methods and we can negotiate with them easily, but tension is always looming when we enter into an agreement with a new venue, where both the venue and the event manager are nervous. Some venues just won't negotiate, but they usually stand out like a sore thumb. Normally these venues also serve other purposes and their main income stream isn't through room hire. For those that we work with regularly, negotiations are a 5-minute conversation and it's sorted. For newer venues, it can take a lot of effort, meetings and phone calls climbing hierarchies etc. It's always worth it in the end. We find it easiest to make an arrangement with a venue as an event management company, that we can repeat with many clients, that way it works for us and the venue in terms of giving them repeat business.

I recently was told that a clause in a contract was that we are liable to pay for staff overtime, because our event is on a Saturday evening . . . in my view payment of venue staff is the venue's responsibility, not the clients. Also, it can be annoying when venues charge for every light switch and plug used as well as charges for 'crew catering' as this is normally four plates of chicken goujons and chips with a little sweet chilli sauce on the side (if we're lucky).

My first tactic when sitting at the negotiating table is always to establish an alliance with that supplier, with a remark insinuating we're one team. Following that, I remind the supplier of the repeat business opportunities, higher spend elsewhere in the budget and as I'm lucky to have high-end corporate brand clients in my portfolio, the affiliation with the brand in their venue, or using their equipment usually gets us over the line. I also find that by mentioning other business that you've got coming up shortly helps, and always ask for more than you actually need so that there's room to compromise if necessary. You'll have to use a lot of your banked favours for your clients, so try and be the yes-man for all your suppliers, so they are always owing you!

9.13 UNDERSTANDING VENUE CHARGES – THE VENUE MANAGER'S PERSPECTIVE

In order to run a venue efficiently, some sort of yield management system needs to be in place at the venue. The system will help the venue manager to achieve the maximum REVPAR possible but it will also help you to identify when you need to alter rates to encourage bookings. Securing a venue booking very far in advance of event day can feel like a great achievement as this is effectively guaranteed money in the bank and progress towards the annual sales target. However, bidding for events and completing RFPs should be done with a strategic plan in place as accepting certain bookings may mean that parts of the venue are going to become very difficult to sell to other users.

In order to secure attractive bookings, such as a large event or a new client, you will need to seriously negotiate with the event manager. Consider what you can add to your offer to incentivise a booking. For example, can you offer additional rooms that would be unsuitable to other events or users at the time of this event? Can you include staff, AV equipment or furniture in the booking? If you are unable to lower the room hire charges, it is important to be able to articulate what you are including in the hire of the venue such as free Wi-Fi, parking etc.

If your venue is residential and accommodation is included in the booking, it is plausible that event attendees can secure better room rates by not booking through the event manager. In order to avoid any confusion or dissatisfaction, encourage the event manager to make it clear to the attendees that by booking through them they secure a variety of extras such as use of the event space, discounted catering, access to leisure facilities etc. This can help event guests to understand how block booking rooms ensures that the overall running cost of the event is kept to a minimum (Lee and Fenich, 2016).

9.14 SUMMARY

Venue hire charges can be complex as they are affected by a number of variables such as when your event is taking place and what activities will be taking place at the event. In addition to room hire, you can expect to pay for a number of additional services, staff or equipment provided to you by the venue. However, most charges can be negotiated and if you are in a position to be flexible with dates, or can include catering or accommodation in your booking you will be in a strong position to ask for charges to be lowered.

The final bill from the venue is likely to be drawn up after event day and it will include the balance of room hire charges as well as any recharges and penalty fees. In order to avoid being presented with an unexpectedly high bill, it is important to work closely with the venue as you develop your event plan so that the venue manager can provide you with an up to date and accurate list of costs. Understanding venue charges can be challenging, even for the experienced event manager. However, the venue's charges, and details of the payment schedule, should be explained in the venue's contract which you will be asked to sign to confirm the booking. Chapter 10 will provide you with an overview of what to expect and what to look for in the contract before you sign.

9.15 FURTHER READING

The following sources are particularly useful for further reading on the subject of understanding venue charges:

Fenich, G. (2012) *Meetings, Expositions, Events, and Conferences: An Introduction to the Industry* (3rd edn). New Jersey: Pearson.

Lee, S. and Fenich, G. (2016) Perceived Fairness of Room Blocks in the Meetings, Incentives, Convention, and Exhibition Industry, *Journal of Convention and Event Tourism*, 17, (2), 159–171.

Rogers, T. and Davidson, R. (2016) *Marketing Destinations and Venues for Conferences, Conventions and Business Events* (2nd edn) London: Routledge.

Planning Pod (blog) (available at https://blog.planningpod.com/2014/09/16/39-Proven-Event-Planning-Strategies-Negotiating-Venues-Hotels-Part-2/)

Hotel Business Review (available at http://hotelexecutive.com)

Contracts and licensing

LEARNING OUTCOMES

By the end of Chapter 10, you should be able to:

* Understand basic legislation and licensing that applies to event and venue management
* Describe the purpose and structure of a standard venue contract
* Understand the typical clauses to be found in a venue contract
* Recognise the ways in which an event manager must meet their contractual obligations to the venue
* Identify the venue's responsibilities and legal obligations to the event manager

10.1 INTRODUCTION

Signing the venue hire contract is a significant stage in the event planning process as it formalises the agreement with one of, if not the, principal supplier to the event. It also signals confirmation of the event date and therefore a commitment to delivering the event and finalising the event plans. Venue contracts can be quite lengthy and detailed documents as they cover all aspects of the agreement between the two parties and the terms and conditions of hire. In fact, a contract issued by the venue can be one of the most complex documents of its kind as it can contain a number of specific clauses (Bladen *et al.*, 2012). As well as confirming the hire charges, the contract stipulates a number of rules and regulations that will govern the event and it will outline the penalties for failing to comply with the contract. Much of this is rooted in the venue's plan to ensure that the event complies with relevant legislation and health and safety guidance. The contract should be read extremely carefully and only signed once the event manager is confident that they understand it fully and also that they comprehend the potential impacts of failing to adhere to the contract. This chapter will therefore cover the purpose of the contract, typical terms and conditions, likely penalties for breaching the contract plus an overview of venue specific legislation and health and safety guidance.

10.2 LEGISLATION AND LICENSING

Venues will be subject to the general legislation that applies to any business or organisation such as employment, sanitation and public safety laws. In addition, some venues may require a licence or certification in order to operate which also sets the maximum capacity of the venue. For example, in the UK the Safety of Sports Grounds Act 1975 was introduced after the Ibrox Stadium disaster of 1971 when 66 football fans were killed in a crush as they were leaving the venue. Under this act, certain sports venues can only operate if they hold a safety certificate which is issued by the local authority.

All venues must meet the specific health and safety regulations as set down by the national governing authority and these are likely to include laws relating to fire safety and risk assessment. Additionally, venues that are used for events are likely to be subject to specific regulations relating to construction, gaming, special effects and the provision of alcohol to name a few (Quinn, 2013, p. 113) and the legislation will usually dictate what is and is not permitted to take place at the venue. A number of typical event activities are often permitted at the venue provided a suitable licence has been sought which many regular event venues will have in place. Figure 10.1 illustrates some of these activities.

Licensable activities can include a number of typical event activities including gambling, the provision of alcohol, the use of children in performances, the playing of music and

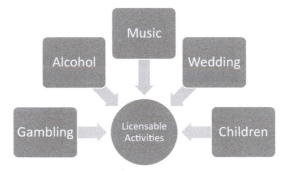

Figure 10.1 Types of licensable activities.

conducting a civil wedding. Many event venues will have licences in place for activities that take place regularly on site. There may be a charge made to the event manager to conduct the activity at the event, even when the licence is in place, as some venues will expect a contribution towards the cost of the licence fee. Where a licence is not in place, the venue will confirm whether or not the activity is permitted on site. If the venue is in agreement, you can then apply for a specific licence at your own expense. Most licence applications are made through the authority that is local to the venue but the venue manager will usually be able to offer detailed advice on this.

The regulation of the provision of alcohol varies considerably across the world. In the UK The Licensing Act 2003 is the principal piece of legislation that covers the supply of alcohol as well as late night refreshment and regulated entertainment in England and Wales. The Act was designed to merge and therefore simplify pre-existing regulations on alcohol, public entertainment, cinemas, theatres, late night refreshment houses and night cafes. Under the Licensing Act there are four types of licence and these are illustrated in Figure 10.2.

A premises licence is required for any venue that is host to one or more of the activities governed by the Licensing Act. Licences are bespoke, in that each venue will apply for a specific premises licence which details the activities that they intend to operate and at which times of the day and night these will occur. Most event venues in the UK have a premises licence in place as the activities governed by the licence occur regularly at the venue. The contract will normally confirm this and provide the event manager with details of what is permitted and until what time of night.

If the venue's licence includes the sale or provision of alcohol, a named individual at the venue is responsible for this activity and they are known as the designated premises supervisor (DPS). The DPS must have a personal licence which is obtained through the local authority but applicants must first obtain a licensing qualification through an accredited organisation such as the British Institute of Innkeeping.

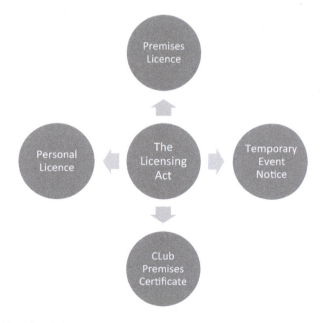

Figure 10.2 The Licensing Act.

CASE STUDY 10.1 THE LICENSING ACT 2003

The objectives of the Act

The objectives of the Licensing Act 2003 are:

- The prevention of crime and disorder
- Public safety
- The prevention of public nuisance
- The protection of children from harm

Licensable activities

All businesses and organisations that undertake licensable activities on a permanent basis must have a premises licence from their local authority. Licensable activities include:

- Sale or supply of alcohol
- Regulated entertainment (entertainment that takes place in the presence of an audience for profit including a performance of a play, an exhibition of a film, an indoor sporting event, a boxing or wrestling entertainment, a performance of live music, playing of recorded music, a performance of dance)
- Late night refreshment (the sale of hot food or drink between 11pm and 5am)

Within England and Wales, any business, organisation or individual wanting to supply or sell alcohol must have a licence and this includes the following types of venues:

- Pubs and bars
- Cinemas
- Theatres
- Nightclubs
- Village and community halls

Additionally, members' clubs (e.g. rugby clubs) intending on supplying or selling alcohol must apply for a club premises certificate.

Types of licence

There are different types of licence:

- A premises licence

This permits the use of any premises (which is defined in the Licensing 2003 Act as a vehicle, vessel or moveable structure or any place or a part of any premises) for licensable activities as defined in section 1 of the 2003 Act.

- A personal licence

Premises licensed to sell alcohol must have a designated premises supervisor, who holds a personal licence. The one exception is a community premises that has successfully applied to waive the DPS requirement under section 41D of the act. Anyone who does not hold a personal licence must be authorised to sell alcohol by a personal licence holder. There is no such requirement for the supply of alcohol in a members' club. Personal licences allow you to sell alcohol on behalf of any business that has a premises licence or a club premises certificate. The relationship is similar to the way that a driving licence permits the driving of any car.

- Designated premises supervisors

A designated premises supervisor (DPS) is the person who has day-to-day responsibility for the running of the business where alcohol is supplied or sold. All such organisations (apart from members clubs and certain community premises) must have a designated premises supervisor. The person chosen to be designated premises supervisor (DPS) will act as primary contact for local government and the police. They must understand the social issues and potential problems associated with the sale of alcohol, and also have a good understanding of the business itself.

Taking responsibility

The Licensing Act requires the DPS and all personal licence holders to take responsibility for the sale and supply of alcohol. This is because of the impact alcohol has on the wider community, on crime and disorder, and antisocial behaviour. Because of these issues, selling alcohol carries greater responsibility than licensing regulated entertainment and late night sales of food and non-alcoholic drinks.

Community premises

If you run or are involved in a community, church or village hall that wishes to sell alcohol or already sells it, you can apply for the sale of alcohol to be made the responsibility of a management committee instead of a premises supervisor. Or you can also apply to replace the designated premises supervisor, if you already have one, with the management committee.

Temporary events

If you're organising a temporary event which is relatively small-scale (under 500 attendees and lasting no more than 168 hours) and you wish to serve or sell alcohol, provide late night refreshment, or put on regulated entertainment then you will need to apply for a temporary event notice (TEN).

Source: www.gov.uk/guidance/alcohol-licensing

Organisations whose members come together for specific social, sporting or political purposes may operate under a specific type of licence called a Club Premises Certificate. Examples of such organisations are political clubs, ex-services clubs and in order to qualify the club must have at least 25 members and the premises must be used regularly for club purposes and not benefit financially from the provision of alcohol.

If a venue does not have a Club Premises Certificate or a Premises Licence, a temporary licence can be granted to permit the licensable activities to take place during the event. This is called a temporary event notice (TEN) and anyone over the age of 18 can make an application to the local authority. It is also possible to apply for a TEN if the venues' existing premises licence does not cover the activities (or the time of the activities) that the event manager requires.

In Scotland, the Civic Government (Scotland) Act 1982 determines that a Public Entertainment or Temporary Public Entertainment licence must be obtained for the venue or site to be used for public entertainment to include dancing, concerts, a variety show or other entertainment where the public are charged an admission fee or they must make a purchase to attend (Bowdin *et al.*, 2011, p. 584).

CASE STUDY 10.2 SAFETY AT SPORTS GROUNDS

The Wheatley Report

The Wheatley Committee was set up to investigate the 1971 Ibrox disaster. The committee reported that the structural failure of the Glasgow stadium had led to the deaths of 66 people when steel barriers on stairway 13 gave way. In addition to those who suffocated to death, many more suffered serious injuries in the ensuing crush. Following the recommendations of this committee, the Safety of Sports Grounds Act 1975 was passed into law. It was the first statute specific to sports venues and it would be applied via the issuing of safety certificates by local authorities to sports venues with a capacity of over 5,000 used by the Football Association premier and football league clubs and sports grounds with a capacity of over 10,000 used for rugby, cricket and international football matches. The certificate would state the maximum number of permitted spectators and it would give information about the venue's exits, entrances, means of access, crash barriers and means of escape.

The Green Guide

In the wake of the Wheatley Report in 1972, the Guide to Safety at Sports Grounds was written in order to provide detailed advice about safety measures needed at sports grounds to those involved in the delivery of sporting events. The guide, known as the Green Guide, has since been revised and republished several times. It covers the responsibilities for managing events including stewarding, crowd control, ground capacity estimates and flow rates. It also contains detailed advice on topics including entrances and exits, the structure of stands and buildings, stairways and ramps, the terraces, crush barriers, hand rails, perimeter walls and fences.

The Taylor Report

In 1989, and after further tragedies at other football stadia, 96 Liverpool fans were crushed to death during the FA cup semi-final at the Hillsborough stadium in Sheffield. Consequently Lord Justice Taylor, a High Court judge, was commissioned by the Government to undertake an investigation and to make further recommendations about crowd control and safety at sports events. In Lord Justice Taylor's Report, published in January 1990, he discussed and criticised a number of issues including the, sometimes, poor behaviour of players, the selling of alcohol at football matches (a potential source of trouble), the attitude of the media, the impacts of segregation and hooliganism and the poor quality of football grounds.

   The Taylor Report concluded with a great many recommendations which included a crackdown on hooliganism and anti-social behaviour, the creation of an advisory council to provide information on ground safety and construction, a limit to the height of perimeter fencing and the end to standing terraces and the introduction of all seater stadia.

Source: www.firesafe.org.uk

10.3 HEALTH AND SAFETY GUIDANCE, LEGISLATION AND INSURANCE

In the UK the primary piece of legislation for any workplace is the Health and Safety at Work Act 1974, which details the principles for the safe management of premises and people. The Act has led to the creation of subsequent and connected pieces of legislation and guidance such as the Control of Substances Hazardous to Health Regulations 2002 (COSHH) and the Reporting of Injuries, Diseases and Dangerous Occurrences Regulations 2013 (RIDDOR). Similar regulations are in place in most parts of the world such as the Occupational Safety and Health Acts in Australia and the USA (Bladen *et al.*, 2012, p. 299).

Essentially, health and safety legislation ensures that venues conduct a **risk assessment** of the premises, a fire risk assessment and have a safety policy in place. All of this is part of their responsibilities to their employees as well as other users of the venue such as members of the public and event attendees.

The venue's risk assessment will be a comprehensive review of the premises to include all equipment and facilities on site. The venue will also conduct and record a fire risk assessment which provides a separate review of fire hazards, such as the storage of dangerous substances, and precautions and control measures such as emergency exits, alarms and fire-fighting equipment. The venue's safety policy should detail the emergency and evacuation procedures that are in place at the venue (Raj *et al.*, 2013, p. 168) and all of these documents should be available to the event manager on request.

Figure 10.3 The venue's responsibilities under health and safety legislation.

THE INDUSTRY EXPERT'S VIEW 10.1

SAFE EVENT OPERATIONS

Andy Grove, HighGrove Events, www.highgroveevents.com

Why is it important to risk assess an event?

The short answer is to keep people safe. Everybody who attends an event should go home in the same state of health as they arrived. Events are dangerous so the only way to ensure you can achieve this is to assess the risks and identify ways of doing what you

continued

do safely. The risk assessment must be suitable and sufficient to the event that you are organising and should only assess significant risks that are reasonably foreseeable. Then, and most importantly, they should be implemented and not forgotten about as a paper exercise.

What are some of the most typical hazards at events?

The most typical hazards at events, like everywhere else are things that cause slips, trips and falls. After that, there are vehicle movements, electrical installations and generators, liquified petroleum gas (LPG), structures (stages and marquees), barriers, people movement, overcrowding, crushing, crowd disorder, food hygiene and severe weather. Sadly, alcohol and drugs are also significant hazards. Many people work long hours and lack sleep and start to follow poor working practices and make bad decisions which makes what they are doing more hazardous.

Why is it important to properly staff events and what do event staff need to be trained in?

Events need to be staffed properly to enable them to function efficiently, effectively and safely. People coming to an event need to be processed and managed as they come into your event, as they take part in it and as they leave. To do this you need the right number of people in the right places doing the right jobs. You can't do it all yourself. They also provide a presence and vigilance around the site that can keep you informed and updated about what is going on. There are, however, many roles within events so it is difficult to say succinctly what they should be trained in. As an event manager, it is your duty to ensure that all staff are competent to carry out the role that you ask them to. It can be as much about finding the right character and personality for the role as it is about training. You could provide the same training to two people but only one may be suitable for the role at the end of it so it shouldn't be about ticking a box and saying somebody is trained. Even within the general terms of stewarding there are many roles within that title, so you must ensure that people are doing the best ones to suit them which isn't necessarily easy. It is also essential to ensure that they are briefed as well as trained as every event is different so they need to know the specific details about your event. You may also need to provide some information to them in writing that they can carry and refer to as they can't and won't remember everything they are told in a briefing.

What are some of the most unexpected situations you've found yourself dealing with at an event?

Here's just some of the things I have encountered:

- Finding no security present when working with a contracted events company for a free, un-ticketed music festival with alcohol on sale
- Having a steward collapse and knock their teeth out on a table during their briefing
- Finding a generator's anti-terrorism device kicked in and shut it down due to an explosion during a battle re-enactment
- Finding a forklift truck left in a firework drop zone with the contractor having parked it and left the site.

Most venues will have employer insurance in place and in many cases this will be a legal requirement. Employers are responsible for the wellbeing of their employees while they are at work. Should staff be injured at work or become ill as a result of their job, then they may try to claim compensation from the employer. Employer's **liability insurance** will help to cover the associated costs of such a claim. The owners and managers of public buildings have a similar responsibility to protect the health and safety of their visitors and therefore venues that are open to the public should also have public liability insurance in place. Most venues will insist that every event is covered by a separate public liability insurance policy which will provide financial support in the event of a claim for compensation by anyone who is injured at the event. The venue hire contract will stipulate if the event manager must take out public liability insurance and it is worth remembering that the insurance policy will only be valid if the event manager has also met their responsibilities under the Health and Safety at Work Act. As Matthews (2016, p. 79) explains further:

> Thanks to numerous stage collapses, crowd crushes, fires, and natural disasters at special events around the world in recent years, event liability insurance and often event cancellation insurance have become mandatory in most jurisdictions. Most venues require proof of adequate insurance before they will allow an event to be booked.

10.4 CONTRACTS

The key purpose of the contract that the venue will issue to the event manager is to clearly outline in writing the terms and conditions of the booking. The contract is a legal tool used to ensure that both parties, the issuer and the recipient, are aware of their rights and responsibilities with regards to the specific booking. The contract will also include the consequences and penalties of not complying with the agreement. The contract is written in favour of the issuer and it is written to articulate the agreement but also to deter the event manager from acting irresponsibly or ignoring the venue's policies. By detailing the penalties that can be enforced if the contract is breached, the venue is trying to minimise the likelihood of something going wrong, but the contract also protects the venue from the effects of poor event management practices.

For a contract to be legally binding there are five key requirements to be met; an offer, acceptance, consideration, intention and capacity.

1. An offer – this is the express description of what is being made available. For example, the venue should make reference in the contract to the specific rooms which are available on specific dates to the event manager. The contract should not just list the rooms that are available to hire.

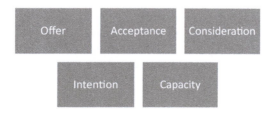

Figure 10.4 The five elements of a contract.

2. Acceptance – the contract requires acceptance of the offer. This is usually made in writing, by signing the contract. Normally the venue will make it clear to the event manager what kind of acceptance they require, such as agreement via email. Acceptance applies to the whole offer and it cannot apply to part of it. This means that the event manager should not sign the contract until they are happy to accept every detail of the agreement. The venue cannot assume that silence indicates acceptance, for example, the venue cannot say to the event manager that they will assume you accept the contract if they do not hear from you within 2 weeks.

3. Consideration – this refers to what will be exchanged between the two parties in order to seal the agreement. This can usually be measured in economic terms such as the provision of money in exchange for goods or services. Therefore, the venue contract will normally indicate the hire charges that apply to the specific booking.

4. Intention – this refers to the notion that the two parties mean to create the agreement and enter into the agreement purposefully.

5. Capacity – this means that both parties must have the capacity to enter into the contract. For example, children cannot enter into legally binding contracts. This means that both the issuer, the venue, and the recipient, the event manager must have the capacity to sign the contract. Of course, for event managers, this usually means that you accept responsibility for the event that you are organising when you sign the contract and not your client. The venue manager cannot offer the event manager the use of rooms that they do not own and operate and the event manager cannot sign if they do not have the authority (e.g., from the client) to enter into the agreement.

In order to ensure that the contract is a legally binding document it should be written by a qualified professional and as the event manager it is important to get a similarly qualified person to read it before you sign it.

10.5 WHAT TO EXPECT IN THE VENUE CONTRACT

Every venue will have their own format for contracts and you can expect to receive a bespoke contract which has been personalised to cover your event requirements. There are a number of entries on the contract which you should expect to see on any venue hire contract to include what the venue is providing and the terms and conditions of hire. Some of the most common entries as listed in Table 10.1.

The name and address of the venue, the contact information for the venue including the name of at least one member of staff and your own contact information should be clearly included in the document. The name of the event, or reference to the type of event or client should be noted. The names of each of the rooms that you are hiring should be listed on the contract and against each, the dates and times of usage to include the get in and get out periods. The contract may detail the agreed room set ups and timings of the event. Although frequently the contract is issued before the event manager is in a position to confirm all of these details. Therefore, it is quite common for this to be agreed and noted via a function sheet or operational schedule much later, although it can be useful if the contract indicates how and when the venue expects to document these arrangements. The contract may list the equipment and services to be provided by the venue, but these may also be added to later documentation.

The contact will specify the venue's rules regarding catering, AV, staffing and stewarding. For example, the contract will indicate if the hirer is obliged to use the venue's own teams and equipment or may choose from a list of preferred suppliers. If the venue is going to provide

Table 10.1 Typical entries in a venue hire contract

Contact information	The name and address of the venue and one member of staff plus your own contact information
The event	The name of the event, or reference to the type of event or client
Rooms	The names of each of the rooms that you are hiring with the dates and times of usage to include the get in and get out periods
Equipment and services	The equipment and services to be provided by the venue (if known at this stage)
Suppliers and staffing	Rules or options for catering, AV, staffing and stewarding (e.g., in-house/preferred suppliers) and minimum charges
Decoration and damage	What is permitted in terms of signage and decoration and penalties for damaging the venue
Temporary installations	Rules concerning loading and unloading, the installation of infrastructure and the collection of rubbish during the event
Licences	Details of what licences are in place and what additional activities will be permitted subject to securing a valid licence
Marketing	The event marketing materials that must be approved by the venue
Health and safety obligations	The event risk assessment and operational schedule must be approved and public liability insurance must be provided
Additional services	What is available in terms of car parking, storage, access for loading and unloading, options for recording the event, details of first aid provision, cloakroom facilities, etc.
Finance	Room hire charges, the arrangement for paying a deposit and balance, charges for services or equipment
Penalties	Details of the penalties for breach of contract

security, stewarding or technical support staff the contract should itemise the hourly charges and the minimum work period (e.g., staff work for a minimum of 4 hours).

The contract will refer to what is permitted in terms of signage and decoration and will include details of the penalties for damaging the venue. For events such as exhibitions and shows, the venue will specify any particular rules concerning loading and unloading, the installation of infrastructure and the collection of rubbish during the event.

Frequently the contract will specify the terms of the licences in place and indicate the nature of licensable activities that may be permitted but that will require the event manager to first secure a valid licence. For example, the venue may permit a disco until 11.30pm under the terms of the premises licence but warn the event manager that it is their responsibility to secure a licence from the Performing Rights Society (PRS) or Phonographic Performance Limited (PPL).

It is not uncommon for the venue contract to stipulate that all event marketing materials must be approved by the venue manager before it is to be used and the process for this may be included in the contract. The contract will also refer to the health and safety obligations of the event manager and the venue hire contract may make it clear that the venue manager must approve the event risk assessment and operational schedule and receive a copy of the public liability insurance cover.

Furthermore, as Silvers (2013, p. 58) reminds us, the contract may reference a number of very specific rules such as:

[the] legal restrictions on what types of special effects are allowed, the construction of temporary structures such as grandstands or viewing platforms, and where smoking may and may not be allowed. There may be venue restrictions on what signage may or must be posted or what sponsor banners may be displayed, which food providers may be used, and which workers are allowed to perform what tasks. There may be specifications on how loud or late music may be played, how many portable toilets must be provided, and where guests are allowed to park.

The venue contract may also make reference to what is available in terms of car parking, storage, access for loading and unloading, options for recording the event, details of first aid provision, cloakroom facilities, etc. Finally, the contract should include detailed financial information including the room hire charges, the arrangement for paying a deposit and balance, and details of the charges for services or equipment to be provided by the venue. The contract will also make reference to the penalties that will be imposed should any aspect of the contract be broken and this may extend to what will happen if the venue breaches the contract.

10.6 UNDERSTANDING THE VENUE CONTRACT

Venue contracts can be long, complex and detailed documents. Reading through a contract can be baffling and overwhelming and therefore it is extremely important to seek professional advice before signing a contract. However, the first step towards understanding the contract is recognising that it is used by the venue to protect their organisation and to mitigate against the poor management of events. Much of the content of the contract, although written using punitive language, is to encourage the organiser to act responsibly in the management of their event.

In the eyes of the law, it can be difficult to identify which party is responsible for the safe delivery of the event; the venue or the event manager. Although the Safety of Sports Grounds Act 1975 make specific reference to the responsibilities of the venue manager, there is no comparable law that expressly points to other types of event venues and the overarching responsibility of the venue manager. Yet, when things go wrong at an event, the venue is more likely to be prosecuted for negligence than the event manager.

Therefore, some of the entries in the contract are to draw the attention of the event manager to relevant legislation and ensure compliance. For example, the Copyright, Designs and Patents Act 1988 dictates that live music performances are subject to a PRS licence and in order to play original sound recorded music a PPL licence must be obtained yet the Act refers to both the venue and the event (Raj *et al.*, 2013). Therefore, the venue's contract may either confirm that these licences are in place or that they need to be obtained in order to comply with the law.

If the venue has a premises licence, then the contract will be worded in such a way as to ensure that the hirer is aware of, and bound to, work within the limits of the licence. Should the terms of the premises licence be broken, it may be revoked and the venue might face prosecution. If alcohol is to be provided at the event then the venue may insist that they appoint security staff to work at the event, at the expense of the event manager. This ensures compliance with the Licensing Act 2003. And, although it can seem strange for the venue to have final approval of event promotional material, this is often a clause of the venue contract to ensure that the venue's reputation is not brought into disrepute. But it is also used as a

CASE STUDY 10.3 THE FIRE AT COLECTIV NIGHTCLUB, BUCHAREST

In 2013, police in Romania arrested the three owners of Colectiv, a nightclub in Bucharest, following a fire in the venue which killed 45 people and injured nearly 200. Most of the victims were in their teens and early twenties and had gathered to attend a concert in the basement venue which was a former factory located close to the city centre.

The fire started when fireworks were set off inside the venue, igniting insulation foam on a pillar. The fire spread quickly and the panicking audience rushed towards the venue's only exit. The ensuing stampede trapped many of the 400 people inside the venue. Evidence collected at the site suggested that improper and highly flammable materials had been illegally installed in the venue in order to keep costs down. The scale of the disaster was further exacerbated by the people managing the venue as they had admitted more people into the club than it could accommodate.

The owners were arrested on suspicion of manslaughter and they later admitted that they had been reckless in failing to follow safety standards at the venue. Prosecutors also went on to arrest the former mayor of the city as there was evidence that he had granted a permit for the club to operate, despite this not being authorised by the city's fire department. Prosecutors confirmed that 'given that several events took place in broadly unsafe public conditions, the lives, health and physical integrity of the audience and staff were permanently put in danger.' There has been much criticism by Romanians of the way permits and licences are issued in the country and fire regulations are not rigorously followed or upheld in Romanian venues. The disaster led to an out-spilling of anger on social media, mostly directed towards the local authorities for failing to properly inspect clubs and other public spaces.

Following news coverage of the disaster a number of other nightclubs have promised to either shut down or improve their safety provision. Andrei Sosa, the owner of Expirat in Bucharest, confirmed that he would permanently close his venue as it only has one exit claiming 'I take responsibility. I have put the lives of thousands of people in danger, weekend after weekend and sometimes during the week.' The owners of the La Baza club in Iasi also apologised for not meeting minimum safety requirements, saying 'we consider we have been ignorant and irresponsible. We were lucky. We don't want to put anyone's life in danger.' And the owners of Rockstadt, a large music venue in the central city of Brasov, announced that it would be shutting for 10 days to replace foam in the venue that was similar to the foam that caught fire at Colectiv. The venue would also be installing sprinklers and focus on meeting other EU safety standards.

Sources: http://www.bbc.co.uk/news/world-europe-34684973;
https://www.theguardian.com/world/video/2015/nov/04/romania-protest-bucharest-colectiv-nightclub-fire-video

mechanism to guard against misrepresentation as, for example, it is illegal to advertise and charge entry to a specific event and then deliver a very different type of event.

Sadly, the multitude of preventable event disasters over recent years, indicates that the greatest risk to human life at events are caused by fire, overcrowding or infrastructure collapse. The venue will take much responsibility for minimising risks in these areas, notably by conducting an annual fire risk assessment and dictating the room capacities. The venue may also insist on providing their own event staff and approving a number of event documents as part of their

Table 10.2 Typical venue requirements

Deposit
Marketing materials
Access and vacate times per venue per day
Approximate numbers of guests
Approximate number of staff
Confirmation of number of security staff
Operational schedule (e.g., room layout requirements, details of activities per room, etc.)
Exhibition plans (to be forwarded to the local council)
Copies of relevant licences
Technical requirements
Copies of riders
Confirmation of catering requirements
Risk assessment (and risk assessments from suppliers)
Copy of public liability insurance policy

responsibility towards minimising the risk of overcrowding and fires. They may want to approve the event operational schedule, which details all of the event activities, for this reason. This is sometimes referred to as a production or event schedule and it is a detailed timetable covering the whole duration of the event. The venue may want to review the event risk assessment and some venues will insist that the risk assessment is conducted via a specific template. Additionally, the local council authorities may also insist on approving plans for installing temporary structures within the venue, such as a shell scheme exhibition. The purpose of reviewing, possibly amending, and ultimately approving event documentation is not to control the event or to find ways to extract more money from the event manager, but to check for early indications of preventable risks.

The venue may insist that they receive copies of riders and technical riders from any performers attending the event. As much of the content of the rider will need to be provided by the venue, this is another safeguarding measure to establish if the venue is able to meet the requirements of the artists and to flag up any additional costs the event manager may incur as a result of the agreement. Similarly, the venue may insist upon reviewing the risk assessments of third party suppliers that the event manager will be hiring to work at the event. Once again this is to alert the venue to any possible problems and so that the venue can be assured that all event staff will be adhering to safe work practices. This is also to ensure that the venue's own insurance policies are not rendered void. Raj *et al.* (2013, p. 300) illustrate this further:

> If an event is held within a venue which has the structure to allow working at height, the venue manager should insist that persons wear a harness when working above head height. Again, if this procedure is not adhered to the venue insurance cover could be invalidated, along with the insurance cover held by the production company.

The venue contract should make the financial arrangement for the hire of the rooms very clear. Typically, this means that the hirer is required to pay a deposit in advance of the event, and often this is payable at the time of booking and signing the contract. The deposit may or may not be refundable and the conditions for this should also be included in the contract. If the event manager is not known to the venue, then it is possible that the venue manager will insist upon full payment in advance of the event. This is sometimes included to deter amateur event managers from making bookings for events that they are not capable of delivering.

Ultimately these clauses ensure that the venue does not make a significant financial loss by accepting the booking and blocking out the use of the venue to other interested parties. The catering requirements will usually be included in the contract if the caterer is in-house or appointed. As with the room hire charges, a deposit may be required well in advance of event day. Often, the full catering charges must be paid in advance of the event and the contract will normally determine the dates by which the catering numbers must be confirmed to the venue. After this date, it may not be possible to make any changes to these numbers but it is particularly unlikely that a refund will be available should the catering numbers go down. This is because the caterer will need to pre-order food and drink, and much of this will be perishable.

All of the financial payments listed on the contract should also make reference to applicable local taxes, such as VAT, and indicate whether the figures shown are net or gross. In some countries, the government may refund certain taxes upon proof of payment and this information should be clearly evident on the contract (Matthews, 2016).

10.7 PENALTIES, FORCE MAJEURE AND INDEMNITY CLAUSES

The contract should clearly detail all of the penalties that apply to both parties (venue and event manager) should either party breach any part of the agreement. A breach of contract can occur when either party fails to fulfil any of their responsibilities listed on the contract or undertakes actions which go against the intent of the contract. Typically, the penalties come in the form of financial charges to either reimburse or compensate the injured party. Cancellation charges should be evident and most venues apply a sliding scale of charges. This means that should the event manager cancel the event, the imposed charges will be greater the nearer this happens to the event date. The same may apply to the catering charges. The contract should also indicate what will happen should the venue cancel the booking.

The contract should include full details of specific costs, such as room hire charges, and estimated costs of variable items such as furniture, equipment, staffing, etc. Any attrition charges should be detailed, listing the charges for the minimum number of accommodation bookings, even if the bedrooms are not occupied. Some venues apply a fine for when the event overruns and you can expect to be charged for any damage done to the venue at any time during the event (including get in and get out periods).

Force majeure (French for 'superior force') is a clause which permits either party to suspend or terminate the contract in the event of circumstances beyond their control. This include acts of God (e.g., flood, hurricane, etc.), war, mass public outcry (e.g., riots, strikes), explosions and government actions. And finally, the contract may include an indemnity or limitation of liability clause. Essentially this clarifies that the event manager assumes all responsibility for the management of the event and thus it protects the venue from any associated harm, loss or responsibility.

10.8 THE VENUE'S CONTRACTUAL RESPONSIBILITIES

Although the contract is primarily designed to protect the interests of the venue, as a legally binding document it also protects the event manager. The contract will stipulate which rooms are going to be provided, on what dates and at what hire charge. It may also list all of the furniture, services and equipment that the venue will either provide or arrange and also at what cost. Although the charges may rise annually in line with inflation (and if so, this should be indicated in the document), the contract provides the event manager with a clear list of charges. Although some will be variable, and dependent on numbers for example, the contract provides the event manager with the means to financially predict and control the event budget and as such it is a useful planning tool. The contract, once signed by both parties, confirms that the booking has been agreed. This should mean that the venue does not offer the same rooms and facilities to another user. Unfortunately, the contract does not provide a cast iron guarantee that the venue will not double book the space. However, it does reduce the likelihood of this occurring and ensures that should the venue make such an error, the event manager will be financially compensated.

The contract also provides the event manager with a useful checklist of what the venue has agreed to provide and what you must arrange yourself. The list of documents that must be provided to the venue, and the payment schedule, are also useful planning tools which enable the event manager to effectively manage the event. Approval from the venue manager of documents such as risk assessments, is a mechanism for getting valuable feedback from an industry professional.

The contract may also detail the operational responsibilities of the venue under the terms of a premises licence or for certain sporting venues, according to the Safety of Sports Grounds Act 1975. And of course, both venue and event manager are jointly liable for fire safety, risk assessment, insurance and health and safety with the onus on the venue meeting these requirements (Raj *et al.*, 2013). Depending on the location of the venue, there may be a number of laws directly applicable to the management of buildings, as Davidson and Rogers (2011, p. 40) illustrate:

> Much of the activity in the area of accessibility is at the level of the individual event venue. Venues are encouraged as a matter of best practice, and required, by legislation, to provide appropriate signage, meeting space, bedrooms, equipment to ensure full accessibility for those with disabilities.

And as Raj *et al.* (2013) remind us, the event manager has a duty to check that the venue has all of their documentation in place and is meeting their legal requirements.

10.9 NEGOTIATING THE VENUE CONTRACT

Although the contract will become a legally binding document, once signed, the terms and conditions of the contract can be negotiated and altered until both parties are content with the final agreement. Upon receipt of the contract, it is wise to get a professional to look at and check the wording of the agreement and to flag up any concerning clauses or penalties or clarify any clauses that you do not completely understand. It is also a good time to negotiate any terms of the contract that are not to your liking or to add in further details. For example, Fenich (2012, p. 199) reminds us that 'everything is negotiable' and Bladen *et al.* (2012, p. 88) suggest that the point of signing the contract should be viewed as an opportunity to negotiate rates and charges once again.

Therefore, just before signing the contract, consider whether it covers all of your event needs. This may be a good opportunity to ask for certain pieces of equipment to be included in the hire or to try to lower some of the room hire charges. Fenich (2012) also advises that you should never sign the contract until the principal room hire charges have been agreed as although you may alter the booking after it has been signed, it will be difficult to negotiate these charges once both you and the venue have signed the contract.

It is worth remembering that the contract can be amended after it has been signed and frequently you will need or want to add or alter details, particularly regarding the number of rooms you are hiring and the hours of usage that you require. But of course, your bargaining powers are reduced once you have entered into a legal agreement with the venue, or indeed with any event supplier.

10.10 TRANSFERRING RESPONSIBILITY TO SUPPLIERS AND GUESTS

One of the fundamental roles of the contract is to set out the obligations of both parties, but also to transfer responsibility from venue to event owner. As previously stated, the contract may include a number of punitive statements, but generally these are used to encourage the event owner to act responsibly in the management of their event. Part of acting responsibly involves understanding the venue's procedures and policies and relaying them to event guests and other event suppliers as appropriate. As Raj *et al.* (2013, p. 168) illustrate:

> The event company has a legal responsibility to relay the health and safety and evacuation procedures presented by the venue to all employees of the event company, suppliers or outside contractual staff working within the venue. This information must be presented and understood prior to any outside employee commencing work within the venue.

It is important to ensure that your event suppliers also act responsibly at the event, partly to ensure that you as the event owner, comply with the terms and conditions of the contract. This means that you will need to convey quite a bit of information to your suppliers to ensure that they work within the venue's policies and provide you with information that you will need to pass on to the venue. This needs to be done in a timely manner, as you may find that the contract details fines for the late provision of information to the venue. Table 10.3 lists some of the key information that you will need to pass on to suppliers to ensure compliance with the contract and it also lists some of the information that you will need to collect from your suppliers and share with the venue.

Of course, you will also need to ensure that your attendees also comply with venue policies and rules so it is important to share information such as the process for parking and the smoking policy. You will also need to go through the contract and draw out any clauses that could be broken by your attendees. Typically, this can include damaging the venue and bringing food and drink on site rather than purchasing it from the caterer. You will need to promote responsible behaviour in your guests well in advance of the event, through means such as establishing your own rules and policies for the event. But on event day, you will also need to monitor your suppliers and attendees to ensure that all of the rules and policies are being upheld. The most effective way of monitoring the behaviour of your suppliers and guests within the venue, is by providing and training event staff to carry out this important role.

Table 10.3 Upholding venue policies

What to Advise
How much time is allocated to the get in/get out
What arrangements are in place for parking, loading and unloading
Permitted/prohibited decorations
What arrangements are in place for the collection of rubbish
Permitted/prohibited special effects, noise levels, equipment etc.
How catering can be arranged
The smoking policy

What to Request
All plans for the installation of temporary structures
Risk assessments for the activity/service provided
Copy of public liability insurance
Copy of licences as relevant to the activity/service provided
Number of staff accompanying each supplier
Technical requirements of each supplier
Copy of rider for each performer

10.11 USING EVENT STAFF AT THE VENUE

Essentially event staff will fulfil two key roles for the event manager; providing customer service and assisting with health and safety requirements. Figure 10.5 illustrates the customer service role of event staff.

Carefully selected and trained event staff will professionalise the event and their customer service role will involve them providing information to guests and suppliers, answering questions, directing people, helping with the evaluation of the event (see Chapter 11) and troubleshooting. Event staff should take on much of the legwork involved in running the event, thus enabling you to focus on overseeing the entire event. Event staff will ensure that everyone is well looked after, but they will also monitor the event for hazards such as monitoring the build-up of rubbish, keeping exits and pathways clear, and checking tickets and monitoring crowds. Your staff can also ensure that the venue and event policies are being upheld, such as making sure that guests are prohibited from accessing unsafe areas, preventing people from smoking and generally being vigilant throughout the event. Of course, the staff can also assist in a crisis and help with an evacuation too.

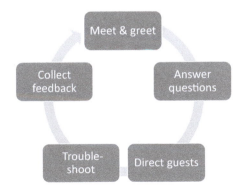

Figure 10.5 Staff roles (customer service).

Figure 10.6 Staff roles (health and safety).

In order to provide excellent customer service and uphold the policies as set down by the venue or by you, event staff must be carefully selected and trained. It is important to conduct at least some of the staff training at the venue so that your staff become familiar with the layout of the site. Many venues will provide staff for you that can fulfil both the customer service and health and safety elements of the role and a number of venues will help you to train your staff in understanding and practising their role on site. Therefore, your event staff should provide you with peace of mind on event day and will help you to comply with the contract by ensuring that your suppliers and guests behave responsibly.

10.12 CONTRACTS AND LICENSING – THE VENUE MANAGER'S PERSPECTIVE

An essential aspect of running a successful venue, is by ensuring that you have a comprehensive written agreement in place with each hirer. It is important to have the contract drawn up by a legal professional although you may be responsible for tailoring each contract to reflect the agreement that you are entering into with regards to a specific event. The contract will confirm your responsibilities to the event owner and it is essential that you are confident about the venue's ability to meet the terms of a legally binding document. The principal reason for issuing a contract to each event manager is to safeguard the venue from the impacts of irresponsible behaviour. As such, the contract must contain a comprehensive list of all of your requirements and all of your rules for using the venue and it must detail the penalties that are in place should these requirements and rules not be met. Of course, you may or may not choose to enforce the penalties but the contract provides you with the right to enact these penalties should you choose to. It may be wise to be prepared to enter into a final phase of negotiations with the event manager after you have issued the contract and before they sign it and these negotiations may require you to add an addendum to the original contract or to alter it. Therefore, it is important to be confident that the contract that the hirer signs contains all of the venue's key requirements.

10.13 SUMMARY

The contract issued by a venue to the event owner is one of the most complicated types of contract as it is likely to contain a number of specific clauses (Bladen *et al.*, 2012). Therefore, it is essential that event managers understand the key terms used in these documents as contracts play a vital role in event management (Goldblatt, 2007). It is therefore important to read the contract carefully and involve the services of a legal professional before signing it. Any final negotiating with the venue should be conducted prior to (and as part of) the process of signing the contract. The contract will make reference to specific legislation, policies and rules that apply to the particular booking. The contract will also outline the payment plan for the hire of the venue and it will give details of the penalties in place for not meeting the terms and conditions of the contract. The contract will also confirm the responsibilities of the venue and it will be signed by the venue manager. The contract can provide the event manager with a useful checklist of information that must be collected and shared with the venue as well as rules that must be upheld on event day. Well-trained event staff can help the event manager to comply with the contract by monitoring the activities of suppliers and guests while at the venue and upholding the venue's and the event's policies. Signing the venue hire contract is a significant stage in the event planning process as it signals confirmation of the event date and therefore a commitment to delivering the event and finalising the event plans. Therefore, once the contract has been received, read and signed the relationship between the event manager and the venue enters into a new and important phase.

10.14 FURTHER READING

The following sources are particularly useful for further reading on the subject of:

Contracts and licensing

Becker, D. (2006) *The Essential Legal Guide to Events: A Practical Handbook for Event Professionals and their Advisors*. Publisher: Author.

Health and safety

HSE publications (available from http://www.hse.gov.uk)
The Purple Guide to Health, Safety and Welfare at Music and Other Events (available at www.thepurpleguide.co.uk)
Silvers, J.R. (2013) *Risk Management for Meetings and Events*. London: Routledge.
Tarlow, P.E. (2002) *Event Risk Management and Safety*. New York: Wiley.
Tum, J. (2006) *Management of Event Operations,* London: Butterworth-Heinemann.

Staffing events

Van Der Wagen, L. (2014) *Human Resource Management for Events* (2nd edn). London: Routledge.

The role of the venue in event preparation, delivery and evaluation

LEARNING OUTCOMES

By the end of Chapter 11, you should be able to:

- Recognise the support available to you from the venue during the lead up to the event
- Draw upon the venue manager's knowledge and expertise in the lead up to the event
- Understand the role of a duty manager and the priorities of the venue on event day
- Describe the event closedown and evaluation process

11.1 INTRODUCTION

Signing the venue's contract is a significant phase in the event planning process and it signals a commitment to the main supplier and confirmation of the event date. When the contract has been negotiated and signed, the relationship between the event manager and the venue enters into a new and important phase. This phase signals the official start of the lead time and the countdown to event day begins. Involving the venue in the final plans for the event is essential as the venue can provide untold expertise and advise on making the most effective use of the site. Although the contract will provide the event manager with confirmation of the information and documentation that must now be provided to the venue there are a number of ways in which the venue manager can contribute to the event plans. This chapter will provide useful tips and advice on how the venue can be a valuable resource in the lead up to event day. It also provides insight into how the various members of venue staff will support you on event day, including the important role of the duty manager. The chapter concludes with suggestions of how and why you should involve the venue in the post event evaluation and how this can provide the basis for a good long term working relationship with the venue.

11.2 INFORMATION REQUESTED BY THE VENUE

As discussed in Chapter 10, and illustrated in Table 10.2, the venue may ask to view and even amend much of the event manager's plans and documentation. This includes marketing material, licences, riders, insurance policies, plans and the event **operational schedule**. Many venue managers will be proactive in liaising with you in the lead up to the event and requesting documentation from you but others will expect you to honour the details of the contract and provide information as it becomes available. Therefore, it is good practice to keep a record of exactly what event documentation you are going to need to show to the venue. You may find that you need final approval from both the venue and your client on a number of key aspects of the event so it is important to have a system in place for recording when you have sought and received approval from these and other key stakeholders. It is particularly important to secure permission or approval for your plans before you begin to share them with your event guests or before you contract third party suppliers.

Even though, by now you will have signed a lengthy and detailed contract which governs what you can and cannot do within the venue, you should not feel wary of asking the venue manager for advice or clarification. The venue manager can be one of your greatest allies throughout the event planning process and on the day of the event, therefore it is important to maintain and develop a good working relationship with the venue over time and in turn this can impress the client (Kirk, 2015). By providing information to the venue in a timely manner, the event manager demonstrates professionalism and gains the trust and respect of the venue manager.

11.3 CHANGES TO THE RFP

Between the time of signing the contract with the venue and the day of the event, the plans for the event will change and this can range from slight tweaks to major alterations to the original concept that was shared with the venue in the RFP. It is extremely important to keep the venue manager abreast of such changes. Where these updates indicate a significant change to what has been agreed with the venue, it is very important to consult with the venue manager before implementing any changes. It may be prudent to do this before agreeing with the client that the changes can be made. For example, if you require earlier, later or longer access to any of the rooms that you have booked, check with the venue manager that this is possible and if so if this is going to alter the hire charges. If you decide to change the way a room is set up also double check that this is not going to be a problem. Remember that many venues have a limited number of furniture items shared across the site. Similarly, if you decide to include or change the plans for how rooms are to be re-set during the event, ask the venue if this is ok as this may be dependent upon (or have a knock-on effect on) the availability of venue staff on event day.

Anything that impacts the length of the hire period of each room and the number of venue staff needed for an event may result in additional charges. Therefore you may request, or may be provided with, an amended quotation for venue hire as your plans for the event develop and change. The new quotation will reflect the changes to the original RFP. You may be able to negotiate the charges, but of course once you have signed the contract, this becomes more difficult. Nevertheless, it is worth discussing the additional charges with the venue manager and employing some of the negotiation strategies discussed in Chapter 9. However, take care not to delay for too long if you are certain that you are going to need more space than you had originally planned for as the venue may become booked up quickly by other users.

As the plans for your event develop and change, be mindful of the auxiliary charges that venues impose. These will usually be provided to you with the contract and booking documentation but remember that anything that the venue provides, such as equipment, furniture and staff, may come at an additional charge. Although the quotation for the room hire charges may be updated to reflect any changes to your event plan, the venue may not continue to remind you of the charges that apply for additional services that you now require. As Malhotra (n.d.) advises, being as clear as possible about your specific event needs with the venue will save time but will also limit any unpleasant surprises with regards to additional charges.

11.4 THE OPERATIONAL SCHEDULE

As discussed in Chapter 10, the venue may ask to see your operational schedule which details all of the activities that will take place at the event. For the event manager, this schedule is a live document that will be developed and amended regularly throughout the event planning process. Therefore for the novice event manager, it can be difficult to judge when to share this document and which version of the schedule is accurate or subject to further change. Once you have a fairly detailed schedule which outlines the principal elements of the event, it can be reassuring to share it with the venue manager and ask for confirmation of viability. Ensure that this is provided to the venue well in advance of event day and in time to allow you to take on board the venue's feedback and implement any changes that they put forward.

Table 11.1 provides an overview of the type of information to include in an operational schedule.

The operational schedule should be as detailed as possible as it is a complete timetable of all the activities that will be taking place on event day. This includes the get in and get out periods and what is happening in the front and back of house areas. Sharing this document with the venue helps them to prepare for the event but also it will flag up any elements of the event that they believe may need attention such as activities that need careful risk management. The operational schedule can be particularly useful for checking timings with the venue. The venue can use this document to assess whether or not you have allowed enough time to set up rooms, to move attendees around the venue and to provide refreshments. Therefore the more information that you can include in the schedule the better, as the venue can help you to ensure that your plans are realistic and achievable.

Table 11.1 Operational schedule template

Entry	FOH/BOH	Responsible	Notes
Arrival of event staff and stewards, first aid personnel, security staff etc.			
Arrival of each supplier to include access and setting up instructions.			
A breakdown of all of the elements of setting up of the event.			
Any activities to be completed before the event begins (e.g. safety checks, staff briefing).			
Doors open to guests and procedures for check in/registration.			
Detailed timings for all activities, performers, catering service etc. Include information about moving or adding furniture or equipment to rooms.			
Detailed entries for notable elements of the event (e.g. arrival or departure of VIPs, speeches, photographs, awards).			
Timings for approaching and reaching the end of the event and all activities associated with guests leaving.			
Detailed entries for the break down (get out/strike).			
Final on-site activities (e.g. debriefs, inspection of the rooms by the venue manager).			

Entry: In this column include timed entries of all event activities such as those listed here. *FOH/BOH*: You may wish to break down the entries according to what is happening front of house and back of house, or per room. *Responsible*: If there is a significant catering element or technical production element of the event, you may wish to split the schedule and list entries by area of responsibility. *Notes*: Include information such as where staff are to report to on arrival, where suppliers should park, if cloakrooms are available etc.

11.5 THE VENUE MANAGER'S EXPERTISE

One of the most important, and underutilised, reasons for working closely with the venue manager is to tap into their wealth of expertise. An experienced venue team will have accrued hours and hours of working with a number of event planners and helped to plan and deliver a huge variety of events, all within their space. This will give them a unique perspective on how to make the best use of the available space and resources. They may have an archive of photos, videos and event documentation that they can draw on and share with you to provide you with inspiration and ideas. The venue manager will also be well connected within the local area and in a position to recommend suppliers who also have experience of working on events in the venue. Arranging follow up site visits during the event planning process can be the best way to get to know the venue manager and to pick their brain for useful information and suggestions. Most venue managers will be only too pleased to be involved in developing the event concept with you as ultimately, their expertise will help you to make informed decisions about using the space. It will also save you time and can help you to avoid making poor decisions about the venue that may prove costly, dangerous or inappropriate.

THE INDUSTRY EXPERT'S VIEW 11.1

HOLDING A FESTIVAL IN AN ACADEMIC VENUE

Judith Heneghan, Director, The University of Winchester Writers' Festival,
www.writersfestival.co.uk

The Writer's Festival is an annual event, first established nearly 40 years ago, that brings new and emerging writers together with literary agents, commissioning editors and established poets, novelists and scriptwriters for three days of workshops, networking and one-to-one appointments. It aims to support, inspire and guide writers towards their professional goals. It also fosters a sense of community for writers who may work alone for much of the year. As well as 750 individual one-to-one appointments we programme over 50 separate events (workshops, all day courses and talks), many of which occur simultaneously, so venue use and timetabling are complex. Each attendee receives a personalised itinerary in advance of the event.

The University of Winchester is the event owner of the Writers' Festival and has two members of dedicated Festival staff that are employees of the University: the Director and the Events Manager/Administrator. The Festival is always held on the campus, which comes with numerous benefits. We have strong, effective relationships with the University's Conferences team and estates managers. We have excellent working knowledge of our venue and we can draw on an enthusiastic pool of students and staff for volunteering. The rooms are set up appropriately, we have access to the auditorium for our keynote speaker, there is accommodation on site, dining facilities, free Wi-Fi and the campus itself is a pleasant environment with a central outside 'quad' area for informal gathering. Having a bar on site also helps!

There are some challenges that come with using the University as a venue for this event. Firstly we are bound by pricing set by the Conferences and Catering departments.

continued

Also the accommodation is 'basic' in that rooms are student rooms. These student rooms are at West Downs, a 10 minute walk from the main event area, up a steep hill, so we are obliged to offer a shuttle bus service. We have, on occasion, needed to work around extensive renovation work on site, and each year we have to negotiate space with other events taking place around the University.

However, our annual event is well-known at the University and communication is constant between ourselves and the Conferences team. We provide information to them about numbers attending, meals and special requirements, accommodation needs, and of course our programme arrangements. The University as a venue supports us in significant ways including promoting the event via social media, events calendars and excellent press office support. On event day the Conferences team are on hand to issue keys, monitor accommodation and dining areas, liaise with Security and deal with any emergencies, for example when an attendee has an accident or falls ill and needs assistance. They will also liaise on our behalf with the University's IT department, and support us with technicians for recording/lighting the keynote event in the auditorium. Having this type of support from the venue is essential as it helps us deliver a fantastic festival for our guests and speakers each year.

11.6 GETTING THE MOST OUT OF VENUE MARKETING OPPORTUNITIES

Unless the event that you are organising is going to be an entirely private affair, it is in your interest and the venue's interest to promote the event through all available and appropriate channels. There are a number of ways that you can market the event with the help of the venue manager as illustrated in Figure 11.1.

Most venues will list the events that they are hosting on their website, particularly if all or part of the venue is open to the public (either free or ticketed). In this case you should be able to add the details of the event, including a link to the website for the event, to this page. Most venues are embracing social media networks and will be keen to tweet or retweet a link to the event, add information about the event to homepages and join in with online discussions and forums about the event. In addition to Facebook and Twitter, venues are also now using electronic newsletters to communicate with consumers and have their own YouTube channels (Quinn, 2013) so explore the options for online event marketing with the venue manager.

Ask the venue for an introduction to the local DMO and explore the ways in which you can get them involved in marketing the event. For example, you may want to list your event on the DMO website, have the event promoted in a newsletter or featured in specific marketing

Figure 11.1 Venue marketing options.

ACTIVITY 11.1

Using a variety of types of venues and types of events, see how many catchy but appropriate hashtags you can create that could be used to engage with potential attendees on Twitter. The hashtag needs to link the venue with the event, be imaginative and quirky but also short and clear.

---

campaigns that are promoting the destination. Although the DMO's relationship with the venue will be a business connection, the DMO will be actively promoting the destination to business and leisure tourists. If your event is going to attract visitors to the area, then the DMO will be keen to promote the event through a number of different channels and they may provide a ticketing facility for all or some of the event activities.

The venue or DMO may also suggest writing and issuing a press release about your event or you may even want to make this suggestion to them. Particularly if you want the event to gain some local publicity. The venue and the DMO will have expertise in this area and good connections with the local and national press. A well timed, interesting news article about the event should bring positive attention to the area, the venue and of course your event. Just try to ensure that the press release, any social media activity, and other marketing materials are getting across the right message and the right image for your event and in terms of what your client has asked you to achieve.

11.7 ASKING FOR HELP AND ADVICE

Even the most experienced and diligent event manager will find themselves faced with unforeseen problems and daunting challenges during the event planning process. During the course of the professional life of an event manager, you can expect to have to deal with difficult and seemingly impossible requests from clients as well as suppliers letting you down and an unending list of demands and requirements from exhibitors and attendees. As you develop as an event manager you will find the skills to cope with each situation as it arises but it can be tempting to try to cover up any mistakes that you make along the way or avoid dealing with complicated or difficult issues. However, if the situation is going to affect your use of the venue then it is important to discuss the problem with the venue manager as early as possible. Some examples of this include underestimating how much space you are going to need for a particular activity, how popular it is going to be or how much time you will need to set it up. You may have made false promises to suppliers or attendees about adequate parking or not budgeted enough to pay for event stewards. Whatever the issue, if it is operational in nature, then it is almost certainly going to have an impact on the venue and the venue staff.

Therefore it is essential that you have an honest discussion with the venue manager about the problem. Remember that most venue managers will be keen to help you to resolve issues as they will want your event to be a success. If you have already invested time in building up a good working relationship with the venue staff, they will support you in finding solutions. You may be forced to accept that the resolution involves a cost, but it is better to know this in advance than on or after the day of the event. This also illustrates the importance of investing time in building a good working relationship with the venue manager. The more they like and respect you, the more inclined they will be to helping you out when you face these challenges!

Similarly, ensure that your event documentation is honest and detailed. For example, there is no point in omitting a high risk activity from your operational schedule or risk assessment for fear that the venue will not approve. If the venue have any concerns about what you are planning on doing on event day, these can be discussed and usually resolved in advance. The venue may ask you to take extra precautions or they may suggest alternative activities. Once again, they may also draw on their expertise to make sensible suggestions as to how a different approach can be just as effective but safer. An example of this could be when you are trying to create a particular ambience at the venue with the use of staging, scenery, props and materials. The operational schedule or risk assessment may indicate to the venue that the scenery will block emergency exits, that the props are too large to get into the building or that the materials are highly flammable. But careful planning and collaboration with the venue can ensure that the right ambience is created by repositioning the scenery, bringing in the props the day before via a different room and applying a fire-retardant spray to the materials.

Working closely with the venue manager in the lead up to the event is a good investment of your time as this helps to reduce the likelihood of problems arising on the day of the event. However, as every event professional will surely confirm, the day of the event can be extremely stressful and full of unexpected problems and challenges and in such situations the venue staff can provide essential support and assistance.

11.8 FINAL VENUE CHECKS BEFORE EVENT DAY

As event day approaches and you begin to pack up all of the equipment and paperwork that you need to take with you to the venue, make sure that you have a final conversation with the venue manager. Go over the arrangements for your arrival including how you gain access to the building. This may seem like an odd question, but as you will be arriving before your staff, suppliers or guests you may not be able to walk into the front entrance of the venue as it may be locked. Therefore, double check things such as where you can park and how you gain access to the venue. If you think it's possible that your client will arrive before you do, let the venue manager know to expect them. It can be very embarrassing if the client arrives at the venue and the venue manager has no idea who they are or why they have arrived so early. Also, if you are expecting to receive keys to rooms that you are going to keep locked during the event, check the procedure for receiving, and also returning, keys from the venue. The same is true for any equipment that you are going to borrow from the venue, particularly portable items such as two-way radios.

Table 11.2 is a useful checklist of items to bring with you to the venue that can be surprisingly useful when you are away from the office for a long period of time.

By now, you will have agreed with the venue how each of the rooms is to be laid out and how much time you need to set up any extra equipment, props, staging etc. in each of the rooms. If you foresee any delays to the plans you have for setting up, it is important to communicate them to the venue beforehand. If nothing else, the venue will appreciate the courtesy as it can be frustrating if the venue team are all ready and waiting to greet the event manager who then arrives an hour later than planned – this is not the best way to start event day! Also ask the venue if they intend to (or would like to) meet with any of your suppliers or staff. Some venues will want to conduct a safety briefing with event staff before any of the attendees arrive in order to go over things like emergency exits and **muster points**. Usually the venue will talk to you about this during the event planning process, but as event day draws near you may feel that you would welcome a briefing from the venue manager once you and

Table 11.2 Checklist of items to take to the venue

Copies of key event documentation	Operational schedule
	Risk assessment
	Contacts list
	Site plan
	Exhibition plan
	Table plan
Stationery	Pens
	Paper
	Drawing pins
	Tape
	Gaffer tape
IT Basics	Extension leads
	Phone charger
	Laptop charger
Refreshments	Bottled water
	High energy drinks
Clothes and toiletries	Change of shoes
	Spare tights
	Deodorant
	Hand wipes
A first aid kit for personal use	Headache tablets
	Plasters

your team are on site. There are some useful tips in the rest of this chapter on what to expect from the venue during the event, but make sure that you know who to go to at the venue should you have a problem.

11.9 THE VENUE'S PRIORITIES ON EVENT DAY

As the event manager, you will have a hundred and one things to do on event day and it can be a tremendously fun, exhilarating but stressful time. The venue's experience of event day and the venue's priorities on event day can however be somewhat different to yours. At most venues, nearly every day is an event day, with one or several public or private events taking place on site. The venue staff will usually start working some time before you are due to arrive and an event day can be fairly routine to them. Their first priority is to ensure that the rooms that you are going to be using are ready. This means making sure that they are clean, ventilated and set up according to your requests. Any furniture or equipment that has been booked will either be in place, or stored and ready to be set up as needed. The level of support available to you during the get in may vary from venue to venue and may be dependent upon what you have agreed in advance. However, a good venue manager will ensure that help is available to you during the get in phase such as staff to advise you (and your contractors) of access routes, the location of service lifts, what equipment is available to use, where items can be stored and so on. A number of problems can often arise such as forgetting to bring stationery with you to needing to print out information such as last minute signage or speeches. Frequently the venue can provide support and assistance with common requests such as these.

Once the get in is complete, the venue will normally want to conduct a thorough check before guests are admitted and this is usually to ensure that emergency exits have been kept clear and aisles or walkways have been preserved so that people can safely and easily move around the venue. Additionally, the catering manager may want to inspect the dining area and check that table plans are accurate and the stage manager may want to complete the sound check and clear the stage. Once everyone involved in the delivery of the event is in agreement with you, the event can officially begin. During this phase of the event, the venue's priority will be to ensure that everyone attending or working on the event is doing so safely. Therefore some venue staff may continue to walk around the event to check that everything is running smoothly, but providing that you are properly staffing and managing the event, the venue may be content to leave you to carry on and conduct minimal checks of just the communal areas of the venue while the event is going on.

However, should the venue have any concerns about overcrowding or any other safety aspect of the event they may keep a heavy presence at the event. This may even lead to the venue moving in extra staff or introducing added safety measures to ensure that the welfare of everyone is promoted and protected. For example, this could involve simple steps such as opening windows to reduce the temperature of a room that is getting very warm to moving and stacking furniture to make a bigger dance floor area if you have underestimated how many keen dancers there are at the event! The venue staff are also likely to refer to the timings of the event as listed on the function sheet or operational schedule. If it appears that elements of the event are running under or over time, they may ask you to verify this as this could be problematic for the venue. This is particularly true when the venue is providing the event catering as it may not be possible to delay or bring forward the serving of refreshments. Similarly, if there are other events taking place in the venue, they may be affected by your event if it overruns or indeed if everyone is going to be leaving early, and at the same time as a number of other event guests. This could lead to a sudden queue for the toilets and the cloakroom, trouble getting hold of taxis or a traffic jam in the car park. And if your event is the last one to finish in the venue, you can also expect the venue team to be visible towards the culmination of the event. They will be on hand to help direct your guests on their way and to help you with the process of the get out. The venue staff will usually stay on site until the get out is complete and they may undertake a check of the site before you leave to ensure that nothing is left behind.

11.10 THE ROLE OF VENUE STAFF ON EVENT DAY

Although the venue's key priority on event day is to ensure everyone is safe, there may be a number of staff at the venue who are able to provide you with support and assistance throughout the event.

Support staff

Depending on the type of venue you are using and the type of event you are delivering, the venue will provide a variety of support staff who will be working on your event, directly or indirectly.

The venue will have a number of its own staff, fulfilling their day to day role on the day of your event. This means that they will be working indirectly on your event and may be called upon to assist you as and when they are needed. This may include reception staff, cleaners, porters, gardeners and building maintenance workers. An effective team of venue staff will have been briefed in advance about your event and therefore will be familiar with what will be going on throughout the event. As such, they should be able to direct attendees that they come into contact with, or answer some basic questions posed by people attending or working on your event. Cleaners, porters and maintenance staff in particular may be on hand throughout the event to help with setting up rooms and changing layouts, moving furniture and equipment and keeping rooms tidy.

At most events there will be a number of catering staff working at the venue. These may be venue staff that form the in-house catering team, an on-site appointed catering company or an external supplier. Similarly there may be in-house stage managers or technicians, or these may be provided by an external company. The venue may also provide their own staff to steward the event. In some cases this means that all of the event personnel will be provided by the venue. At other times there will be a mixture of staff that work for the venue and staff that have been hired in for the day of the event and in most cases, all of the staff working at the venue on event day will report to the duty manager.

The duty manager

The duty manager is the term for the person who assumes overall responsibility for the venue and all venue operations. This therefore extends to all of the permanent venue staff as well as any personnel working on site. The duty manager is also responsible for the safety and welfare of all event staff, suppliers and attendees.

The duty manager is therefore a key contact and an important source of support on event day, and this role is often rotated among permanent venue staff, including the venue manager, but check with the venue as to who the designated duty manager or managers will be for your event. If possible, try to get to know them before event day. The duty manager can be a particularly strong ally as they will typically be a highly trained and experienced senior member of venue staff. Duty managers fulfil a dual role of providing customer care but also ensuring the safety of operations within the venue. Figure 11.2 gives further examples.

Often duty managers have first aid, security, food hygiene and licensing qualifications. They can step in to resolve conflicts, take control of difficult situations and troubleshoot throughout the course of an event. If the venue you are using has duty managers, make sure that you know how they can be contacted and where they are likely to be stationed on event day. If you find

Figure 11.2 The role of the duty manager.

yourself dealing with a difficult situation on event day, or perhaps you are in a scenario that is a diplomatic nightmare, call on the duty manager to help resolve it. For example, you may find that two of your suppliers are falling out over who gets to park closest to the entrance, or your client is determined to start the event earlier than the get in will be complete. The duty manager will have the authority, the experience, and the impartiality to resolve awkward or difficult situations. Furthermore, they are your first port of call if you have any problems or issues with any of the rooms or facilities that are being provided by the venue and a good duty manager will occasionally check in with you during the event to ensure that you are satisfied with how the event is proceeding.

The venue manager

It is worth noting that sometimes the person that you have been working with at the venue in the lead up to your event, has very little contact with you on event day. Sometimes this can be very disconcerting, as the person at the venue who knows most about your event, and helped you to make decisions about the event, is not necessarily going to be there on the day. Therefore, it is worth asking the venue about this beforehand and getting to know some of the operational staff who will be on hand to assist on the day. However, a good venue manager will welcome you on arrival at the venue on event day and will check in with you from time to time to ensure that the operational schedule is on track. They will make sure that you are pleased with the way the rooms have been set up and that any equipment or furniture is in the right place. A good venue manager will be visible during the get in period as this can be a particularly stressful part of the event. They will also take time to introduce themselves to your client and to check that your suppliers have everything that they need to begin to get ready for the event. They will liaise with all the venue staff and all of the members of event personnel so that the preparation for the start of the event goes as smoothly as possible.

You may find that the venue manager will undertake a number of checks during the get in phase. This could include reviewing your event risk assessment, to ensure that appropriate safety measures are being put in place, talking to your suppliers and monitoring the unloading and installation of equipment. The venue manager may ask to brief your event staff about safety procedures on site and they may want to double check that you have the appropriate number of stewards and security staff in place before the event begins. Remember that one of the venue manager's key priorities is making sure that the event goes ahead safely, and lots of these checks are to ensure that this happens. Once the event is underway, the venue manager may become less visible as they take a back-seat role and let the operational staff look after the running of the event.

When something goes wrong

Figure 11.3 provides an overview of some of the situations that can occur at events that require the immediate involvement of the venue.

Should there be an accident or an incident during the event, it is important to involve the venue staff as soon as possible. The duty or venue manager can ensure that the emergency services have clear and immediate access onto the site, and if they are first aid trained they can tend to the person in need of help in the meantime. Even if a guest, supplier, performer or member of event staff has a minor accident or feels slightly unwell, it is important to make the venue aware of what has occurred. The venue will want to keep a record of all accidents, injuries and illnesses. This written document may be requested by the police or an insurance company

Figure 11.3 Incidents that require the involvement of the venue or duty manager.

should there be an investigation into what happened at a later date. The venue may also have a list of useful phone numbers such as an emergency dentist, late night pharmacist and on-call doctor.

If there are any instances of anti-social behaviour, including any threats of violence, made by anyone at the event or to anyone at the event, these should also be reported to the venue staff. Once again, many duty managers are certified security professionals and will step in to take control of any potentially hostile situations. But even in venues that do not have a duty manager, it is important to make the venue aware of any unreasonable behaviour directed towards or coming from any of the event staff or guests. The venue may choose to involve the police and they may want to record in writing the details of any unpleasant incidents at the event.

From time to time the venue may be visited by the police, the licensing authorities, the fire brigade or environmental health officers. Usually these visits are part of a routine check of the area but occasionally the visiting officer may ask to enter the event and inspect all or part of the venue. Should such a request be put directly to you, or to a member of your event team, then redirect the request to the duty manager, if there is one, or to the nearest member of the venue team.

In the very unlikely event that there is a fire during the event, or that a part of the building or a temporary structure collapses, the venue staff will probably be aware of the issue before you are. However, it is possible that a small fire can be put out without too much drama, or that you or one of your staff or guests may notice that some equipment, staging or roof tile, for example, has come loose. In all such cases it is vital that the venue is informed straight away. Such incidents will need to be recorded and investigated as they may be symptomatic of a more serious problem.

If something goes wrong during the event and you are not sure whether you need to involve the venue, then it is usually best to make them aware of the situation. Much of the time the venue staff will be only too happy to help out and will probably have experienced similar problems and issues many times in the past. Bear in mind that the venue is very unlikely to want to stop the event when there is a problem. Even if it's an issue that requires investigation or even the involvement of the emergency services. The venue will not want to stop or interrupt an event that is underway unless this becomes absolutely essential. Therefore do not hesitate to involve the venue staff in minor as well as major problems on event day.

Terror attacks

Unfortunately, the number of events being targeted by terrorists has significantly increased in recent years, particularly in the West. Venues are a clear target because of the potential to create significant harm to a high number of people in a confined space. Some of the worst atrocities in venues include the shootings and taking of hostages at the Bataclan concert hall in Paris in 2015, and the suicide bomber who detonated an improvised explosive device in the foyer of the Manchester Arena at the end of an Ariana Grande concert in May 2017. Consequently, venue managers are constantly looking at ways to improve the security of buildings and sites. They work closely with the police, the emergency services and the local authorities to keep abreast of these issues and together they prepare for a coordinated action plan to deal with any terror related incident or threat. This may mean that the details of your event, your operational schedule and your strategy for staffing the event, may be shared and scrutinised in the lead up to event day. However, the venue will be on hand to both guide you and reassure you about any concerns you may have about venue safety. You shouldn't expect any unrealistic demands from the venue in terms of preparing for a terror attack and as Ibrahim (2016) explains, although security measures must form part of your event safety plan, proportionality is essential.

11.11 EVENT CLOSEDOWN

Once the event has ended and the attendees have left the venue, the get out or the breakdown can begin. Shone and Parry (2010) suggest that this should be planned in as much detail as the rest of the event with a detailed schedule of all the activities and sequences involved in closing down the event as this helps to ensure a safe and efficient get out period. Try to ensure that all of your suppliers, performers and staff check in with you or a member of your team before they leave the venue. This in turn enables you to check that they have fulfilled any responsibilities to you (and to the venue) such as leaving no damage or rubbish behind and returning any borrowed furniture or equipment.

Once you are completely sure that the get out is complete, walk around the entire venue and double check that everything has been taken down including signage and decorations both inside and outside the venue. Gather up items that you may wish to keep such as table decorations and items used to brighten up dressing rooms and toilets (flowers, tissues etc.). When you are satisfied that you have everything ask the venue or duty manager to inspect the rooms with you. Should they not be available, take photographs of the rooms that have been used, thus providing you with a record of how you are leaving them. By being this methodical at the end of the event, you should avoid receiving unexpected bills for repairing damage or removing excess rubbish.

If time permits, have a debrief with the venue or duty manager. It can be really useful for both parties to have a quick conversation about the event shortly after it has finished and the details of the event are still fresh in the minds of those involved. Ask the venue for their feedback on how the event went and check if they dealt with any issues or complaints that you were not aware of during the event. Try and record in writing any key points that come up in the discussion as they could be useful for the more detailed event evaluation to come.

Of course, the relationship with the venue manager will continue after event day as you can expect the final invoice to be sent to you some time after the event has concluded. Table 11.3 lists the items that may appear on the final invoice from the venue.

The venue's bill will include the balance payable for the hire of the rooms, including any rooms that were added to the booking during the planning process. All chargeable items of equipment, furniture, electricity, phone calls, photocopying, printing, Wi-Fi and any borrowed items of stationery may appear on the invoice. If the venue has provided event staff, these charges will be included. Also if the venue or duty manager deemed it necessary to bring in

Table 11.3 The final venue invoice

The balance of room hire charges
Hire charges for equipment
Hire charges for furniture
Charges for electricity etc.
Charges for phone calls, photocopying, printing, Wi-Fi, stationery etc.
Staffing charges (stewards, security, cloakroom etc.)
Charges for the use of a box office/ticketing facility
Charges for selling merchandise on site
Charges for licences (music, alcohol etc.)
Catering costs (including table decorations, printing menu cards, corkage and staffing)
Charges (and fee) for organising services or supplies for the event (e.g. technical support, extra furniture etc.)
Penalty charges (e.g. repairs, removal of excess rubbish, storage of early deliveries, provision of last minute staffing)

additional staff to manage the event, for example if the event manager failed to recruit an adequate number of stewards, these charges will be included. The invoice should not contain any surprise entries but will reflect all applicable charges plus the cost involved of providing services such as the use of a box office facility, or commission for merchandise sold on site. Agreed contributions to licensing will appear on the bill as will the catering charges, if the venue has an in-house team, otherwise the invoice for all of the outstanding refreshment charges will be provided to you separately and directly from the caterer.

The venue manager may contact you in advance of sending you the invoice to discuss any penalty charges that are going to be added to the bill. They may want to take the opportunity to gently remind you of their policy for charging for the removal of excess rubbish, for example. They may also want to discuss with you what they believe to be a reasonable charge for making good any damage done to the venue during the event. Should the venue get in touch to discuss the invoice, this is an opportunity to negotiate the penalty charges. The venue will need to ensure that they recoup any costs that they have incurred as a result of hosting the event, but most venue managers will not want to impose unreasonable costs particularly if they are looking to work with you again in the future. This is also therefore, a good opportunity to begin the discussion and negotiations of all charges for any future bookings that you may wish to make with the venue. If the event has gone smoothly, this too is a useful bargaining tool in the renegotiation of the venue as you have demonstrated to the venue manager that you are a competent and trustworthy client and this should gain you ground for future bookings.

11.12 EVENT AND VENUE EVALUATION

A significant element of the closedown process is the evaluation of the event and a 'proper event evaluation and follow up really completes the "circle of life" that is a special event' (Matthews, 2016, p. 208). Ideally the evaluation of the event should take place as early as possible once the event is complete, so that the views and experiences of everyone involved in the event can be accurately recorded. This should include obtaining and discussing feedback from the venue staff and also recording the views of all of your suppliers, staff, performers, attendees and client with regards to the event and the venue.

Figure 11.4 Who to involve in the evaluation of the event.

You may wish to ask your event stakeholders for their assessment of how you used the space as well as their evaluation of the venue's features and services. You may wish to seek specific feedback on people's interaction with venue staff and their experience of using the venue's equipment. As (Matthews, 2016, p. 208) goes on to explain, occasionally there may have been minor conflicts between subcontractors and venue for example that you were not aware of and should disputes not be resolved with the venue this could lead to strained relationships with the venue in the future.

It is important to gather, analyse and reflect on the feedback and to share relevant feedback with the venue manager as illustrated in Figure 11.5. Similarly, the venue should collect feedback from their staff on their views and experience of working on the event, and this should be shared and discussed with you also because sharing feedback is essential dialogue between key event stakeholders that helps all those involved in event delivery to assess performance (Ferdinand and Kitchin, 2012). Furthermore, understanding what has and hasn't worked well during the event helps both the event and venue managers to plan for future events.

Ideally the venue manager will specifically seek out your feedback on the entire process of working with the venue from booking through to event delivery. This is an important part of venue management, and helps the management team to identify and address areas that they can improve upon. Giving and receiving constructive feedback can be the basis for establishing genuine long term relationships with venue managers. Continuing the dialogue with the venue manager after the event has ended is important at least until all of the event administration (invoices, reports, evaluation etc.) has been completed and any issues have been resolved. But it is also a good time to discuss future plans that you may have to use the space again and it is an opportunity to begin an early negotiation of dates and hire charges.

After the event there is also an opportunity to discuss a post-event press release with the venue which could be advantageous to both sides by drawing attention to the strong partnership that has been created by hosting a successful event in a great venue. And finally, you, your client, and the venue may wish to record testimonials, highlighting the positive relationships that have been created through working together and recommending each other to the rest of the event management community. In an industry that is people driven, such

Figure 11.5 The process of event evaluation.

endorsements can have a lot of influence on future business and providing testimonials is a great method for demonstrating to other event managers the importance and benefits of developing and maintaining strong working relationships with venues.

11.13 THE ROLE OF THE VENUE IN EVENT PREPARATION, DELIVERY AND EVALUATION – THE VENUE MANAGER'S PERSPECTIVE

Once the event manager has signed the contract booking the venue, the countdown to event day can officially begin. Some event managers will be very proactive in providing you with key information about the event that will help you to prepare the venue and your staff. Others will be less aware of what sort of information you need in the lead up to event day and they will need to be chased for information. Checking the operational schedule and marketing materials for an event is essential to ensure that the plans are going to make effective and appropriate use of the venue and there are no deviations from what has been agreed and reflected in the contract. Any operational issues regarding the event are going to have an impact on the venue and potentially on your staff and your reputation. Therefore, it is best to raise, address and resolve any issues before event day particularly if they relate to the potential safety and wellbeing of guests or staff.

On event day, it is important to be the first person that the event manager meets on arrival at the venue. This is going to be a stressful day for them and being greeted by a familiar face will help to soothe their nerves. Having a visible presence during the get in and during the early phases of the event is similarly important as you will normally be in a strong position to step in and resolve queries or offer advice. If the event manager has a strong working relationship with you, they will value your input and respect your attempts at supporting them through potentially difficult and diplomatic challenges. It is also important to fully brief all of the venue staff who will be working on event day, regardless of whether they are directly or indirectly involved in delivering the event. Ensuring that your staff deliver excellent customer service starts with giving them full details of what is happening at the event including how many suppliers and attendees are expected on site, the timings of all activities, details of room turnarounds and information about any VIPs.

11.14 SUMMARY

Working closely with the venue in the lead up to the event is essential. Try to provide them with clear and detailed information about the event as early on in the planning process as possible. This will contribute to making sure that your plans for event day are sound and this can reduce the number of challenges that you will find yourself facing on the day of the event. The venue manager will have lots of experience of working with clients and they can offer advice and support particularly when you find yourself having to make difficult decisions about event operations. It is particularly important to build a good relationship with the venue manager over time because they can be one of your greatest allies on event day. Should you find yourself facing a crisis on event day, such as being let down by one of your suppliers or being forced to mediate between guests, the venue manager is often your greatest source of practical support. This is also true of venues that have a duty manager for event operations. The venue or duty manager is often the best person to turn to when you need immediate help therefore invest time in getting to know them before event day. Remember too that as Kirk (2015) points out, venue managers work with many event organisers and therefore their opinions can carry great sway as how they compare you to others can influence your reputation as well as your relationship with your client. Once the event is over, take time to engage all of your event stakeholders in a process of event evaluation. Make sure that the venue is involved in giving and receiving feedback and use this tool to continue to develop a strong working relationship with the venue manager as you may want to, or find yourself, working with them again and again in the future.

11.15 FURTHER READING

The following sources are particularly useful for further reading on the subject of:

Event evaluation

Ferdinand, N. and Kitchin, P. (2012) *Events Management: An International Approach* (2nd edn). London: SAGE.

Crowd management

Silvers, J.R. (2013) *Risk Management for Meetings and Events*. London: Routledge.
HSE publications (available from http://www.hse.gov.uk).
The Purple Guide to Health, Safety and Welfare at Music and Other Events (available at http://www.thepurpleguide.co.uk).

Site and operational planning

Matthews, D. (2016) *Special Event Production: The Process* (2nd edn). London: Routledge.
Tum, J., Norton, P. and Wright, J.N. (2006) *Management of Event Operations*, Oxford: Butterworth-Heinemann.
The Purple Guide to Health, Safety and Welfare at Music and Other Events (available at http://www.thepurpleguide.co.uk).

Terror prevention

Counter Terrorism Protective Security Advice for Major Events (available at http://www.ukcma.com/wp-content/uploads/2016/06/Major_Events_Reviewed.pdf).

Venue-based employment

LEARNING OUTCOMES

By the end of Chapter 12, you should be able to:

- Recognise types of venue-based employment
- Identify the key skills required to work in an events venue
- Create a professional development plan aimed at securing venue-based employment

12.1 INTRODUCTION

The final chapter of this book culminates by reviewing the different types of roles that are based in venues for people aspiring to join the dynamic events industry. A significant amount of industry employment is available within the many different types of events venues now in operation. Obviously, purpose-built conference, exhibition and event venues will have a dedicated team of highly trained venue staff. But even academic, sporting and unusual venues as well as hospitality providers will have dedicated events staff based at the venue to focus on attracting and servicing the needs of amateur and professional event organisers. There are a number of key employability skills essential for anyone wishing to work in the events industry.

Venue-based employment also requires a particular skill set and in return it can offer a rewarding career. This chapter will help you to identify the type of experience and the skills needed to be a successful venue-based industry professional. The 'roles, titles, salaries and job descriptions are not yet standardised in the industry' (Bowdin *et al.*, 2011, p. 41), so therefore this chapter is an excellent resource to guide you through where to look for work and will help you to create a career development plan that focuses on securing a role within a venue.

12.2 VENUE-BASED ROLES

Event venues, whether they are purpose-built or have a different primary purpose, are a huge source of industry employment. Venues employ a range of people to fulfil all sorts of roles from receptionists and porters to gardeners and cleaners. In terms of event-specific employment, broadly speaking, employment in venues is within one of three areas: marketing, sales or operations. This means that you would be either working to attract event bookings or working to deliver events within the venue, although in smaller organisations or venues you may have a role that covers all three of these areas. Plus, all three roles overlap and therefore there are often shared responsibilities between the people undertaking each role.

Figure 12.1 Venue-based employment.

Depending on the size of both the venue and the organisation, as well as the type of venue, there may be a number of different event-related jobs. For example, large venues or organisations may have personnel who work purely in a marketing role focusing on publicising the venue as an event space. Some venues will have a dedicated wedding co-ordinator, others will have a business events only professional. Venues with an in-house caterer will often have a banqueting manager or food and beverage (F&B) manager and all of these roles are discussed in more detail later in the chapter.

Specific jobs at venues can have a variety of titles that do not always explicitly indicate that the role is related to event management. For example, an operations manager or a duty manager may not have the word 'venue' or 'event' in their title, but the role will be focused on the operational management of events held at the venue. It is important to bear this in mind when looking for venue-based employment and more tips for finding suitable roles are covered further on in this chapter.

12.3 VENUE MARKETING ROLES

As there are now thousands of venues vying to attract events, venues must work hard to market themselves and stand out in a densely competitive industry. There are an increasing number of state of the art purpose-built conference and exhibition centres being built around the world and the number of new and emerging destinations is also rising. Also, there are more and more

Table 12.1 Venue marketing job description

Design and execute a marketing plan for the venue to include print and online advertising, direct mail, email, sales promotions and partnerships, social media and PR campaigns

Establish relationships and negotiate with external publications, associations and websites in order to develop optimum external coverage for venue

Manage the venue's online listing portfolio, ensuring that all content is up-to-date, accurate and features the latest venue offers

Develop a creative strategy for attendance at trade exhibitions and sales events and deliver each to an exemplary standard

Implement a social media strategy to promote the venue and manage the venue's Twitter feed and overall social media presence

Ensure that the venue's corporate identity and brand is adhered to in all marketing materials and to ensure standards are upheld across the venue itself

Ensure that all copyright issues are checked and adhered to, and that the venue is not subjected to any legal misrepresentation

Stay up to date with the latest marketing techniques, trends and policies and identify opportunities for the venue to exploit or implement them

Produce reports, analysing the effectiveness of campaigns and making informed recommendations for their strategic development

venues that historically have not been used for events, but are diversifying to take advantage of a significant secondary income from event bookings. In either case, marketing staff must work hard to raise the profile of their venues. The marketing team must focus on maximising the occupancy of their event spaces and persuade event organisers to select them, consequently the role of the marketing manager is one of the most important jobs in any venue (Davidson and Hyde, 2014).

Typical venues will have a website and an active presence on social media and will also produce traditional marketing materials such as a brochure. Therefore, the marketing staff will need to be confident in a range of marketing approaches and possess a variety of skills. Table 12.1 lists some of the typical responsibilities of a venue-based marketing manager role.

A venue-based marketing role will require a range of standard marketing skills and experience of designing, delivering and evaluating a marketing campaign. Therefore, knowledge of the events industry, potential clients and competing venues will be essential too. Table 12.2 is a sample of a job description for a venue-based marketing position which further illustrates the type of skills and knowledge needed for the role.

12.4 VENUE SALES ROLES

In a number of venues, and indeed in other industries too, the sales and marketing role will be merged and both areas will be the responsibility of one person or one dedicated team. However, there are differences in the type of work involved in marketing a venue and selling the event spaces. Within the context of venue management, sales can incorporate a number of different areas including selling the use of the space to amateur or professional event organisers as well as other individuals or companies. This could be for a one-off event, a series of events or for a more permanent leasing or use of some of the building. Most commonly

Table 12.2 Essential skills for venue marketing roles

Excellent verbal and written communication skills and a track record of creating compelling and effective communications

Experience of integrating marketing across different channels and working to commercial objectives, gained in either a venue or a creative-events role

Strong analytical marketing and negotiation skills

Excellent copywriting and proofreading skills and attention to detail

Experience in managing digital campaigns including display, social ads and email marketing

Highly effective communication and interpersonal skills including the ability to communicate at all levels including with clients and high-profile sponsors

The ability to motivate and manage team members

Project management and organisational skills including the ability to manage simultaneous projects to tight deadlines

Computer literate with good knowledge of IT including Office packages, Word, Excel, PowerPoint, Access and Outlook

Budget management skills

An enthusiastic and proactive person who is imaginative and creative

Table 12.3 Venue sales job description

Research, create and lead new activities/initiatives to generate potential venue hire clients, e.g., by attending networking events, exhibitions, etc.

Manage new enquiries to include responding to RFPs

Manage the venue diary to maximise yield

Arrange and lead site visits and building tours with potential clients and proactively seek to upsell occupancy, equipment and catering

Complete credit checks on all new clients

Upon confirmation of a booking, issue a contract and deposit request

Report on the monthly and yearly sales targets for the venue, undertake competitor analyses and report on the performance of the venue

Raise the final invoice after the event has been held and manage the customer account to ensure repeat bookings have been explored

Collate testimonials for future marketing campaigns and assist the marketing manager with online reviews

the venue sales manager will be responsible for working on identifying potential clients for the venue, leading a sales campaign and taking responsibility for converting enquiries into bookings. Table 12.3 illustrates some of the responsibilities that a venue sales manager will have.

A venue-based sales role will require a certain level of confidence when communicating with people over the telephone, in person and via email. Experience of designing a sales campaign and taking a leading role in a variety of sales activities such as attending trade shows and leading fam trips will be essential and a good knowledge of the events industry, potential clients and competing venues will be vital. Table 12.4 is a sample of a job description for a venue-based sales role which further illustrates the type of skills and knowledge needed for this type of employment.

Table 12.4 Essential skills for venue sales roles

Confident communicator (verbal and written) and presenter with the ability to influence over the phone and face to face

Excellent interpersonal skill and able to quickly establish connections with a variety of organisations and individuals

Experience of planning and delivering engagement/sales activities and initiatives

Able to effectively manage multiple projects simultaneously and thrive under pressure and when working to tight deadlines

Organised, energised, with entrepreneurial flair and able to develop creative solutions/ideas

Flexible approach to working outside of normal office hours (e.g., able to work evenings and weekends)

Very good administrative and financial management skills with a high attention to detail

Computer literate and preferably skilled in maintaining a venue diary

A team player who is also able to work on their own initiative

12.5 VENUE OPERATIONS ROLES

In most venues, once the sales person has converted an enquiry into a booking, there will be a process of transferring the client and the responsibility for the booking to a member of the team who has a more operational role. Operational staff have the responsibility for working with clients in the lead up to their event. They ensure that the event can take place safely and effectively on site and this can involve overseeing some of the event preparation that the client (the event manager) is undertaking. Table 12.5 illustrates some of the typical responsibilities and requirements of an operational role.

Frequently an operational role can also involve an element of sales, particularly for trying to upsell the venue in terms of room, equipment and catering bookings. Operational staff also often fulfil the event day role of the duty manager which is a highly responsible role. As such, operational staff often need to be very experienced and possess specific skills as shown in Table 12.6.

12.6 DUTY MANAGER ROLES

As indicated in Table 12.6, operational roles usually require a high level of competency in delivering safe events and the responsibilities of the duty manager often forms part of a broader, operational role. However, some venues, particularly ones with high levels of public activity taking place regularly, will appoint trained duty managers with a specific function within the operational team. This is common in theatres, hotels, attractions and other venues that are often visited by members of the public. The duty manager will usually have a strong presence in the front of house area of the venue. They will oversee all of the day-to-day activities in the venue, including any public or private events. As discussed in Chapter 11, the duty manager assumes overall responsibility for everyone on site and for all the activities taking place in the venue. Therefore, previous experience of supervising a diverse workforce (e.g. caterers, receptionists, porters, technicians, etc.) is essential. Typically, the duty manager will be a highly trained individual and will have accrued much front-line customer service experience in a venue role.

Table 12.5 Venue operations job description

Liaise closely with clients and contractors to ensure that all event details are obtained, checked and properly acted upon both in advance of and during the event

Produce key event documentation (e.g. operational schedule, pre- and post-event briefings and reports, risk and fire risk assessments)

Set, communicate and maintain timelines and priorities on every project ensuring maximum customer satisfaction for clients

Undertake presentations and site visits and maximise ancillary revenues

Advise clients on the feasibility of room/furniture/equipment configurations, the operation of PA and lighting equipment, health and safety and fire regulation issues, venue procedures and relevant legislation

Monitor the venue's nominated contractors/preferred suppliers (e.g. standards of service they provide to clients)

On event day, meet and greet clients, have responsibility for and ensure that all their needs are met during their event

Fulfil the role of duty manager (e.g., take responsibility for the health and safety management of events)

Manage the financial closure of an event (e.g., reconciling orders, compiling recharges and providing the finance department with the details for the final invoice)

Update and maintain the floor plans and the technical specification of the venue

Conduct post-event reporting and analysis including client evaluations

Maintain an accurate inventory of all furniture, equipment and fittings in the venues and report on their condition to the venue manager

Table 12.6 Essential skills for venue operations roles

Several years' experience within a similar role

A passion for delivering exceptional service in a client-facing role

Highly organised with strong negotiation and decision-making skills

Strong project management and administrative skills with meticulous attention to detail

Experience in managing budgets and forecasting results in a similar sized venue

Possesses strong commercial acumen, with experience in increasing profitability in a tight market sector

Excellent leadership and communication skills

Calm, efficient with the ability to work well under pressure

Good knowledge of health and safety and security procedures (ideally with a current Institution of Occupational Safety and Health certificate)

Personal licence holder

Qualified first aider

It is common for duty managers to be qualified first aiders, to hold a personal licence, to be a certified door supervisor and to have obtained a health and safety qualification. As such it can take a while to build up the necessary skills, experience and qualifications to secure work as a duty manager but much of this can be gained in an operational role.

12.7 SPECIFIC VENUE ROLES

A number of venues that target specific types of events, will frequently appoint a member of the venue team to work purely with certain clients. For example, a number of venues now have a dedicated, in-house wedding co-ordinator. This person will work closely with couples who are having their wedding or reception at the venue. This can be quite a complex role, particularly if the venue is licensed to host wedding ceremonies, as the coordinator may be required to offer advice on the legalities of organising a civil wedding service. Similarly, some venues will have an in-house business events specialist or conference co-ordinator. This person will focus on working with clients who are organising meetings, conferences and other corporate events. Different skills are often essential to some of these roles as, for example, a wedding coordinator will work closely with many couples who have no experience of organising events at all. Additionally, as a wedding is a highly personal and emotional event, a wedding coordinator needs to be diplomatic and caring as well as able to deal with the high stress levels often felt by couples as their wedding day nears. On the other hand, a business events specialist will need exceptional organisational and negotiation skills and will become adept at working with busy and often demanding professional conference organisers. Venue staff who specialise in working with particular clients, or on specific types of events, will often have a mixture of marketing, sales and operational roles and will fulfil many of the responsibilities outlined in Tables 12.1 to 12.6.

Venues with an in-house catering function will usually have specific members of their management team dedicated to looking after the catering operation. Frequently this role is called the food and beverage manager, banqueting manager or simply the catering manager although sometimes the title of duty manager also applies to this role. The skills required to fulfil this role will include experience of catering operations, menu creation and working with clients, as well as the ability to manage a large team. Knowledge of food hygiene regulations as well as alcohol licensing are also prerequisites for employment in a senior catering role.

Some venues will also have a dedicated technician on staff and this is particularly true of venues that own a lot of AV equipment. This is often a complex and specialised role as it involves a knowledge of lighting and sound design, production, stage management, electrical testing and health and safety practice and legislation. Prerequisites for such a role can include an in-depth knowledge of specific health and safety guidance, regulations and best practice as well as experience of using specific equipment and software. Technicians often have financial management responsibilities and oversee teams and are required to have an electrical qualification and advanced IT skills.

As illustrated in this chapter, venues often employ a range of highly trained and qualified individuals to fulfil very specialised roles and these are summarised in Figure 12.2.

Figure 12.2 Specialist roles.

12.8 KEY SKILLS FOR VENUE STAFF

Although most of the roles of the various members of the venue staff are specific and require a particular set of competencies and knowledge, there are a number of key skills that are common to nearly, if not all, venue-based roles.

IT proficiency is a basic requirement of most jobs today and venues will often use a mixture of standard and bespoke software. Microsoft applications including Word, Excel, PowerPoint and Outlook are used widely and candidates for venue vacancies will usually be required to be proficient in their usage. Most venues use specific software for the management of their accounts as well as their diary or room booking system. While knowledge of specific packages can be advantageous, new staff can often be trained on the job in how to use the software.

The ability to negotiate is frequently listed as a key requirement of any new venue staff. This is because of the nature of the events industry, which involves working with others, often in an advisory capacity. In most venue-based roles, you will find yourself negotiating with a variety of clients, contractors and suppliers and the ability to work with and persuade others becomes an essential tool of the trade. Similarly, given the customer facing nature of the events industry, experience of working with people, and particularly customers and clients, is essential

Figure 12.3 Key skills for venue staff.

if you want to secure a role in a venue. Demonstrable skills in teamwork and the ability to work alone, is a typical dichotomy of employment in any industry today. Many venue-based jobs are solo roles, in that you will be the only person at the venue with your responsibilities. However, you will be part of a larger team either through being a member of a specific department or because you are a part of the venue personnel. Budget, or financial management skills are also a common requirement of venue staff. Most venue employees are either responsible for spending or making money and, in some cases, both. Therefore, you may be asked to manage a budget that is to be spent on advertising, for example, or you may be asked to take responsibility for reaching certain sales targets. In either case, you will need to have had some relevant experience that you can highlight in your job application.

Many of the skills required to be an effective venue employee are referred to as 'soft skills'. These are more recognisable as personal attributes, and possessing them is an indication of your ability to interact effectively and harmoniously with other people. Tact and diplomacy are examples of such skills and these are highly regarded qualities because both event and venue managers will often find themselves dealing with tense situations and difficult clients and suppliers. Additionally, attitude and flexibility are important assets in venue staff as you will need to demonstrate an ability to get on with a range of different people, sometimes when you are working closely with them on challenging events. Also, as the events industry is not a nine to five sector, a commitment to working evenings, weekends and sometimes long shifts is another essential attribute.

12.9 ACADEMIC QUALIFICATIONS FOR VENUE STAFF

Although there are no entry requirements for people wishing to join the events industry, the route into employment and up the career ladder is certainly easier if you have both experience and relevant qualifications. Although you do not need a degree to become an event or venue manager, many job adverts now indicate that a relevant degree is a prerequisite. Given the broad nature of the events industry, there are a number of degree courses that would be deemed relevant for particular roles. Subjects including sports management, psychology, sociology, tourism, hospitality and business management as well as stage production or arts management are just some of the subjects that are relevant to roles in venue and event management.

There are, however, a growing number of specific undergraduate and postgraduate degrees in event or venue management and these began to appear in the early 1990s (Getz, 2012). This was part of the trend in western countries in particular for developing and adapting degrees to meet the growing demand for vocational programmes (Jarvis, 2000). The majority of these courses are offered by universities who focus on providing degrees that offer preparation for a profession (Brooks and Mackinnon, 2001), and the increased political attention toward higher education degrees which support a growing workforce has contributed to their growing prestige (Gray and Griffin, 2000).

From university to university, the classification of event management varies, with some institutions offering it as a Bachelor or Master of Science and others as a Bachelor or Master of Arts. Similarly, some universities locate event management within a faculty of arts and others within social science or business. There can be quite a variation in what is offered as part of a degree in event or venue management too. But most degrees reflect the broad nature of the events industry and the discipline can include the study of sociology, semiotics and anthropology as well as event planning and delivery.

THE INDUSTRY EXPERT'S VIEW 12.1

EVENT MANAGEMENT DEGREES

Kiri Collymore-Hunter, BA (Hons), Event Management Graduate

In one way or another I have always been involved in events but I never saw it as an industry. That was until I was studying business at college and I had an event management module. Learning about the different kinds of events and the process of what's involved convinced me to start applying for event management courses with universities. I have always been a natural organiser, it's not so much a skill but a characteristic, and the content of an event management course complimented my skills, my passion and it was something I knew would work for me.

The course I picked had a venue management module which I took to instantly. It demonstrated elements of event management that were intricate, the things that make it tick. I enjoyed the sophisticated level of detail behind the planning of events such as looking at contracts. It really made me appreciate the finer, background work that goes into an event. I also had the opportunity to plan an event for a real client. This allowed me to put into practice all the skills and knowledge I had accrued and I learnt so much from tackling team conflict to conducting meetings with a client – it was a valuable experience.

I truly can't say enough about the lecturers I met at university! I count myself as fortunate to have had such passionate lecturers who gave us access to details about the events industry some could only dream about. They knew their subject and they were very easy to connect with. They were always honest as they wanted us to see the industry for what it is, there were no false impressions about what we were taking on. And they were incredibly supportive. They really believed in our potential and they were so easy to talk to.

The course was generously planned to allow time during the week for both study and work experience and I volunteered at conferences, charity, entertainment and sports events and took on two intern positions to really embrace the practical side of events as much as the academic side. This also taught me time management skills which we all know are an important factor in event management. The whole time we were being prepped for when we ventured out into the industry.

Now that I have graduated I am working for a housing organisation charity as a conference and facilities assistant. I'm also working with a friend to start up a wedding consultancy business using an online platform. We've recognised that the UK has adopted many trends from the US and linking this to how hectic people's lifestyles are, we found ourselves creating My Wedding Planner. Whether a couple wants wedding planning support throughout the whole journey or help here and there, we can support their needs and requirements. It's an exciting development! We have a very long way to go but we are thrilled at undertaking a venture that we're both very passionate about. The wonderful thing about events is that regardless of the sector or purpose, they're about creating special moments for other people and that just cannot be competed with. It's a challenging industry to work in but it's equally rewarding.

12.10 PRACTICAL QUALIFICATIONS FOR VENUE STAFF

As well as there now being an array of degree level courses in venue and event management, there are a number of practical qualifications that are particularly useful for anyone wanting to develop a career in the industry as illustrated in Figure 12.4.

A valid first aid certificate is particularly useful for anyone seeking to work in an operational or front-line role at a venue that will involve coming into contact with the public and there are a number of organisations that offer first aid training, occasionally free of charge. For anyone interested in a hospitality related role, such as an F&B manager, a food hygiene certificate is essential as this will cover the basic food storage, preparation and service regulations. A personal licence and a door supervisor's licence are also useful if you are looking to work in a licensed venue, particularly if you are going to have an operational role and will be present at functions such as dinners and celebrations. NEBOSH (the National Examination Board in Occupational Safety and Health) is one example of a practical qualification that is related to risk management in the workplace. This type of qualification is also particularly useful for operational staff including duty managers and technicians.

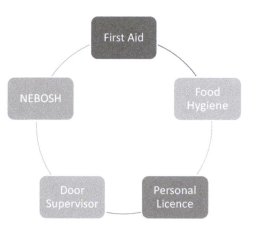

Figure 12.4 Practical qualifications for venue staff.

12.11 GETTING EXPERIENCE

One of the challenges of securing any type of employment when you are just entering a profession, is being able to demonstrate that you already have relevant experience. However, there are a number of ways of building up your experience of working in venues and on events. Volunteering your time can be a very easy way to secure relevant experience as there are a number of venue and event managers that would be very amenable to requests to help out for free. This can be particularly true of non-profit making venues such as church halls and museums as well the number of charities and associations that frequently put on events. There are also a number of venues that will take on casual staff to help out during their busiest times of the year. For example, attractions add to their staffing levels during the summer when they are in peak season. Similarly, hotels will often recruit extra staff over the summer and also Christmas holiday period. Academic venues such as universities, will often be very busy during the summer vacation period when there are no students on campus. Their rooms are often filled with conferences and summer schools and therefore extra staff are needed to help out with these events. Many theatres run busy summer seasons of shows and will take on extra staff at this time as well as during their exceptionally busy pantomime season in winter. And sporting venues will usually employ a high number of casual staff to fulfil stewarding and catering roles on event days, whether that's for a concert or sporting competition. Vacancies for casual roles will often be advertised on the venue's website or via local job centres, volunteering bureaux and in local papers, so a targeted search for jobs in a particular geographic location can be fruitful in the run up to busy times of the year for specific venues.

12.12 LOOKING FOR VENUE-BASED EMPLOYMENT

Once you are ready to begin the search for employment there are a number of ways to identify and target venues in particular. An increasing number of specialist recruitment agencies now operate within the events industry and have a vacancy search facility on their website. Some sites will put all venue roles into a particular category, others won't but it is usually obvious from the job description if the post is based in a venue. Table 12.7 lists some of the specialist recruitment consultants.

If you are keen to focus your search on a particular geographic area, then it can be useful to build up your own list of websites to check for vacancies on a regular basis. Most venues advertise their vacancies on their website. Therefore, identify all of the types of venues in the area that you are interested in and look for the careers/jobs/vacancies or about us section of their website. Don't forget to consider universities and other academic institutions, attractions and other unique venues, hotels and hospitality providers, sporting venues as well as any purpose-built conference and exhibition centres. A number of umbrella organisations will

Table 12.7 List of event management recruitment agencies

Albany Appointments	www.albany-appointments.co.uk
Caterer	www.caterer.com
Dragonfly Recruitment	www.dragonflyrecruitment.com
Eligo	www.eligo.co.uk/events-recruitment
ESP Recruitment	www.esprecruitment.co.uk
JB Event Recruitment	www.jbeventrecruitment.com
Live Recruitment	www.live-recruitment.co.uk
Reed	www.reed.co.uk
Regan and Dean	www.regananddean.com

Table 12.8 List of industry publications

Attractions Management	www.attractionsmanagement.com
BizBash	www.bizbash.com
Conference News	www.conference-news.co.uk
Event Industry News	www.eventindustrynews.com
Event Magazine	www.eventmagazine.co.uk
Exhibition News	www.exhibitionnews.co.uk
M&IT (Meetings and Incentive Travel)	www.meetpie.com
MeetingsNet	www.meetingsnet.com
Sports Management	www.sportsmanagement.co.uk
The Stage	www.thestage.co.uk
Stand Out	www.standoutmagazine.co.uk

advertise on behalf of their members, for example, www.jobs.ac.uk allows you to search for roles in UK academic institutions and www.gov.uk/jobsearch allows you to search for public sector work.

There are of course a number of general recruitment agencies and national and local newspapers that will advertise jobs too. However, industry specific sources can be more effective for identifying specific venue-based roles and Table 12.8 lists some of these industry publications.

12.13 CAREER DEVELOPMENT IN VENUES

Despite the growth of the industry and also the popularity of event management degrees, rather little is known about career development in the events sector (Getz, 2012). However, as you begin to accrue skills and experience there is the potential to grow your career and seek promotion. Typically, entry level roles in the industry will be supportive in nature but as you gain experience and skills you can look to follow the typical route to co-ordinator, executive, manager and then director. There are a number of online resources to help you to develop a career plan and to identify and target roles that you aspire to reach. Industry sources such MPI (www.mpiweb.org/portal/career) offer much professional development and career planning advice. ESP Recruitment offers a salary calculator facility and reports on average salaries by role and sector (www.esprecruitment.co.uk/salary-calculator.asp).

To be successful in the events industry, you must identify your own skills and interest and match these to the needs of the employer (Bowdin *et al.*, 2011). Therefore, career planning begins with understanding what your short- and long-term goals are. Identifying your goals, as well as recognising what type of roles you enjoy as well as do not enjoy, are the first steps towards professional development planning. Subscribing to industry publications is one way of identifying future opportunities, searching job vacancies and also reading profiles of leading industry professionals; all of this can be inspirational in terms of helping you to think ahead to what you would like to achieve in the future. The next few pages are devoted to sharing with you some of the success stories of industry professionals who are enjoying a venue-based career. They may just provide you with some tips or inspiration to find the sort of role that you might enjoy yourself in the future!

THE INDUSTRY EXPERT'S VIEW 12.2

WORKING IN A HOTEL

Amy Leitch, Conference and Events Manager, The Holiday Inn

Working in a hotel is great fun! Each day offers a new opportunity to interact with new clients. From corporate clients, booking training sessions and meetings, to the general public booking events such as weddings, family parties and festive celebrations; every day is different.

In some cases, your client may be the person holding the meeting, in other cases it may be someone's PA or an event agency placing the enquiry on behalf of another company. Most have experience with booking venues, but from time to time there are

---

continued

people who need guidance and help. Brides and grooms can be extremely challenging as they are putting their trust in you to deliver their special day paid for by their hard-earned money. Their demands can be frequent and quite often they are not organised as this is a one off event they haven't had experience of planning before.

Showrounds of the hotels facilities forms part of the daily routine and are imperative when it comes to securing new business. Knowing the hotel well and how it works operationally as well as behind the scenes is key to ensuring an event goes well and that we meet the client's expectations.

It is often good to gain work experience or part time work within a hotel to help establish yourself and gain a greater understanding of the industry. If the opportunity arises, working on reception or in the food and beverage department of a hotel will give you some operational experience and will help you understand the industry.

Hotels are often open to taking on work experience candidates; this can enable you to spend several weeks in various hotels – something which is helpful if you are unsure of the type of property you are looking to work in; whether it be a boutique hotel, branded hotel, independent or budget hotel.

With hotels comes the opportunity to work as part of a large team. Different departments are reliant on one another for information. For example, the events team liaises with chef for menus, reservations and housekeeping for bedrooms and the food and beverage operations team for event requirements and set up.

Being so reliant on other departments can sometime be frustrating, especially with those departments who work shifts. It is also challenging as events take place throughout the day and sometimes it's not always possible to be on site to meet your clients.

Overall, working in hotels is really enjoyable and is great especially if you can't decide which events you want to spend your time planning! If you're looking for a varied role where you can be involved in lots of different aspects of the event then this could be your venue of choice!

THE INDUSTRY EXPERT'S VIEW 12.3

WORKING IN A UNIQUE VENUE

Katrina Rodier, Receptionist and Facilities Coordinator at the House of Commons

Working in the Palace of Westminster has so far been a very exciting and unique opportunity within my career. In my current role, I am constantly dealing with a diverse range of people, including members of the public, press, Members of Parliament, Members' Staff and House Staff. My team specifically deals with the logistics of the building; we are the glue that holds everything together. It is not unlike that of being behind the scenes of a theatre production. We run the main reception desks, committee events corridor and arrange onsite office accommodation for Members and other staff. We deal with any faults reported around the building and ensure all offices are equipped with the correct materials. We've dealt with issues such as staff being locked out of their offices, flooding in the more medieval parts of the Palace and events being over-capacity due to MPs inviting too many friends!

I started working at the Houses of Parliament back in 2014 as a part-time Visitor Assistant where my main role was assisting members of the public with access into the Palace and on guided tours. I simply applied for this job on the House of Commons careers website and I was a strong candidate due to having previous experience working in various venues and on events which attracted a diverse range of customers and therefore gave me strong customer service skills. My current role was offered on the same website, and having been previously security checked and an internal candidate meant I easily transferred across within Parliament. Starting in one role and building up my knowledge and skills worked to my advantage greatly.

The challenge of being a member of a team within this venue is having to deal with strong and often challenging members of staff, partly due to traditional services that are slowly being phased out or kept in place. What is also challenging is the vast size of the Palace. It often can take up to fifteen minutes to get to a specific room or place; especially when the House of Commons are sitting and certain areas become out of bounds. When you are pushed for time, you have to often do a bit of running.

One aspect of my job that I love is being surrounded by such beautiful architecture and interior design. I am constantly learning about the history of the building and I tend to find a new shortcut or route every day when completing a job.

One tip I would give to anybody when working in any venue is to be courteous and friendly to everybody you encounter within your workplace. Treat everybody with the same level of respect and kindness you would wish to receive yourself. You never know what kind of friends or contacts you can build just from being friendly, open and polite to those around you. I have found within my role that other members of staff are more willing to help you and work with you if you are approachable.

THE INDUSTRY EXPERT'S VIEW 12.4

WORKING IN A SPORTING VENUE

Laura Tringham, Marketing Executive, Northampton Saints RFC, www.franklinsgardens.co.uk; www.northamptonsaints.co.uk

From my time working in the events industry, I have thoroughly enjoyed being part of a brand that is a venue. With that, everything is under one roof. You have endless content at your fingertips and you are able to fully immerse yourself in the brand, understanding the ins and outs of the venue. That helps when you come to host an event at the venue. You have the knowledge of the building – its history and future plans – and that, alongside the needs of your client, allows you to stage a successful event. Being onsite and having that knowledge means you can be proactive to deal with any potential barriers, and be on hand to resolve any issues that surface. With different types of venues comes varying demographics and a whole range of customer expectations but, regardless

continued

of what project you are working on, you stick to the same basic principles. All venues have unique USPs and, to be successful in your job role, you need to discover those, focus on them, and understand how they can both benefit and hinder your client's event. The way you approach your work, and how clients approach you, will vary with the different characteristics of the venue. For example, if you work in a hotel, the client may be at a business event but staying at the hotel as a leisure guest. This will require different needs compared to those delegates whose event is at a sports venue, and may wish to be associated with not only the brand but also the professional sports figures as part of their event day. Keeping people happy is vital. Working in a venue means that last-minute changes are prevalent, so flexibility and adaptability is key. You need to be able to support all of your colleagues within the venue and ensure you have the basic knowledge of all departments in order to address all issues, from both an operational and commercial perspective. You must understand the priorities of your client as well as the restrictions you may face as part of working in a venue – consider everything from health and safety limitations to data protection. There is no hiding behind the unknown when working at a venue. Needless to say, what I enjoy most about my job is supporting a variety of departments, adding to my experience. This ensures my day is never the same, from one to the next. You are able to build on your knowledge by learning something new every day. Working in a venue, you should always expect the unexpected.

THE INDUSTRY EXPERT'S VIEW 12.5

WORKING IN A PURPOSE-BUILT VENUE

Ashley Simcox, Assistant Director, Experience Management Suntec Singapore Convention and Exhibition Centre

Once reserved and introverted, Ashley Simcox now spearheads the experience management team in the world's leading meetings and conference centre. Still a few years shy of 30, Ashley is already a veteran in the hospitality industry with more than 10 years of experience. Upon completing his event management studies in university, his subsequent stints managing sales and corporate events in hotels paved the way for his big break with Suntec Singapore, his first international role away from the UK, where he is from. Three years on, Ashley is more passionate than ever for the industry, and has managed multiple international conferences, conventions, pop concerts and corporate dinners for an extensive portfolio of clients in the venue. In this interview, Ashley shares his insights on the industry, his experience and his advice to aspiring event management professionals.

How did you get into hospitality/event management?

I started early while I was still in school back in the UK. I was only 14 then, and I worked part-time at a golf club doing a variety of junior roles – everything from banquet service to kitchen porter. When I turned 18, I also did a little bit of bar work.

This exposure to the hospitality industry fuelled my passion and naturally led me to take an events management degree at university where I had the opportunity to conduct a number of events internships and I've not looked back since. My subsequent roles in various luxury hotels involved managing event sales for corporate meetings, weddings and social events.

What's the biggest difference between managing events in a hotel and a convention centre?

Event management has the same set of fundamentals across venues, however, hotel events are usually smaller and more intimate, while events at convention and exhibitions centres are often much grander which gives you greater exposure to work with the big players within the industry and work on flagship events which are on an international scale.

Not forgetting the faster pace in Singapore. I thought dealing with 80 weddings a year in a hotel was crazy enough within the UK, but I actually managed a record eight events in a day here in Singapore. Then again, I probably wouldn't want a job that needs me to be sitting around in the office from 9 to 5.

How do you manage effectively when you have multiple events on hand?

Good planning is king – without a systematic approach during the planning stages, the event will never go to plan. It is also important to keep things simple and have good time management skills. If you do adequate preparation during your pre-event planning, you minimise the chances of mistakes or interruptions when it comes to on-site execution.

Given the number of events held at our convention centre, we build functionality and processes into our DNA to ensure consistency for our client.

Is event management something you see yourself doing in the next 10 years? What do you enjoy most about it?

I think I found my forte in event management. Knowing that not one event is the same gives me a sense of achievement and fulfilment when I see it through. The fast-paced industry consistently energises you and keeps you on your toes as there's always something new to learn.

Your best advice to aspiring event management professionals?

Our industry is built on the fundamentals of people meeting – always push yourself to meet new people and never shy away from an opportunity to learn or network.

THE INDUSTRY EXPERT'S VIEW 12.6

WORKING IN AN ACADEMIC VENUE

Peter Duckett, Events Assistant, the University of Northampton

As an Events Assistant in the Marketing and International Relations department at the University of Northampton, I support the Event Manager with any marketing, student recruitment and PR related events. Day-to-day tasks include answering the main events inboxes, creating marketing documents that will be used at events, working with wider university departments to support their events and working on various projects. One of my main ongoing jobs is managing the student ambassadors. This includes their recruitment, training, timesheet approval, posting of jobs and being their main point of contact to the university.

I found my job by being on the mailing list of a general university jobs website, which would regularly email me when marketing related jobs became available. This led me to the University of Northampton's website, where I applied using the online form. Whilst studying event management at university, I would regularly take voluntary event assistant opportunities presented alongside my study. The majority of these were one-off events assistant roles, however I did also complete a 4-month placement at a hotel as part of the course. Working on the placement allowed me to understand how a venue uses its different teams to ensure their customers got the service they were expecting. Upon graduating, before my current role, I worked as an administrator for a residential activity centre. Overall, having experience of handling enquires by phone and email, programming planning, interacting with guests and previous work experience whilst at university, enabled me to develop transferable skills that I showed my current employer during the interview process.

The main skills I have developed during my time at the University of Northampton have been leadership and management skills. Due to the level of responsibly given to me when managing 100 Student Ambassadors, it is crucial that I know each of them has the relevant training to perform the tasks required of them to comply with the law and internal policy. This means I must spot when issues could arise and solve problems before they get out of hand or making tough decisions that are for the greater good of the organisation. These transferable skills will help me later in life when applying for other roles as I progress in my career.

One of the best things about the job is that no two days are the same. Whilst like every job there are routine day-to-day tasks, each individual project or event has its own objectives that need to be achieved. Working with the wider marketing team and other university departments requires good communication to ensure the unmoveable deadlines are met. My role provides opportunities to problem solve both in the planning stages and whilst the events are occurring. Even though problems during events are not desirable, I enjoy the sense of achievement that comes when I resolve them under a time-pressured situation.

In a competitive jobs market, to get a job, you have to have done the job before. My advice to undergraduates is to take every opportunity that they feel may advance their career, whether paid or unpaid. You don't want to work for free upon graduating because you don't have the transferable skills and experience required to get the job you desire. In the future, I would like to progress my career within the area of events marketing as it allows the creation and implementation of events that endeavour to achieve a greater objective. Additionally, you get to work with a variety of internal and external stakeholders, as well as notable VIPs.

12.14 CONCLUSION

The events industry continues to expand year on year and this growth provides a range of employment and career development opportunities for aspiring professionals. Much of this employment is venue-based, with a number of specific marketing, sales and operational roles. Venue managers and their teams need to have a range of skills, experience, knowledge and competencies to fulfil the demanding but rewarding nature of the role. Venues are an excellent foundation for career development as these roles can be more stable than the episodic nature of event specific roles, which often result in professionals frequently changing jobs (Getz, 2012). Working in a venue can be challenging and demanding and high levels of tact, diplomacy and flexibility are essential traits of successful venue managers. Venue staff need to be creative, organised and confident negotiators, familiar with the quirks of their building and able to attract and inspire event managers. The rewards of working in a venue is that every day will be varied, every event that you work on will be unique and will leave you with lasting memories of what you have helped others to achieve.

12.15 FURTHER READING

In addition to all of the websites listed throughout this chapter, the following sources are particularly useful for further reading on the subject of:

Roles in venue marketing

Rogers, T. and Davidson, R. (2016) *Marketing Destinations and Venues for Conferences, Conventions and Business Events* (2nd edn). London: Routledge.

Roles in venue sales

Davidson, R. and Hyde, A. (2014) *Winning Meetings and Events for Your Venue*. Oxford: Goodfellows.

Roles in venue operations

Schwarz, E., Hall, S. and Shibli, S. (2015) *Sports Facility Operations Management* (3rd edn). London: Routledge.

GLOSSARY

Acoustics The properties of a venue that determine how sounds are transmitted within it

Apron The part of the stage which protrudes through and beyond the proscenium arch

Attrition A fine for failing to use all of the rooms that were booked for an event

Auditorium The seating area of a venue (usually a theatre)

AV Audio-visual (equipment for sound and lighting)

Back of house The backstage area of an event or venue

Bed stock The number of hotel rooms

Blackout facilities The ability to block natural daylight (filling a room)

Bureau An office (plural: bureaux)

Business tourism Travel for business related purposes

Cherry picker Hydraulic crane for raising/lowering people

Commission An amount of money paid to an agent

Corporate social responsibility A form of corporate self-regulation involving assessing an organisation's impact on society and evaluating their responsibilities

Dais A raised table or low platform for a lectern

Day delegate rate The venue hire charge per attendee (usually to cover the use of one room and refreshments)

Demographic Statistical data related to groups within a population

Dock door The entrance to a loading area of a venue

Evacuation chair A chair that facilities the safe evacuation of a less able bodied person down stairs

Experience economy An economy based on creating memorable events or experiences for customers

Fam trip A familiarisation visit (e.g. to a destination)

Floor loading limit/capacity The amount of weight that can be placed on the floor of a venue at any one time

Floorplan A map of the venue showing the layout of rooms

Flown Hung (e.g. The scenery is flown on stage)

Force majeure French for *superior force* meaning an unexpected and disruptive event

Front of house The public area of an event or venue

Get in/get out Period of time before and after an event for setting up and dismantling equipment etc.

Globalisation The process by which businesses or other organisations develop international influence or start operating on an international scale

Gobo A stencil used to shape or alter the pattern of light

Green room A lounge provided to performers to use before and after their performance

Hospitality The provision of refreshments and/or accommodation

Induction loop Equipment to help people with hearing impairments by reducing the effect of background noise by converting sound into a magnetic field

Infra-red system Equipment to help people with hearing impairments via a transmitter that converts sound to infrared light that is transmitted to the receiver

Infrastructure Physical attributes (of a destination) such as venues, transport systems etc.

Latticework A structure or pattern made with crossing strips

Lavalier A type of microphone that is usually attached to clothing

Lead time Period of time between starting to plan an event and event day

Lectern A stand for a speaker to use to stand against/rest papers on

Liability insurance Insurance that protects the purchaser from lawsuits and similar claims

Licensable activities Activities for which a licence must be obtained before they can go ahead

Lighting rig A structure that holds lights in place

Merchandise Products for sale

MICE Meetings, incentive travel, conferences and exhibitions

Moulding A decoratively shaped piece of material such as wood or stone

Muster point The place where everyone must assemble in the event of an emergency

Operational schedule A written record of all the event day activities

PA system A public address system (enabling announcements etc.)

Pinch point A part of the venue which is likely to get congested

Proscenium arch The frame that divides the stage from the auditorium or seating area

Rack rate The advertised price of a hotel room

Raked stage A stage that slopes upwards

Residential event An event at which attendees will stay overnight

REVPAR Revenue per available room; the maximum amount of money that can be made from hiring out rooms

RFP Request for proposal

Rider The contract provided by a speaker, performer or other artist

Rigging Fixing lighting, sound and scenic devices to the theatre structure

Risk assessment A systematic process of evaluating the potential risks that may be involved in a particular activity or undertaking

Roving microphone A wireless microphone that can be held as the speaker walks around the room

Service lift A (usually large) lift to enable the movement of goods or equipment

Service road A usually private road giving access to deliver items to a venue

Shell scheme Built exhibition stands, clipped together and divided by walls

Sound desk A mixing console or piece of kit for controlling the sound

Sprigs Trestle tables

Subvention An offer of support (usually financial)

Sustainability The avoidance of the depletion of natural resources in order to maintain an ecological balance

Tabs Curtains

Technical specification A list of equipment available at the venue and staging/room information

Trade pitch A stand or space for a vendor to sell items at an event

Trade show An exhibition relating to a particular industry or type of business

Truss A means of lifting equipment (a truss can be flown or supported from the ground)

Wash A general use of coloured light across a stage

Yield management A technique for altering charges in line with demand

BIBLIOGRAPHY

The AA (2016a) *Accommodation Star Ratings*. Available at: www.theaa.com/travel/accommodation_restaurants_grading.html#tabview%3Dtab1 (accessed 1 August 2016).

The AA (2016b) *Common Standards for Hotel and Guest Accommodation*. Available at: www.theaa.com/travel/accommodation_restaurants_grading.html#tabview%3Dtab0 (accessed 1 August 2016).

Adongo, R. (2011) Quality Grading of United Kingdom Meeting Venues. *Journal of Convention and Event Tourism*, 12, (3), 206–231.

Andrews, H. and Leopold, T. (2013) *Events and The Social Sciences*. London: Routledge.

Ascot (2016) *Short History*. Available at: www.ascot.co.uk/Short-History-Ascot (accessed 9 May 2016).

Athens and Epidaurus Festival (2009) Home Page. Available at: http://greekfestival.gr/en/ (accessed 19 July 2016).

Baggs, S. (2013) *Brainstorming Extraordinary Events (Part One)*. Available at: https://lateralevents.com/brainstorming-extraordinary-events-part-one (accessed 26 July 2016).

Ball, C. (2011) *12+ Meetings Technology Trends to Watch for 2012*. Available at: www.corbinball.com/articles_technology/index.cfm?fuseaction=cor_av&artID=8756 (accessed 9 December 2015).

BBC (2015) *Bucharest Nightclub Fire Leaves Romania Stunned*. Available at www.bbc.co.uk/news/world-europe-34684973 (accessed 17 July 2017).

Beldona, S., Morrison, A. and Anderson, D. (2003) Information Exchange Between Convention and Visitor Bureaus and Hotels in Destination Marketing, *Journal of Convention and Exhibition Management*, 5, (1), 41–56.

Berger, J. (2005) *Profiting with Yield Pricing*. Available at: www.wiglafjournal.com/Pricing/2005/12/Profiting-With-Yield-Pricing (accessed 18 June 2016).

Berridge, G. (2007) *Events Design and Experience*. London: Routledge.

Bladen, C., Kennell, J., Abson, E. and Wilde, N. (2012) *Events Management: An Introduction.* London: Routledge.

Bonnerud, T.E. (2008) The Peripheral Value of Bluetooth Low Energy Wireless Technology, *Wireless Design and Development,* 16, (11), 10–12.

Bowdin, G., Allen, J., O'Toole, W., Harris, R. and Mcdonnell, I. (2011) *Events Management* (3rd edn). London: Routledge.

Bret, A. (2016) *When TFI Visited South Africa*. Available at: http://tfigroup.com/when-tfi-visited-south-africa-2 (accessed 10 August 2016).

British Standards Institution (2016) ISO 20121 *Sustainable Events Management Case Studies*. Available at: www.bsigroup.com/En-GB/Iso-20121-Sustainable-Events-Management/Case-Studies (accessed 21 June 2016).

Brooks, A. and Mackinnon, A. (Eds) (2001) *Gender and the Restructured University*. Buckingham: Open University Press.

Broome Civic Centre (2017) Available at: www.broomeciviccentre.com.au/ (accessed 7 June 2017).

Brown, S., Getz, D., Pettersson, R. and Wallstam, M. (2015) Event Evaluation: Definitions, Concepts and a State of the Art Review, *International Journal of Event and Festival Management*, 6, (2), 135–157.

BVEP (2016) *Subvention Funding Key Area for Event Organisers Finds BVEP Research*. Available at: www.businessvisitsandeventspartnership.com/news/bvep-press-releases/480-subvention-funding-key-area-for-event-organisers-finds-bvep-research (accessed 28 January 2017).

Callow Event Management (2017) Available at: http://callowevents.co.uk (accessed 7 June 2017).

Case, R. (2013) *Events and the Environment*. London: Routledge.

Clancy, H. (2015) *Mobile Apps Change the Face of Corporate Events*. Available at: http://web.a.ebscohost.com/ehost/detail/detail?sid=e6b70a69-5766-4fd5-bad7-1b93aa651e5e%40sessionmgr4001&vid=12&hid=4109&bdata=JnNpdGU9ZWhvc3QtbGl2ZQ%3d%3d#AN=109064512&db=bth (accessed 9 December 2015).

Colston, P. (2014) *CYE Group Reports Rise in Popularity of Unusual Venues*. Available at: www.conference-news.co.uk/2014/08/Cye-Group-Reports-Rise-In-Popularity-Of-Unusual-Venues (accessed 25 July 2016).

Communities and Local Government (2003) *Planning and Access for Disabled People: A Good Practice Guide*. Available at: www.gov.uk/government/uploads/system/uploads/attachment_data/file/7776/156681.pdf (accessed 21 June 2016).

Croke Park (2017) Available at: https://crokepark.ie (accessed 7 June 2017).

Davidson, R. and Hyde, A. (2014) *Winning Meetings and Events for Your Venue*. Oxford: Goodfellows.

Davidson, R. and Rogers, T. (2011) *Marketing Destinations and Venues for Conferences, Conventions and Business Events*. Oxford: Elsevier.

Dingley, R. (2016) How Venue Technology Standards Are Changing. Available at: https://ungerboeck.com/Blog/How-Venue-Technology-Standards-Are-Changing (accessed 17 June 2016).

Disney Weddings (2016) Home page. Available at: www.disneyweddings.com (accessed 9 May 2016).

Dowson, R. and Bassett, D. (2015) *Event Planning and Management*. London: Kogan Page.

Edwards, D., Foley, C., Dwyer, L., Schlenker, K. and Hergesell, A. (2014) Evaluating the Economic Contribution of a Large Indoor Entertainment Venue: An Inscope Expenditure Study, *Event Management*, 18: 407–420.

Egan, J. (2013) What to Look for During a Site Inspection. Available at: www.hoteldesk.co.uk/posts/what-to-look-for-during-a-site-inspection/ (accessed 16 June 2016).

EVCOM (2016) Event Market Trends Survey. Available at: www.evcom.org.uk/Uk-Events-Market-Trends-Survey (accessed 10 May 2016).

Event Manager Blog (2017) Available at: www.eventmanagerblog.com/audiovisual-questions-to-ask (accessed: 7 June 2017).

Events Scotland (2016) Chapter 9 – Event Production: Operations, Equipment, Facilities, Health and Safety. Available at: www.eventscotland.org/Assets/183 (accessed 16 June 2016).

Fenich, G. (2012) *Meetings, Expositions, Events, and Conferences: An Introduction to the Industry* (3rd edn). New Jersey: Pearson.

Ferdinand, N. and Kitchin, P. (2012) *Events Management: An International Approach* (2nd edn). London: SAGE.

The Fire Safety Advice Centre (2015) Available at: www.firesafe.org.uk/ (accessed 7 June 2017).

Fisher, T. (2012) How to Live-Tweet from an Event. Available at: www.socialmediatoday.com/content/how-live-tweet-event (accessed 29 January 2017).

Fullard, M. (2016) Technology and Sustainability Lagging Behind when it comes to Events. Available at: www.conference-news.co.uk/2016/10/technology-and-sustainability-lagging-behind-when-it-comes-to-events/ (accessed 7 June 2016).

Getz, D. (2012) *Event Studies: Theory, Research and Policy for Planned Events* (2nd edn). London: Routledge.

Ghazali, M. and Ghani, M. (2015) A Theoretical Framework of Organization Senior Management's Choice of Convention Venue, *International Conference on Trends in Economics, Humanities and Management*, March 27–28, 14–21.

GL Events (2017) Available at: www.gl-events-venues.com/gl-events-venues-renewed-the-iso-14001-certification-for-the-event-venues-in-france (accessed 7 June 2017).

Goldblatt, J. (2007) *Special Events: The Roots and Wings of Celebration* (5th edn). New York: Wiley.

Gomez, C., Oller, J. and Paradells, J. (2012) Overview and Evaluation of Bluetooth Low Energy: An Emerging Low-power Wireless Technology, *Sensors*, 12, (9), 11734–11753.

Gordon, A. (2014) *How Venues Are Adapting to Meet Planners' Needs*. Available at: www.bizbash.com/How-Venues-Are-Adapting-To-Meet-Planners-Needs/New-York/Story/28732/#.V2fxpzv8-4Z (accessed 15 June 2016).

Gray, D.E. and Griffin, C. (2000) *Post-Compulsory Education and the New Millennium*. London: Jessica Kingsley Publishers.

The Guardian (2015) *Thousands March in Romania after Bucharest Nightclub Fire*. Available at: www.theguardian.com/world/video/2015/nov/04/romania-protest-bucharest-colectiv-nightclub-fire-video (accessed 7 June 2017).

Guinness World Records (2016) Available at: www.guinnessworldrecords.com/World-Records/Oldest-Purpose-Built-Cinema-In-Operation (accessed 25 July 2016).

Haywood, L., Kew, F., Bramham, P., Spink, S., Capenerhurstt, J. and Henry, I. (1995) *Understanding Leisure* (2nd edn). Cheltenham: Stanley Thornes.

Heipel, M. (2012) *How are Venues Adapting to New Industry Trends?* Available at: https://michaelheipel.wordpress.com/2012/06/08/How-Are-Venues-Adapting-To-New-Industry-Trends (accessed 16 June 2016).

Hennessy, M. (2015) *The Top 10 Things to Look for When Choosing a Venue for Your Next Corporate Event*. Available at: http://specialevents.com/Blog/Top-10-Things-Look-When-Choosing-Venue-Your-Next-Corporate-Event (accessed 16 June 2016).

Hischier, R. and Hilty, L. (2002) Environmental Impacts of an International Conference. *Environmental Impact Assessment Review*. 22, 543–557.

Historic UK (2016) History Magazine. Available at: www.historic-uk.com/CultureUK/The-History-of-the-Wimbledon-Tennis-Championships (accessed 8 May 2016).

HM Government (2007) *Fire Safety Risk Assessment – Open Air Events and Venues*. Available at: www.gov.uk/government/uploads/system/uploads/attachment_data/file/14891/fsra-open-air.pdf (accessed 21 June 2016).

HM Government (2013) *Alcohol Licensing Guidance*. Available at: www.gov.uk/guidance/alcohol-licensing (accessed 7 June 2017).

HSE – Health and Safety Executive (2016) *Venue and Site Design*. Available at: www.hse.gov.uk/Event-Safety/Venue-Site-Design.Htm (accessed 15 June 2016).

Ibrahim, M. (2016) *Terrorist Attacks are a Constant Threat for the Events Sector*. Available at: www.raconteur.net/business/terrorist-attacks-are-a-constant-threat-for-the-events-sector (accessed 27 May 2017).

Iwamoto, K. (2016) Drive More RevPAR from Group Meetings. Available at: http://hotelexecutive.com/business_review/4397/drive-more-revpar-from-group-meetings (accessed 18 June 2016).

Jakobson, L. (2015) iBeacon Adoption Grows, *Successful Meetings*, 64, (1), 24.

Jarvis, P. (2000) Lifelong Learning, an Agenda for a Late-modern Future, in: Gray, D.E. and Griffin, C. (Eds) *Post-Compulsory Education and the New Millennium*. London: Jessica Kingsley Publishers.

Kear, J. (2014) *39 Proven Event Planning Strategies for Negotiating with Venues and Hotels – Part 2*. Available at: http://blog.planningpod.com/2014/09/16/39-Proven-Event-Planning-Strategies-Negotiating-Venues-Hotels-Part-2 (accessed 21 June 2016).

King, E. (2015) *Pop Up Venues are a Flexible Route to Success*. Available at: www.conference-news.co.uk/2015/12/pop-up-venues-are-a-flexible-route-to-event-success (accessed 15 May 2016).

Kirk, R. (2015) *Planning an Event? Here's how to Make Venue Managers Love You*. Available at: https://blog.propared.com/Planning-An-Event-Heres-How-To-Make-Venue-Managers-Love-You (accessed 17 June 2016).

Laing, J. and Frost, W. (Eds) (2015) *Rituals and Traditional Events in the Modern World*. London: Routledge.

Ledger, A. (2013) Venues Failing to Understand Clients' Event Technology Needs. Available at: www.citmagazine.com/article/1210253/venues-failing-understand-clients-event-technology-needs (accessed 17 June 2016).

Lee, S. and Fenich, G. (2016) Perceived Fairness of Room Blocks in the Meetings, Incentives, Convention, and Exhibition Industry, *Journal of Convention and Event Tourism*, 17, (2), 159–171.

Lee, S. and Slocum, S. (2015) Understanding the Role of Local Food in the Meeting Industry: An Exploratory Study of Meeting Planners' Perception of Local Food in Sustainable Meeting Planning, *Journal of Convention and Event Tourism*, 16, (1), 45–60.

Lee, S., Close, A. and Love, C. (2010) How Information Quality and Market Turbulence Impact Convention and Visitor Bureaus' Use of Marketing Information: Insights for Destination and Event Marketing, *Journal of Convention and Event Tourism*, 11, (4), 266–292.

Lindsey, K. (2011) *Planning and Managing a Corporate Event*. Oxford: How To Books.

Lloyd, T. (2013) *Choosing the Right Venue for Your Event*. Available at: www.ignitiondg.com/choosing-right-venue-event (accessed 18 June 2016).

Lord's (2016) History. Available at: www.lords.org/history/ (accessed 9 May 2016).

Malhotra, B. (n.d.) *How to Find the Perfect Destination and Venue for Your Next Event*. Available at: www.cvent.com/En/Company/Find-The-Perfect-Event-Destination-And-Venue.Shtml (accessed 16 June 2016).

Marina Bay Sands, Singapore (2017) Available at: www.marinabaysands.com (accessed 7 June 2017).

Masterman, G. (2009) *Strategic Sports Event Management* (2nd edn). London: Butterworth-Heinemann.

Matthews, D. (2007) *Special Event Production: The Resources*. London: Routledge.

Matthews, D. (2016) *Special Event Production: The Process* (2nd edn). London: Routledge.

McKinley, S. (2015) *10 Venues Embracing Sustainability*. Available at: www.eventmanagerblog.com/sustainable-venues (accessed 18 June 2016).

McNeill, A. (2012) *7 Tips for Ethical Fam Trips*. Available at: http://meetingsnet.com/corporate-meetings/7-tips-ethical-fam-trips (accessed 10 August 2016).

Meeting Tomorrow (2017) Available at: https://meetingtomorrow.com/hybrid-events (accessed 7 June 2017).

Milano Congressi (2017) Available at: www.micomilano.it (accessed 7 June 2017).

Morell, K. (2010) *High-Tech Meetings*. Available at: www.meetingstoday.com/Articledetails/Tabid/136/Regionid/0/Articleid/14438/Default.Aspx (accessed 17 June 2016).

Naipaul, S., Wang, Y. and Okumus, F. (2009) Regional Destination Marketing: A Collaborative Approach, *Journal of Travel and Tourism Marketing*, 26, (5), 462–481.

One Events (2017) Available at: http://one-events.co.uk/ (accessed 7 June 2017).

Page, S. (2012) *Tourism Management* (4th edn). London: Butterworth-Heinemann.

Parent, M. and Smith-Swan, S. (2012) *Managing Major Sports Events: Theory and Practice*. London: Routledge.

Park, J., Wu, B., Shen, Y., Morrison, A.M. and Kong, Y. (2014) The Great Halls of China? Meeting Planners' Perceptions of Beijing as an International Convention Destination. *Journal of Convention and Event Tourism*. 15, 244–270.

Paskaleva-Shapira, K. (2007) New Paradigms in City Tourism Management: Redefining Destination Promotion, *Journal Of Travel Research*, 46, (1), 108–114.

Pipe and Glass (2016) About Us page. Available at: www.pipeandglass.co.uk/about-the-pipe-and-glass.aspx (accessed 2 August 2016).

Powell, C. (2013) *How to Deliver Outstanding Corporate Events*. Publisher: Author.

Practically Perfect PA (2012) *How to Negotiate When Planning an Event*. Available at: www.practically perfectpa.com/2012/how-to-negotiate-when-planning-an-event/09/14/ (accessed 7 June 2017).

Proudlock Associates (2016) Home page. Available at: http://proudlockassociates.com (accessed 12 August 2016).

The Purple Guide to Health, Safety and Welfare at Music and Other Events (2017) Available at: www.thepurpleguide.co.uk (accessed 7 June 2017).

Quinn, B. (2013) *Key Concepts in Event Management*. London: SAGE.

Raj, R. and Musgrave, J. (Eds), (2009) *Event Management and Sustainability*. Wallingford: CABI.

Raj, R., Walters, P. and Rashid, T. (2013) *Events Management: Principles and Practice* (2nd edn). London: SAGE.

Ramchandani, N. (2016) Singapore Tourism Industry to get S$700 Million Boost Over Next Five Years. Available at: www.businesstimes.com.sg/government-economy/singapore-tourism-industry-to-get-s700-million-boost-over-next-five-years (accessed 10 May 2016).

Robertson, A. (2013) 10 Steps for Achieving the Perfect Atmosphere at Your Event. Available at: www.eventmanagerblog.com/Event-Atmosphere (accessed 16 June 2016).

Rogers, T. (2013) *Conferences and Conventions: A Global Industry* (3rd edn). London: Routledge.

Rogers, T. and Davidson, R. (2016) *Marketing Destinations and Venues for Conferences, Conventions and Business Events* (2nd edn). London: Routledge.

Ronnie Scott's Jazz Club (2017) Available at: www.ronniescotts.co.uk/ (accessed 7 June 2017).

Ruth Pretty Catering (2017) Available at: www.ruthpretty.co.nz/ (accessed 7 June 2017).

Salter, R. (2013) *The Audio Visual Relationship that Every Event Planner Needs*. Available at: http://blog.socialtables.com/2016/04/13/audio-visual-relationship-every-event-planner-needs (accessed 17 June 2016).

Schwarz, E., Hall, S. and Shibli, S. (2015) *Sports Facility Operations Management* (3rd edn). London: Routledge.

Sekula, A. (2013) *Site Inspection Checklist: 11 Things Event Planner Should Never Forget to Ask*. Available at: www.bizbash.com/Site_Inspection_Checklist_11_Things_Event_Planners_Should_Never_Forget_To_Ask/New-York/Story/25302/#.V2l2ijv8-4Y (accessed 17 June 2016).

Shapiro, M. (2009) Hybrid Events: How Meetings are Blending Virtual with Face-to-Face. Available at: www.meetings-conventions.com/News/Features/Hybrid-Events (accessed 17 June 2016).

Shone, A. and Parry, B. (2010) *Successful Event Management: A Practical Handbook* (3rd edn). Hampshire: CENGAGE Learning.

Silvers, J.R. (2013) *Risk Management for Meetings and Events*. London: Routledge.

Sloan, P., Legrand, W. and Chen, J.S. (2013) *Sustainability in the Hospitality Industry* (2nd edn). London: Routledge.

Smith, A. (2012) *Events and Urban Regeneration: The Strategic Use of Events to Revitalise Cities.* London: Routledge.

Sox, C., Kline, S., Crews, T., Strick, S. and Campbell, J. (2015) Virtual and Hybrid Meetings: A Mixed Research Synthesis of 2001–2012 Research, *Journal of Hospitality and Tourism Research*, May 5th, 1–40.

Sumners, C. (2015) *Five Reasons to Always Use a Venue Finder for Your Event Planning*. Available at: www.fiftyonedegrees.uk.com/Five-Reasons-To-Always-Use-A-Venue-Finder-For-Your-Event-Planning (accessed 17 June 2016).

Teng, C.-C., Horng, J.-S. and Hu, I.-C. (2015) Hotel Environmental Management Decisions: The Stakeholder Perspective. *International Journal of Hospitality and Tourism Administration,* 16, (1), 78–98.

Tompkins, T. (2016) *Take Your Event Virtual: Recent Trends and Strategies with Virtual and Hybrid Events, Part 1*. Available at: www.associationadviser.com/Index.Php/Virtual-Events (accessed 17 June 2016).

UKCAMS (2017). Available at: http://ukcams.org.uk/published%20ukcams%20reports/index.html (accessed 15 January 2017).

Unique Venues of London (2016) Home page. Available at: www.uniquevenuesoflondon.co.uk (accessed 7 August 2016).

United Nations Environment Programme (2012). Available at www.unep.org/publications/ (accessed 7 June 2017).

Universities UK (2016) Available at: www.universitiesuk.ac.uk/Pages/Home.Aspx (accessed 9 May 2016).

Upchurch, R., Ellis, T. and Seo, J. (2003) A Case Study of the Yield Management Conundrum: Usage Versus Competence, *Journal of Hospitality and Tourism Research*, 27, (1), 124–137.

Van De Wagen, L. (2007) *Human Resource Management for Events: Managing the Event Workforce*. Oxford: Butterworth-Heinemann.

Venue Cymru (2013) *Choosing the Right Destination for Your Event*. Available at: http://conference. venuecymru.co.uk/choosing-the-right-destination-for-your-event.html (accessed 16 June 2016).

Victoria and Albert Museum (2016a) Available at: www.vam.ac.uk/Page/G/Great-Exhibition (accessed 12 May 2016).

Victoria and Albert Museum (2016b) Available at: www.vam.ac.uk/Content/Articles/0-9/17th-Century-Theatre (accessed 12 May 2016).

Whitfield, J. (2009) Why and How UK Visitor Attractions Diversify their Product to Offer Conference and Event Facilities, *Journal of Convention and Event Tourism*, 10, (1), 72–88.

Whitfield, J., Dioko, L. and Webber, D. (2014) Scoring Environmental Credentials: A Review of UK Conference and Meeting Venues Using The GREENER VENUE Framework, *Journal of Sustainable Tourism*, 22, (2), 299–318.

Whova (2015) *10 Things to Consider when Choosing Your Event Venue*. Available at: https://whova.com/blog/things-consider-when-choosing-event-venue (accessed 16 June 2016).

William McDonough Architects (1992) *The Hannover Principles*. Available at: www.mcdonough.com/writings/the-hannover-principles/ (accessed 7 June 2017).

INDEX

Entries in *italics* indicate a publication title. Page numbers in **bold** refer to information in tables, *italics* to figures.